Praise for

Well, This Is Exhausting

"Not only is it one of the funniest books you'll read this year, but it's also one of the most important. . . . It is, in a word, delightful."

—*Shondaland*

"Tired of talk about burnout? Well, sometimes the best way to get through something is just to talk about it—endlessly. *GQ* columnist Sophia Benoit shares her experiences with burnout, starting with her adolescence and having to grow up fast in taking care of her younger siblings; trying to balance life between her divorced parents' homes, part-time jobs, and school on top of it all. As Benoit illuminates, trying to do everything to please your parents is a condition we carry into adulthood, manifesting itself in a variety of ways, from impostor syndrome to fear of missing out by trying to do too much."

—*Fortune*

"Humorist, Twitter star, and *GQ* columnist Sophia Benoit tracks her journey from classic good girl to feminist as she examines how to be 'good' these days. (I mean, do any of us really know?!) Weaving in anxiety, dating, reality TV, and more, these essays pack a memoiristic punch."

—GoodMorningAmerica.com

"A riotous collection. . . . Heartening and hilarious, this is prime summer reading material."

—*Publishers Weekly*

"Benoit's writing style is like a witty, long-form tweet—familiar, pithy, and off-the-cuff. . . . Benoit brings her A game in her first book, a new addition to the recent spate of brutally honest memoirs. Recommended for fans of Samantha Irby."

—*Library Journal*

"Sharply observed."

—*Kirkus Reviews*

"Sophia Benoit is that rare combo of wisecracking friend and tough older sister."

—*BookTrib*

"Sophia Benoit is smart, funny, and extremely good at short-form writing. The translation from short form to longer form [. . .] is sometimes exhilarating, sometimes transformative, and criminally interesting."

—Medium.com, *The Pour Over*

"I've known for years that Sophia Benoit is funny. *Well, This Is Exhausting* shows that she is also wise, insightful, and has a Terry Pratchett–esque talent for footnotes."

—Mara Wilson, author of *Where Am I Now?*

"*Well, This Is Exhausting* is a delightfully conversational, funny essay collection that digs right into the heart of what it is to be a woman coming to terms with her personhood. Benoit explores what it means to be a 'good girl' by diving into parental divorce, body issues, crushes, sex, love, standing up for yourself, hostile workplaces, and the tired line between 'chill' and 'too much,' peppering her advice with humor, poise, pop-culture references, and a couple of one-liners that had me literally laughing out loud. Readers might find themselves hoping they're secretly Benoit's sister, and therefore the direct recipient of some of her best life advice."

—Rebecca Fishbein, author of
Good Things Happen to People You Hate

"Sophia Benoit is hilarious and sharp in this vibrant collection of essays about what it means to be a woman in a world that won't stop telling us we're doing it wrong. . . . Give yourself a break with this funny, honest, and relatable book."

—Sara Schaefer, author of *Grand*

Well, This Is Exhausting

essays

Sophia Benoit

G

GALLERY BOOKS

NEW YORK LONDON TORONTO SYDNEY NEW DELHI

G

Gallery Books
An Imprint of Simon & Schuster, Inc.
1230 Avenue of the Americas
New York, NY 10020

First Gallery Books trade paperback edition June 2022

GALLERY BOOKS and colophon are registered trademarks of Simon & Schuster, Inc.

Note to reader: Some names have been changed.

For information about special discounts for bulk purchases,
please contact Simon & Schuster Special Sales at 1-866-506-1949
or business@simonandschuster.com.

The Simon & Schuster Speakers Bureau can bring authors to your live event.
For more information or to book an event, contact the Simon & Schuster Speakers Bureau at 1-866-248-3049 or visit our website at www.simonspeakers.com.

Interior design by Michelle Marchese

10 9 8 7 6 5 4 3 2 1

The Library of Congress has cataloged the hardcover edition as follows:

Names: Benoit, Sophia, 1992– author.
Title: Well, this is exhausting : essays / Sophia Benoit.
Description: New York : Gallery Books, 2021.
Identifiers: LCCN 2020049501 (print) | LCCN 2020049502 (ebook) |
    ISBN 9781982151935 (hardcover) | ISBN 9781982151959 (ebook)
Subjects: LCSH: Benoit, Sophia, 1992– | Journalists—United
    States—Biography. | Internet personalities—United States—Biography. |
    Conduct of life—Humor.
Classification: LCC PN4874.B425 A3 2021 (print) | LCC PN4874.B425 (ebook)
    | DDC 070.92 [B]—dc23
LC record available at https://lccn.loc.gov/2020049501
LC ebook record available at https://lccn.loc.gov/2020049502

ISBN 978-1-9821-5193-5
ISBN 978-1-9821-5194-2 (pbk)
ISBN 978-1-9821-5195-9 (ebook)

For Mom and Papa.
I know I don't say this enough:
this is all your fault.

Contents

SECTION TWO,
in which I try really hard to impress shitty men,
discover Skinnygirl piña colada mix,
and learn how to do eye makeup.

SECTION THREE,
in which I get very tired of trying so hard,
realize I was wrong about almost everything,
and save my boyfriend's life.

"It's a decision a girl's gotta make early in life, if she's gonna be a nice girl or a cunt."

—Tony Manero, *Saturday Night Fever* (1977)

"I'm gonna be real with you, 90 percent of the time when there's a quote at the beginning of the book, it's v[ery] esoteric and it makes no fucking sense and doesn't seem to relate to the book at all—and even if it did, I haven't read the book yet so what the shit do I know."

—Sophia Benoit, Twitter (2020)

Introduction

When I was about six or seven years old, my dad gifted me *The Phantom Tollbooth*. This was thrilling because (a) gifts from dads are always thrilling and (b) it was a book. I was a huge reader* and I felt very ready to dive into this Important and Grown-Up chapter book. I began reading almost immediately. At least, I tried to. There was one huge problem: *The Phantom Tollbooth* was boring as *shiiiiit*. Every few months I would open the book up again and try and try to get into it. My older sister, Lena, had already read it and loved it. My dad had recommended it. I couldn't understand what I was missing. I felt stupid and embarrassed for not liking the book, for not *getting* the book. The back cover said it was about a bored white boy on a journey, which is what approximately 82 percent of kids' books were about until the '90s, but despite reading and rereading the synopsis, I couldn't figure out what the hell was happening in the story.

I put the book aside and went back to *The Baby-Sitters Club*, but it remained my white whale. I held out hope that *someday* I would be

---

* Loser.

like Lena and Papa and *I* would understand *The Phantom Tollbooth*. A year or two went by.* I finally decided to try again. I cracked open the book, flipped past the dedication, and landed on a page titled "Introduction," and I started to read it again, except this time I realized something. Something important. I realized what the hell an introduction is. I had been under the assumption that the introduction was *part of* the story. I had never before read a book that had to introduce itself. I had been trying and trying to get into this book, thinking that this was chapter one; meanwhile, I was reading a bone-dry introduction from the author about his time in the military and how he'd asked some other guy, Jules Feiffer, to do the illustrations for the book. I just didn't realize that an introduction was a whole separate thing. I know!!! Dumb bitch alert!!! Once I skipped ahead and got to the *actual* story, I loved *The Phantom Tollbooth*.

From that point on, I had quite the vendetta against introductions. For many, many years I simply leapfrogged right over them, assuming, often rightfully, that I wouldn't need the information therewithin. Then I grew up some more and figured reading the intro was the right thing to do, so I forced myself to. Some of them are still bone-dry. Sometimes authors use the intro to just lay out everything you're going to learn in the book and then what's the point of even reading the book? The best introduction in my mind would be one that shares a juicy piece of gossip or drama, although authors don't usually do that. On the whole, I think we could live without intros.

Well, guess what? I'm finally publishing my own book and I'm going to do what I want. No one can stop me!† I'm a rascal! And also

---

* Maybe more, maybe less—I don't know—I was a child. Children have a birthday and then like thirteen days later they're like, "Okay . . . when is my birthday coming again?" Time is immeasurable for children. They're not bright.

† Many, many people can stop me.

my editor explicitly told me: "You have to have an introduction." So now I just have to transition from this meta diatribe against introductions into the *real* introduction, where I outline the Big Themes, reminisce about my military career, and tell a raucous tale of how Jules Feiffer declined to do illustrations for this book.

Perhaps because of my historically anti-intro stance, I was a bit lost on how to actually introduce my own book, so I made a semi-frantic call to my aforementioned editor and said, "Okay, so . . . be honest . . . what the fuck am I supposed to write?" (Note: it is not the job of the editor to tell you what to write.) And she was very kindly like, "The introduction should serve as a meditation on who you are and why you wrote this book." So let's do that. I think I was supposed to be more subtle than this—in fact, my editor explicitly was like, "Don't come right out and say it"—but if this part is in the book you're holding, I can assume that my editor felt she'd allow this to pass, that there were bigger fish to fry. Someone had to talk me out of titling the book *The Da Vinci Code 2: Guess What, You Can Name Your Book Anything*, so you can imagine there was a lot of work to be done behind the scenes.

About five years ago, when I first set out to write this book, most of the funny nonfiction books I'd read by women—of which I have read *many*—were chockablock full of women being a mess. They were stories of disastrous one-night stands, raucous parties with minor celebrities, "charming" (insanely privileged) tales of twentysomething white women getting fired from shitty jobs and moving back home for a month before getting offered a salaried gig with health insurance in the big city. Everyone, I felt, had a story about a bad breakup, mountains of cocaine, a sketchy hostel on a European vacation, the alienation of people you love, and the morning-after pill; sometimes that was all one story. To me, this was the template. Take your craziest, funniest stories, the stories that painted you in a kind-of-bad-but-not-*too*-bad light, put 'em in a bag, shake 'em up, and you've got a memoir. You're a person to whom things have *happened*.

I don't have those stories.

A couple of years ago, at my friend Tam's house, her cool artist-musician friends were planning that they were going to do cocaine at Tam's bachelorette party the next week, where we were all going to get together and go to a Chippendales show.* Someone took an informal poll of who was going to do coke, and they asked me if I was going to join and I said no because I'm a little baby and I had never seen cocaine in real life before let alone done it, and they kept encouraging me to try coke for the first time next week before we went to the show and I got so overwhelmed that I cried.

I cried when offered cocaine *a week in advance.*

And somehow I spent years trying to write a book about all the funny, crazy, wild things that happened to me. The truth is, those things *didn't* happen, because the reality is: I am a careful person. I weigh risks, and when in doubt, I err on the side of staying home and watching *To All the Boys I've Loved Before* for the thirty-eighth time. Once I finally admitted to myself that I'm not exactly a Wild Fun Person and therefore cannot write a book about being a Wild Fun Person, a lot of things opened up. I realized the very obvious concept: You Should Write the Truth, Sophia, Not What You Want the Truth to Be. I realized I had all of these actual stories and viewpoints and philosophies inside that I had been thinking (complaining) about for years and years. Most of what they amounted to is this: no matter how good you are, no matter how well you behave, no matter how few risks you take, you will get hurt. You'll feel left out. You'll be lonely. You'll wish you had more friends as an adult. You'll get acne on your chin. You'll feel like

---

* The show ended up being one of the most rewarding experiences of my life. Male strippers are . . . [*chef's kiss*]. The corniness? The camp? The costumes? Unmatched.

your boss hates you. You'll get a bunch of parking tickets. You'll never get it right.

You can't beat the system just by behaving, and society sure has a whole lot of ideas about how you should behave if you happen to be a woman—and even stronger and more restrictive prescriptions if you're also part of any other marginalized community. No matter how closely you follow the guidelines, how stringently you appeal to the straight cis male gaze, you will not win. Look at Anne Hathaway, for example: she has it all.* She's done everything right. She's rich, has perfect teeth, can walk in heels, has won an Oscar, has been in a Nancy Meyers film, is friends with Emily Blunt, is the Queen of Genovia *and* Catwoman, and looks great with short hair. (My only knock on her is that she named one of her sons Jonathan and then the next son Jack, which is a nickname for Jonathan.) After she won an Academy Award a lot of people just started hating her for all kinds of strange reasons: for being *too* into acting, for trying too hard, for seeming insincere in her humility. Some people simply hated her for no discernible reason at all. Some people still hate her! And if Anne Hathaway is an object of this much baseless criticism, then you know the rest of us are.

I felt pressure in my life to be more fun, to write a book that had more *wild* stories. Stories that included risk and danger and unexpected hijinks. Stories that would have made me look bad if they didn't make me look so cool. Long before I was trying to mine my life for stories that would make me seem fun, I felt pressure to be thinner. I felt pressure to be quieter. I felt pressure to not be such a know-it-all. I felt pressure to drink, to dance, to be easy to talk to and hard to get into bed.† I felt pressure to like good TV and hide the romance novels I read behind other, more "intellectual" books

---

* At least, she has it all in terms of what our capitalistic society says women should want. I'm not saying that *I* want her life, just that she's successful on almost every front.
† But not *too* hard, you know. A challenge. But an easy one.

on my shelf. I felt pressure to be a good daughter, a good student, a good girlfriend, a good employee. And I tried really hard, because what if all it takes to be like Anne Hathaway is trying really, really hard to please everyone around you?

Well, spoiler: it did not work. I am not succeeding on almost any front that Anne Hathaway is doing well in; I don't even have a garbage disposal or air-conditioning in my apartment. I tried really hard to please other people and all I got was tired.* Maybe you've felt the same way—like you have tried really hard and been good and it hasn't always paid off and you're not always sure what the point of trying that hard *is* or who you're even trying for anymore. I feel you. This is the story of a girl named Lucky. Just kidding,† but it *is* the story, loosely, of how I went from being an anxious Goody Two-shoes kid to an anxious insecure wannabe-slutty college student to a still-anxious but now very tired adult who gave up on pleasing people so much. It's the story of how I learned how to be good for myself rather than for other people. A little bit. I'm not doing perfectly; let's not get crazy.

---

* I'm sure Anne Hathaway is tired too.

† If you didn't get the reference in the last sentence—or don't get any of the ones in the coming pages—don't worry. Almost none of them are essential to understanding me; they're more like little inside jokes with myself. (You can always google them, too.)

SECTION ONE,

in which I try really hard to be a good kid for my parents,
miss out on a normal youth because I was fat,
and then date someone who sucks.

Bless You, Brendan Fraser

Like most people, I experienced my sexual awakening during the horse scene of the award-nominated film *George of the Jungle* (1997). If you don't know the scene, let me explain: Leslie Mann takes Brendan Fraser—whose body is *BANGIN' HOT* and whose long hair is *LUSTROUS*—to her ritzy engagement party to another man, Thomas Haden Church. George/Brendan is wearing an impeccably tailored (for the '90s) suit, which is already enough to get anyone's engine (vagina) going, but *then* he leaves the party to go hang out outside with animals (relatable as hell). He climbs into a pen with some horses that are on the property, because rich people always have horses, and he starts running around with them like he's in a horny perfume ad. Naturally, all the hot single women at the party come watch this sexy display. A couple of men scoff and ask, "What is it with chicks and horses?" which is a valid, if sexist, observation. I maintain this is the first time in cinema that women's sexuality was fully understood. It can be no coincidence that *Sex and the City* premiered the following year, building off what *GotJ* had already laid down.

I was only about four or five when I first saw this movie, and yes, that does feel young for me to have my sexual awakening, but it's never too early to get horny. After I saw this magnificent film, I was destined to be thirsty forevermore. Actually, I don't know how much it has to do with Brendan Fraser; I was just a horny kid. Strictly speaking, when *GotJ* came out, I was already getting in trouble for masturbating during nap time at preschool, even though I had *no idea* what I was doing. I was just humping things constantly, which is a fairly normal thing for kids to do, it turns out. I didn't know that, though. It's not like you can tell a four-year-old that it's normal to want to hump things but that they can't because of society's complex, horrid relationship with sex. I eventually got the message that I wasn't supposed to be jerking off in public, even though no one really explained it to me. What I *did* glean from the adults around me was that there was supposed to be shame around whatever it was that I did before bed every night; I often tried to quit. I would go weeks or months, proud of myself for having given up my nightly ritual, only to relapse. This was not long after Dr. Joycelyn Elders, the first Black surgeon general of the United States, was asked to resign after saying that masturbation was "part of human sexuality." In 1994, by Bill Clinton. The famously sexually appropriate president.

When I was about thirteen, my mom sat me down for the number one most mortifying conversation of my life and informed me that what I had been doing every night since I was a child was masturbating and that that's what sex felt like. I, of course, was fucking pissed. *That's it? That's what sex is like? What a total scam!* Here I thought I had *another* cool thing to experience on the horizon, but nope! I'd already been doing it since preschool. Seeing my disappointment at this, my mother assured me that sex would be so much better because it was with another person, and I rolled my eyes and was like, *Yeah, fucking right, Mom. There's no way anyone knows how to do this better than I do.* And for the most part, I have been right about that. Sex has rarely been better—or at least more reliable or easier—than masturbating, in my personal experience. Another total scam.

I didn't grow up in a household that shunned sexuality. There used to be a magazine rack at my dad's house that held dozens of magazines; I believe my dad and stepmom had it custom-made since my dad subscribed to so many. There was one magazine that was on the rack that I loved. It had Tyra Banks on the cover, topless, with her long hair covering her boobs. The cover said, "Tyra, please pull back your hair." I would often sneak into the living room when no one was around to look at it. I remember a pinup calendar in my dad's basement office that featured a naked woman wrapped in cellophane for December (she's an object—get it?). I remember December because that calendar stayed up on the wall in the basement for years after my father moved his office up to the attic. Only once did I work up the courage to take the calendar off the wall and peek at the other months before setting it back to December.

My mother, for her part, was even *less* of a prude. In a hyperrational move typical of her, my mom never minded sex scenes in movies, as long as there wasn't violence; at age ten I saw my first R-rated movie, *Love Actually*, where we see quite a bit of Martin Freeman and Joanna Page (at least there are no guns). When my older sister Lena and I asked what sex was when I was about six, Mom calmly explained (in an age-appropriate way) about bodies and babies. She never found sex repulsive or embarrassing. She wasn't crossing weird boundaries with Lena and me or anything; she was just clear that safe sex isn't a big deal.

No one in my house was selling the lie that sex *ought* to be shameful, but I still got the message anyway. You can't live in America and not get the message that sex is wrong. I got it from the way movies were screened for children and what we were allowed to talk about at recess, and most of all, I think, I understood sex is shameful because of the general silence and discomfort around the topic. Children have a keen sense of what is Not to Be Discussed.

On top of the normal American puritanical shit, I had another reason to feel disgust with my sexual appetite: I was fat. And in my filled-with-internalized-fatphobia-mind, fat people—especially fat teens—were *not allowed* to be sexual. When I saw *Hairspray* in theaters with a group of my size 0 friends, I remember burning with resentment that Carly Wooldridge loved the movie. She wasn't fat! A movie starring an overweight and horny teenage girl?! This movie was *mine*. I bought the soundtrack immediately simply to express to everyone that I liked the movie more than Carly did; unfortunately, she already owned the CD and no one else was keeping score. She was obsessed with Zac Efron, and I with the idea that a fat teenager could be attractive to someone as hot as Zac Efron. The relationship between Tracy and Link in the movie was the ultimate fantasy for me. Unfortunately, in real life, perhaps because I didn't end segregation on my local TV station or have an amazing singing voice—not that either of those things would have likely impressed the guys at my school—I was destined to be alone. This was a particularly heartbreaking prospect since I was constantly in love with and wildly horny for everyone around me.

My father similarly grew up a fat kid and as such placed an oversize importance on people being attracted to him. I don't think he's been single-single—like not dating *anyone*—since he lost weight at nineteen. His best friend Jim once commented, "I don't think he'd be like this if he'd just been asked to one Sadie Hawkins dance." And I think Jim's right, both about my father and about me. The longer I went without getting sexual attention, the more I got into watching and reading about it, and the media I was consuming only reinforced the belief that I needed to be thinner in order for someone to ever want me. There is something about youth, at least as we see youth in media, that promises sexual experiences, even if they be rushed and unsatisfying, and when you don't get those experiences, you feel like a FREAK.

This is *especially* true for women. There is no shortage of messages, both explicit and implicit, screaming at you that the most sexually desirable thing you can be is a teenage girl (so fucked-up). This just made me even more hurt and angry that as a teenage girl I *wasn't* sexually desirable to anyone around me. It wasn't just my perception, either. It's not like that problematic but highly catchy One Direction song where I just didn't know that I was beautiful, thus making myself desirable to men. No, media and fellow ninth graders were *very* clear on the issue of fat women: not hot. Funny, sure. Slobbish? Yeah. But not hot.*

In recent years, there have been two rom-coms made about hot guys falling for overweight women, but only *AFTER THEY GOT HIT IN THE HEAD AND ENDED UP AT THE HOSPITAL.* Meanwhile, there are hundreds of movies about a schlubby guy somewhere between fourteen and fifty-four years old trying to hook up with someone way out of his league, and in none of them did the protagonist even have to go to urgent care. The messaging is clear: if you're a girl who isn't under 135 pounds, you would have to have a traumatic brain injury to think you could get with an attractive guy. If you ever want to have sex, ladies, your job is to be hot. (And by *hot*, we mean thin.) And, boy, did I ever want to have sex! Even if it *was* the same as jerking off.

My sister Lena, who is three years older and hundreds of times bolder than I am, started buying *Cosmopolitan* magazine when she was fourteen. I immediately started stealing them from her room, which rightfully drove her nuts, and often led to blowout screaming matches. My mom would try desperately to mitigate these fights by saying, "Lena! It's not like she's going to read the words off the page!" Which is true, but to be fair, stealing them was fucked-up of me. The thing was: *Cosmo* is horny, and once I found that out, there

---

* This is not the case, by the way! Media and ninth graders are wrong!

7

was no way I wasn't going to steal it. *Cosmo* was the only "person" willing to talk to me about sex; everyone else avoided the topic with me aggressively. It's *wild* to me that the horniest mainstream magazine for women is mostly just sex tips on how to make sex feel better for men, when men get to watch and read all kinds of porn directed right at them. Because we are required to be virginal and pure *and* adventurous sexual objects who exist solely for the pleasure of men. That's why our sex advice is about making *him* come. So while I loved *Cosmo*, she also let me down. Where was the porn for *me*?

Do you realize just how few depictions there are in popular culture of young horny women? Or even adult horny women? *Fleabag* felt like a revelation because it depicted a woman wrestling with her sexual desire in a deeper way than the broad strokes of horniness they gave Samantha in *Sex in the City*. Women who are nuanced, competent individuals who want to have sex that makes them feel good and who aren't the butt of a joke? There are like four movies total that have characters like this, and they're all indie movies that didn't do well commercially but should have. Pretty much every other movie on earth is about a horny dude, with the possible exception of the *Harry Potter* films, because there's no sex at all in them, which is boring *as fuck*. (How did y'all make it through *SEVEN* books about teenagers where no one fucks and sucks? I truly cannot fathom this.) There is a truth universally acknowledged that men are constantly thinking about sex, and not just thinking about it, but seeking it out. Well, guess what, society? Ladies are horny, too!

But that's not something we're supposed to talk about. When I was younger and somehow both much smarter (I got As in AP calc, bitch!!) and much dumber (I wasn't a feminist yet) than I am now, I spent a lot of my time around guys joking about female masturbation owing to the simple fact that no one else was talking about it, and it therefore got me attention. None of my female friends and I talked about it with each other, other than perhaps a one-time timid exchange of "Do you . . . ?"/ "Yeah? Me too." But I loved talking about it to guys because they were so shocked and, at least in my mind, excited to hear that women indeed did want to have sexual experiences. Looking back, I think I mostly just made everyone super-duper uncomfortable, but I thought that was a key part of jokes, because I watched too much *Chelsea Lately* at the time. I promise I'm better now.*

Honestly, though, masturbation jokes and the reaction they got reinforced the idea that as someone who was both fat and a woman my enjoyment of sex—my simple desire to have sex with another person—was a type of transgression. Something to tell jokes about, if I wanted to talk about it at all. Something profane. The jokes were my way of trying to normalize my own voracious sexual appetite. This was before the days of Twitter and "Spit on me, Rachel Weisz," or "Hit me with a bus, Michael B. Jordan." I didn't know other women were also *desperately* horny. Even *Cosmo* often framed sex as something nice to do with a partner rather than an all-consuming preoccupation.

While I was embarrassed by my seemingly insatiable desire for sex, there was one thing that went even *beyond* that shame: my interest in love. Up until at least college I could more easily watch TV in the same room as other people when someone was getting railed than I could when two people were declaring their love for one another. (Honestly, I still often find it squirm-worthy.) Masturbating and having sex were things I could, and did, joke about. They were cool but transgressive, I felt. Love was not. In no way was love cool. I was under the impression that it was feminine and, therefore, icky. While someone might put up with a thinner, hotter person wanting love from them, as a fat woman it felt like way too much to ask for. I convinced myself for many, many years that I actually found romantic love gross and overrated.

---

* Please mentally insert that gif of Natasha Rothwell saying "Growth" here.

That did not stop me from desperately consuming every single book, movie, and television show I could find about the topic. I have seen almost every single mainstream rom-com made since 1980, and many from before then. I read dozens of romance novels a year, usually within a day, and I have since I was about fourteen. Yes, I wanted to **** Brendan Fraser's ****, but I also thought that I could really end up marrying Heath Ledger someday, if I simply lost weight, and *only* if he agreed to give up smoking. In real life, I maintained a crush on at least one person virtually nonstop from age five (Michael Bernard) on. Clearly, on some level, I was still into the idea of love, even if I acted disgusted and above it. This was self-preservation. I suspected love was not coming for me.

In sixth grade, I stupidly let one of my friends tell Ben Cannon that I liked him. I think I mostly liked him out of a sense of protection or pity for him, because a friend of mine, Annie Manwaring, was *obsessed* with him to the point of being creepy—she saved a Kleenex he threw at her once—and I thought he deserved better, which perhaps morphed into *me* liking him. Or maybe Annie just talked about him so much that I became preoccupied, too. Either way, when Ben found out that I liked/was scared for him, he looked up across the room of Mr. McGee's sixth-grade science class and let out a simple yet effective "Ew." I turned bright red and my whole body got hot. Like on-fire hot. Like a sunburn, but everywhere. It felt like I was being incinerated. What the fuck had I even been thinking letting someone tell him that I liked him? Never. Fucking. Again.

But then seventh grade came along and I liked Dominic Coultrip, who was always super nice to me—*of course* I liked him. Unless I was in a group project, no guy *ever* talked to me.* Guys talked to my friends, I joked around awkwardly on the periphery, the guys

---

* You're welcome for taking the reins on every single PowerPoint from 2004–2007, Nipher Middle School boys.

laughed and then returned their attention to my friends, girls who emitted polite giggles and fit into denim skirts. One day in computer lab Dominic Coultrip found out that I liked him—*Serial*, please do a podcast to find out who told him. I carefully avoided him for the rest of the day until he approached me in Mrs. Goeke's science class (WHY IS IT ALWAYS SCIENCE CLASS?) and told me super, super kindly that he didn't like me at all but that I was very funny, which was *so* much worse than Ben's response, because while I agreed with Ben's assessment of me, I did not agree with Dominic's. I assured Dominic that I didn't actually like him—that someone had given him bad information—a lie, which he very generously let me tell.

After that, I stopped telling friends about my crushes. What was the next person going to do when they found out I liked them, vomit? I'd barely survived disgust and condescending kindness. I didn't need any further confirmation that I was an ugly piece-of-shit hag whom no one would ever be horny for, the very thing I wanted *most*. At that time, I truly believed the zenith of human experience was someone being attracted to you.* This belief caused me absolutely zero problems at all.

Just kidding.

---

* Frankly, I still kind of believe this.

Too Many Servings of Ketchup

A doctor broke the news to me when I was in fourth grade. More accurately, a doctor broke the news to my mother, who then broke it to me: I hated myself.

He was an ear, nose, and throat doctor named Dr. S, whom I've always associated with cotton balls, although I have no explanation for that. Both my sister and I had ear surgeries young, so maybe he was the first person to show me a cotton ball. I don't know. This isn't about him!

I had gotten out of school (thrilling!) for a few hours in order to get an appointment with Dr. S, which went normally, as far as I remember, until the end, when he sent me out to the lobby while he talked to my mother. I felt this was weird, but I didn't know enough about ears, noses, or throats to know what was happening. When my mom came out, she was crying and she shuttled me out to our waiting Honda Odyssey. My mom crying is pretty standard fare—everyone in my immediate family cries early and cries often—but every time she cries I am paralyzed with fear that I have Done Something Wrong.

This time, she was crying because Dr. S had informed her that I hated myself. My presenting symptoms: I had black nail polish on and

I was wearing all black and I was fat. First of all, I wore all black *because* I was fat and black is supposedly slimming.* (Also, my entire dad's side of the family wears all black because we're Italian; I don't know what to tell you, Dr. S.) And I was fat not because I hated myself but because I loved eating and couldn't stop and my metabolism is certifiably slow.

Until Dr. S, it did not occur to me to hate myself. I didn't think that was really an option, since, you know, I was stuck with myself. That's like hating the sky. Like, okay, cool, now what?

Here's where I *could* give Dr. S a break and presume that he meant well, but I really don't care. He's a white dude who probably made six figures for decades and had free health insurance the whole time, so I don't give two shits about making sure we all think well of his intent. I get the idea behind telling a parent that you're concerned about their child as a medical professional. However, (a) first of all, YOU'RE AN EAR, NOSE, AND THROAT DOCTOR, BUDDY. And (b) second of all, the reason that Dr. S presumed that I hated myself and pulled my mother aside to chitchat about that was simply because he believes fat people hate themselves. There is no way he would have confronted my mother if I'd been thin. Even if I'd been *too* thin.

Before the revelations of Dr. S, I'd certainly disliked my body. It wasn't like I didn't notice and *feel* the differences between my body and other kids'. I was the slowest to run a mile in gym class, I didn't look as "good" in clothes, and Natalie Buckner stopped being my friend in first grade because I was "getting fat." I knew what was happening, but I was also innocently self-absorbed enough, as many kids are at age nine, to not have considered self-hatred an option.

My mother was caught off guard by having a fat kid. At the time she met my father, he was in the best shape of his life, obsessively exercising and carefully dieting to stay fit. I'm sure she knew his ori-

---

* While we're listing things that can fuck off, the idea of dressing to "slim" yourself is right up there with Dr. S's antics.

gin story of being a fat kid; he refused to dance at their wedding or go swimming *ever*—two very common aversions for ex- or current fat people. As Guy Branum described in his book *My Life as a Goddess*, "Fat people are told we are supposed to be obsessed with our bodies but never take pleasure in them." When my dad got remarried after they divorced, he and my stepmom had an accordion player at their wedding in lieu of a band or a DJ, I presume so that no one would expect any dancing. I still don't think it occurred to my mom—a tiny, birdlike woman who passed on to me her delicate wrists and *nothing else!*—that her child would be overweight. I know it had to have occurred to my father, for whom fatness and youth are inextricable. When I started getting fat around the same age he had exactly forty years earlier, I suspect it felt like fate. I was already like him in just about every other way (shy, unibrow, very expressive dresser).

It took a while after my seminal appointment with Dr. S for me to be concerned that something might actually be "wrong" with me. I was sitting in the front seat of my mom's car outside of Subway while my sister Lena ran in and got a sandwich before she had to head to choir practice. I'd gotten french fries from somewhere. I would say McDonald's, but these were crinkle-cut fries, which we *all* know McDonald's doesn't serve, and which I think we can all agree SUCK.* Anyway, I had already eaten dinner, and I started eating this cardboard tray of shitty fries and my mother told me to stop, that I'd already had enough. I agreed wholeheartedly with her. I was full. I didn't need any more food. I *wanted* to stop. I *knew* fries weren't good for me, but more than that, I thought these fries tasted like shit and I wasn't hungry. But I couldn't stop. I kept watching my hand feed my mouth, but I had no control. I felt like scream-

---

* French-fry types ranked from best to worst: McDonald's fries, seasoned fries, curly fries, sweet-potato fries, shoestring fries, regular fries, waffle fries, steak fries, crinkle-cut, potato wedges (which are bad potatoes masquerading as fries).

ing, but I knew that would freak my mom out. (Yelling, "HELP, I CAN'T STOP EATING FRIES, IT'S AN OUT-OF-BODY EXPERIENCE RIGHT NOW, PLEASE HELP!!!!" is not chill, and my mother is a worrier). So instead, I picked the least weird option, which was to keep eating the fries even as my mother tried to get me to stop. Even as my own brain tried to get me to stop.

I knew then that I had a problem. Around the time I entered middle school, people around me got a lot more bold about my "weight problem." Let's be clear: my weight was in no way a problem for literally anyone, other than possibly me. My stepmother, another naturally thin woman in my life, swore that what I had was "baby fat" and that she had hers until nineteen.* By age twelve, it was pretty clear that it was more than baby fat; I could and often would eat an entire large pizza by myself. People—parents, medical professionals, aunts, really any adult I came in contact with for long enough—came up with some pretty great theories as to why I'd gotten fat, which they of course shared with me:

1. My parents let me have too many treats.
2. My parents never let me have any treats, so when I *did* get them, I went overboard.
3. My body never felt full.
4. I was punishing my body.
5. I had too little going on in my life.
6. I had too much going on in my life.
7. I wasn't *mindful* enough when I ate, which was evinced by the fact that I often danced while eating or enjoyed the food too much.
8. I was upset about my parents' divorce.
9. I simply didn't know about healthy choices.

---

* Disputed claim.

The last one was one of the most ridiculous. It's not like I didn't *get* what eating healthy was all about. Here's my moment to sound like a total ass, but I was scoring in the 98th percentile of my state in standardized testing and everyone thought I couldn't figure out that eating a second breakfast of a soft pretzel with cheese and *four* sugar cookies when I got to the cafeteria in the morning was bad for me. At one point, my mom literally called the school and told them to stop selling me breakfast, and then I tried to scam and lie to the poor lunch ladies, who did not need to add "Keep my kid from gaining weight" to their job. I fucking *knew* what the problem was.

The problem was I couldn't stop eating.

The first person to describe what was actually happening to me internally was a friend of my mother's. She was a school nurse with purple hair, purple glasses on a beaded chain, tattoos, and the best gap-toothed smile in the world. And she was a food addict. She'd also been a drug addict before, so if anyone is going to know what addiction was like, it's her. Food is a particularly shitty thing to be addicted to since, you know, you can't exactly quit. At a dinner once, she told me about the time at a party where she ended up eating dozens of carrots, and how upset she was by it. A friend of hers failed to understand the problem: "But carrots are healthy!" My mom's friend explained: "Yes, but I didn't *want* to eat them; I just couldn't stop."

I remember thinking, *That's me. That's me. That right there is me.* My heart was racing because I was so thrilled to have an answer to why I ate everything that my friends didn't like in their lunches, even after I'd eaten my own. Why at camp I got thirds and fourths from the buffet when no one else did. Why I saved my allowance to add money to my lunch account. It wasn't something as poetic as loving food: I loved *eating*.

My mother, being both extremely compassionate and extremely worried, tried to force me into therapy, an exercise and healthy habits class for teens, and then, finally, a nutritionist's office. She tried to appeal to me with everything she could think of. She told me stories of a friend of hers whose brother had lost his foot to diabetes—not because she thought that might sway me into eating healthier, but because she was terrified. She reminded me frequently how scared she was for me, but it's not like you can just picture losing a foot every time you're about to eat a whole bag of Reese's and then put it down and walk away. I couldn't. My mother's imagined future for me at age twelve (diabetes) was about as real to me as my father's imagined future for me (NASA physicist).

The dietician my mom sent me to lasted the longest. Possibly because we did what I already liked to do—talk about food. She missed the point *entirely* and probably cost my mother a lot of money and time away from work, but she would explain in buttery tones that matched her buttery blonde hair that if I simply swapped salami in my sandwiches for turkey, I'd be healthier. That was more fun to talk about than my parents' divorce, which every other mental health professional thought was The Issue, but which I saw as normal since it had happened when I was two.

I think the dietician's name was Becky, but she also looked exactly like my mom's friend Becky, so I might just be transferring the name-memory over. Anyway, I didn't really have a choice about visiting Becky; my mother believed strongly that sometimes you didn't give kids an option *not* to do something. You just told them, "You're going to therapy." The moment I knew Becky was bullshit was when she tried to teach me about portion sizes of ketchup. BECKY!!!! ME EATING TWO SERVINGS OF KETCHUP INSTEAD OF ONE IS NOT THE ISSUE!!! It's like when women's magazines tell you that you can have a handful of almonds as a snack or a square of dark chocolate as a treat. Bitch, if I could stop at one square of chocolate we wouldn't be here!

The problem was that no one knew what they were doing. My mother didn't know how to help. Becky didn't know how to help. The therapists I tried didn't know how to help. I wasn't sad or self-loathing (take that, Dr. S). They all refused to confront the problem I described to them. I wasn't a binge eater so much as I was *always* eating and couldn't stop. I wasn't ignorant of healthy habits. I was simply addicted to eating, and *every single* time I started to eat, I began the struggle of when I'd be able to stop myself. Every meal was a binge. I wasn't throwing up; I simply didn't feel full *ever*. And even when I *did* eat healthily, I gained weight. I wasn't eating my feelings, I was just eating everything.

I think about my childhood as a fat kid a lot, how I was parented and helped, corrected and cajoled, and what the adults could have done differently. I don't know what the answer is. I asked a friend of mine who has struggled with weight her whole life, who was sent to fat camps and therapists, nutritionists and personal trainers, what she wishes her parents would have done. "Nothing." That's what she said, and she said it without pause. "I wish they'd done nothing. I'm still fat now, so clearly it didn't help them reach their goal; all it did was ruin our relationship." (We both agreed that while we could wish that now, had they really said or done nothing, we might still resent our parents.) There is no winning when your focus is on getting your child to lose weight, even if you feel *certain* that it's for all the right, good, moral, healthy reasons.*

What I know is this: As a fat person, I became my body and my body became everything. Not just to me, but for the people around me. It became uncomfortable for them to be around, and people like to fix or avoid discomfort. Being fat became part of my personality, it became all my worth. My body became a conversation piece and the metaphorical elephant in every room I entered, the breath held every time I sat on a too-small-for-me chair or tried on a top in a size

---

* SPOILER: It is probably not!!!! You probably have a lot of unexamined fatphobia coursing through your veins. Most of us do!

that was not mine out of misguided hope. Eventually, at the behest of social acceptability, I shifted my obsession from eating to my body.

At some point, probably with the aesthetically obsessed* Greeks, we started conflating self and body. White cis men, of course, have mostly escaped that fusion. They've had enough nuanced narratives about them to fill the next two thousand years, and those narratives helped to establish that white men are more than just bodies. They are leaders, innovators, and intellectuals. They can sin and be forgiven because they are more than simply bodies. Everyone else . . . not so much.

For women, and minority women especially, as well as for non-cis people, bodies are given value only because (or whenever) they are consumable by the people in charge.† That is what is at the core of our objections to objectification: I'm not *for* you. I'm not here to be jerked off to, fantasized about, yelled at on the street, derided, fucked, commented on, rated on a scale of one to ten, or assaulted when I decline any of the above. I'm mostly here on planet Earth to read crappy romance novels and get sick to my stomach from eating too much cookie dough,‡ okay? Not for human consumption.

Of course, when you're fourteen and eighty pounds heavier than your peers, you aren't swayed by even the best self-love/self-worth arguments. You want your body to have worth like other kids' bodies have worth. At least, I did. I was very, very, very, very exhausted from buying ugly one-piece swimsuits with skirts to hide as much of my body as possible while my friends got to buy two-pieces. I was exhausted from not being able to swap dresses after school dances. I

---

* Horny.
† White cis men, in case you're lost.
‡ Let me be extremely clear: I do not think that you can get salmonella from cookie dough. Yes, the FDA says you can, and so does science. But science is a little bitch sometimes. So the stomachaches in this situation are from consuming too much sugar and not from being betrayed by my true love: raw dough.

was exhausted from never getting asked to dances in the first place. While hilarious now, I was burning with shame when my friends were all members of the Spice Girls for Halloween and I dressed up as a garden gnome. No one asks you to be in the Spice Girls—real or fake—when you're two hundred pounds.

I was so starved for someone to like my body in any way, to pay it any positive attention. Once, in Mr. Drury's algebra class—a class I was *very* happy to be in because my crush at the time was also in the class—said crush and a bunch of his friends sat in the back of the room and pointed at me "sneakily" and gestured to the fact that I had really big boobs. Which I did. Like really massive boobs. Big titters are great, and once you lose weight you lose weight from your boobs first and that's how I know God is a fake bitch. Anyway, despite the fact that I also overheard their assessment of the rest of my body (gross), I was *thrilled* by the idea that they'd thought about my boobs at all.

Growing up, I lived in a town that boasted of having "the oldest football rivalry west of the Mississippi." Think *Friday Night Lights* but in Missouri instead of Texas and with a lot fewer hot people. The point is that Friday nights revolved around high school football. Our field was surrounded on three sides by hills. Two of those three sides had bleachers where parents, the marching band, and high schoolers watched the games. But the middle schoolers spent the football games on The Hill.* The Hill was . . . well . . . a steep grassy hill with no seating and scant lighting, situated right behind the concession stand, an enclave that went mostly unpatrolled by authority figures.

---

* This is not to be confused with the Italian neighborhood in St. Louis called "The Hill," where my family goes to get staples like panettone and salted cod from rival Italian grocers, John Viviano & Sons and DiGregorio's.

I often didn't go to The Hill, or football games in general. Partially, I didn't go because I was with my dad every other weekend and couldn't go those weekends. Partially, I didn't go because watching football didn't sound like fun. This was before I understood that we weren't going to the game; we were going to the social event taking place next to the game. Anyway, on The Hill once I met a guy who was a grade older named Danny, a very, very popular hot guy *who went to a different school*—which somehow makes people more popular and more hot. A friend of mine who was also hot and popular, who was trying to be kind and show me around the football game, introduced us. She told him my name and he replied with "Oh, I'll remember that. I have a poster of a naked girl named Sophia on my wall with soapy titties." Something in me must have come alive with the tiniest speck of male attention because, high on adrenaline, I replied, "Oh, me too." Everyone loved it. At least, that's how my memory re-creates this moment. More likely, a few people who had never talked to me before laughed politely. But I had finally—*finally*—found a loophole in being a nobody: I could be funny. That's one thing people let you be when you're a fat woman: you can be funny. Especially if you're willing to make fun of yourself.

I wanted attention; I craved it. I tried being funny, because if you're funny at least you're getting some attention, but a lot of the time my "funny" was really mean or obnoxious. I *knew* I was often being mean or obnoxious but I couldn't stop myself, because it was the only time I got attention from someone who wasn't a teacher. And even bad attention is attention. I never got to text with a guy friend or even really *have* a guy friend, like the rest of my female friends did. I therefore never got invited to events by guys, only by the girls whom they'd invited. The few times guys talked directly *to* or *with* me that wasn't a part of a group project, I tried to shock them and impress them. I'd take any dare, eat any disgusting food, say any profane thing I could think of, to hold their attention just a little bit longer.

Pretty much every woman who has ever grown up fat has stories like this, of feeling desperate of being overlooked. I'm not saying I had it the worst; I wasn't the saddest or the most bullied teenage girl. In fact, I was mostly okay. But I have the markers of a fat female childhood both literal (stretch marks, which I ironically mostly got from *losing* and not gaining weight) and figurative (BODY DYS-MORPHIA!!!). The bullshit part—well, one of about 24,048 bull-shit parts—is that women are reminded that they're only valuable if they're young and if they're thin, and if you spend your youth being fat, you've wasted all your good years, according to society. The years you might be worth something to someone else. And as much as I would have loved for fourteen-year-old me to *get* that you can also just be valuable to yourself and that's "enough," being beloved and cherished by ninth graders is a heady fucking drug.

Exactly the Woman I Thought
I'd Be When I Grew Up

I thought I'd be married by now, not because I'm romantic, but because I thought I'd be divorced by now, and in order to be divorced, you must have at some point gotten married. Almost everyone in my family is on their second spouse. Some are up to their third or fourth. I always thought being divorced was glamorous, adult, sophisticated. What could be more grown-up than the end of a rocky marriage? To me, it was like owning a car or having a 401(k). I thought—I *know*, actually—that I would be a fabulous divorcée. I would go through it with wine and Fleetwood Mac albums. Which is not all that dissimilar from how I've gone through my normal life, now that I think about it. I would have close female friends come over and we'd shit-talk my ex-husband and do bad karaoke in my living room, and then a month later I'd start a brief albeit fulfilling affair with a slightly younger guy.

I assumed I would have lots of money. I know this is both a stupid assumption and an inevitable one after growing up in American Dream Land. You don't fantasize about growing up and think, *Hey, maybe I won't be able to afford to go out to eat more than once a month and I'll have to really budget for it.* I thought I'd be able to walk into any store and purchase anything and everything I wanted; I assumed there would be shopping trips in my future where I came out of the mall arms laden with purchases. I also assumed I'd still be going to malls, so I was wrong about a lot of things, I suppose. I thought I'd have a nice apartment with one of those tobacco-brown leather couches from West Elm and a sunny balcony like all good Italian apartments have.

Speaking of Italians, I figured—hoped—that I'd speak fluent Italian, useful for my biannual months-long trips to my pied-à-terre in Siena. Also useful for my trysts with my rotating cast of Italian lovers. Sorry to use the word *lovers*, but there really aren't enough good words for that. Am I supposed to say "fuck toy"? No, it's crass. I'll get a letter of complaint from one of my aunts about it, and I don't need that headache.

I figured I would have bimonthly manicures. I don't know; I thought nice adult ladies all had professionally maintained acrylic nails. I thought I'd wear perfume every day like my aunt Suzanne and that I would clean the house with a kerchief tied around my head like my aunt Karen.

I thought I would have lots of rings. Every adult woman I knew had lots of rings. Looking back, I think the women in my family just got engaged a lot and therefore owned a lot of redundant jewelry. Also, my aunt Patti is a jeweler, so perhaps that's the source. Either way, I assumed my fingers would be decked out. As it stands, I think I own three rings that aren't from Target, and I get too nervous to wear them anywhere.

I assumed that I'd live in New York City when I grew up. I listened to the Jay-Z and Alicia Keys song "Empire State of Mind" while working out in high school, preparing for my inevitable future in the Big Apple. New York, it seemed, was the place to be if you wanted to be glamorous and wear all black and rush to the subway holding a cup of coffee, which to me was the height of human adult experience. You know the opening of *The Devil Wears Prada?* Where the KT Tunstall song plays as a bunch of models get ready for the day? Of course you do. I assumed—not wanted, not desired, assumed—that my life would go like that. That I'd be rolling out of a bed (*with a frame* and a heavy white duvet), leaving a hot shirtless guy behind, telling him to let himself out as I put on heeled boots and rushed to catch the F train or something like that. I have no idea what the subway lines are called in New York and I don't want to spend my life right now looking up which one would make the most sense to reference.

Everyone of style and substance that I could imagine lived in New York. By this I mean the characters from Nora Ephron movies, Nora Ephron herself, and Holly Golightly. I've seen the movie *Breakfast at Tiffany's* only once or twice because it's so glamorous that it makes me sad.* I can't really explain it, but that movie makes me feel like someone beautiful died young. It feels the same way as Grace Kelly or Heath Ledger's death, like something untouchable is gone. For Grace and Heath, the loss is about a person; for *Breakfast at Tiffany's* it's that I simply cannot ever *be* Audrey Hepburn, gliding around 1950s New York, gorgeous enough to get away with anything and naive enough to want to.

I feel this way about a lot of movies, people, stores, cities, etc. *Breakfast at Tiffany's* isn't even a particularly strong trigger for longing for me, other than, of course, the song "Moon River," which could make even the most stoic person face the truth of mortality with sentimentality. I just used the movie as an example because we all know about *that* New York. And it's a New York that I assumed I'd be a part of.

---

* Also, obviously, it is very racist (see: the entire character of Mr. Yunioshi), which is incredibly disturbing to watch.

I felt I had seen enough of New York in the movies to understand what the deal was and the deal was this: walk the streets in a glamorous coat while on your phone, drinking expensive coffee. Occasionally attend a gallery opening (something no adult I know has ever done in real life). Vacation in a friend's Hamptons mansion over the summer. Smoke on a fire escape. Hail a cab in a sequined dress. Cross the street openmouthed laughing with friends to get to a crowded bar. I needed no more information about New York; I got the deal.

For as long as I can remember I've known that I would grow up to be a famous actress.* Perhaps this started the day that my mother told me that Julia Roberts owned five horses and ten dogs. Ten dogs seems like a lot. Maybe it was ten horses and five dogs. I don't even know if that number was true, or where my mother read that if it was. I just remember my mother telling me that and me thinking, *Okay, being the highest-paid actress in America seems like the most reliable route to owning a bunch of dogs and horses*, which was, of course, my ultimate goal at age six.

I suppose that I assumed I'd be on set for certain stretches of time. Or doing some acting here and there. I definitely assumed I'd be hooking up with famous costars and attending the Oscars in gifted haute couture gowns. The only other career I could possibly fathom—and it took effort—was being in academia, but being the kind of professor who teaches abroad during the summer (international travel is clearly a theme for me), and who sleeps with the married department chair (sex also *clearly* being a theme for me). Mostly, though, I assumed I would be famous or at least somewhat wealthy, which is basically the same thing.

My idea of fame was mostly that you were in magazines, a medium I venerated. I practiced my interview answers frequently. I

---

* I was, of course, wrong as per usual.

also figured I would be going to high-society parties in apartments with crown molding *and* wainscoting *and* built-in bookcases. Apartments with nine-foot ceilings and kitchens hidden away because my God who goes into their own kitchen? I didn't expect myself to be so ungodly rich as to *own* an apartment like that in New York, but I did certainly think my friends or acquaintances would be. Going to a sumptuous party once a month or so seemed doable. Likely, even. When I traveled, I expected to stay in hotels that provided robes.

One of the hardest presuppositions of mine to let go of was the idea that as an adult I would be extremely fit and incredibly hot. I did not, for some reason, assume that the stretch marks of my youth would carry over into the fantastical world of adulthood. I thought I would have long, lean legs that I showed off in miniskirts. (I also assumed I would know how to get out of cars gracefully without showing off my undergarments, something I'm still mediocre at.) I did not imagine working out or eating with any level of discipline, really. I just assumed I would be, well, someone else entirely, and that included my body.

I thought I would cook elaborate dinners for my many, many friends. In my assumed adult life, I would be an excellent cook—the kind of person who deep-fries things on their kitchen stove and doesn't follow recipes and owns a blowtorch for crème brûlée. You can't imagine how many friends I assumed I'd have. I figured I'd be the elegant type, a person who would pen meaningful handwritten notes to friends that they'd keep for years. I would be generous and funny and people would look forward to my yearly New Year's Eve party (or whatever holiday I decided I was big enough to eclipse). I would have my friends' children and my children's friends over to stay with me often, and I would never worry if they spilled orange soda all over an expensive rug. I'd laugh and pour my own glass of wine on the rug, too. "It's just stuff!" I would say, and they would feel so welcome and loved. "Your aunt/mom/neighbor/ex-wife is so cool," they'd whisper, awed.

I vacillated on the children in my future. When I did imagine them, I had them with an Italian man and we never spoke English at home. Or I married André 3000 and we had however many children he wanted; I was (and still am) willing to compromise on anything to marry André 3000. Usually, though, in my crystal-ball future, I was alone and childless, a Stevie Nicks replicant sans musical talent and with fewer gloves, no offense to her fashion sense. I felt I was done with the idea of kids after doing so much with my younger siblings. I felt exhausted by the very *thought* of being asked to play dress-up or to help with science homework. Being a cool aunt seemed more doable, more likely. I fancied myself quite nomadic, when really I just had seen *The Lizzie McGuire Movie* a few too many times and wanted to go get sexed up by a hot guy in a foreign city.* Honestly, I thought I would be too busy having fun to consider children.

I did not imagine getting married to stay married. I didn't imagine my wedding much outside of thinking about pigs in a blanket (which are really just a delightful thing to think about) or funny things to do instead of the traditional wedding ceremony. Like getting married in a parking lot or walking down the aisle to the song "All Star" by Smash Mouth as an homage to *Shrek*. I did not imagine homeownership in the traditional American sense; certainly I never imagined owning a yard. Gag me. I did not think I would ever own a car with more than two seats. Maybe I wouldn't even need a car at all!

I figured I'd be extraordinary, that everyone would want to be

* Also, as any Lizzie-Head will tell you, the hottie she gets with in Rome is actually a liar and a *fraud* and it's her best friend from regular-ass America whom she's really in love with.

me or fuck me—sometimes both. I thought I would become less of a people pleaser, but more liked. I thought opportunities and friendships and careers would land in my lap.

I have to say, I really, really, really thought I would use weekender bags a whole lot more.

How to Use Your Parents' Divorce
to Get Kicked Out of Gym Class

My parents split up pretty swiftly after I arrived. I have one image that I *believe* is a memory of us together as a family; however, I once read that when you revisit a memory, you're actually just revisiting the last time you remembered it, and human memory is decidedly fallible, so I don't know. Even in that "memory," my parents are not together in any kind of romantic way—they're just in the same room, the kitchen of our old house, feeding my sister Lena and me. I remember the tile floor mostly, but I asked my mom about the floor in the old kitchen once, pre-renovation, and it did not corroborate my memory.

Sometimes, as a teenager, when I was home alone, I would go into my mom's armoire and get down the oldest photo albums I could find and try to find photos of the two of them together. I tried to make their marriage feel real, or at least plausible. Seeing them together felt like how I would imagine it would feel if you came home and Lady Gaga was sitting on your bed. It didn't compute. I don't know why, but I always associate my father moving out with the John Denver song "Sunshine on My Shoulders." I would sit on the floor of my mother's bedroom and look at photos from when they were still married and just *think* about the lyrics, "If I had a day that I could give you / I'd give to you the day just like today." Most of the photos of both of them together—there weren't many; my father is camera-averse, and why would you keep photos post-divorce?—had my sister in them. A few photos feature one parent as the subject with just pieces of the other. My dad's hand hovering in the corner of a picture of my mom and the new baby. My mom's shoulder in a distinct ultra-'90s sweater visible on the couch next to my father. Lena had *a lot* of baby pictures because she was the first kid and also because they weren't getting divorced when she was new on the scene. I don't know of any photos with just me and both of my parents.

My parents don't talk. They didn't talk when I was little and they don't talk now. When they jointly walked Lena down the aisle for her wedding last year I kept thinking, *It's weird that they know each other*. My mom and dad weren't ever like the modern divorced parents who try to do birthdays and holidays together for the sake of the children. My father likes moving on from certain things and never looking back, probably because he got too into stoic philosophers in grad school. Honestly, everyone in my family is too sensitive for post-divorce chill togetherness to have worked, so I'm mostly glad we didn't try.

Their lack of communication meant that Lena and I were often operating with limited or confusing instructions, a complicator of our living-out-of-bags life. It was difficult to know what to pack for when we spent weekends with my dad. Most things weren't planned or communicated well, and we didn't keep clothes there. Lena and I had a shared room and, much to my deep embarrassment, a shared bed until she left for college. I don't know why that's so embarrassing to say; it shouldn't be—lots of people around the world share rooms and beds with siblings. But it felt shameful to me.* Anyway, we didn't have a closet or a dresser at my dad's, really, which meant we didn't keep separate clothing or shoes there. The only items that were ever at my dad's house were weird gifts that relatives had given us from Christmases long, long ago or things we'd forgotten from the last weekend.

We stayed with my dad every other weekend and every Tuesday night. Everything we wore each weekend and on Wednesdays had to come over to his house in a bag. The problem with packing and the living-out-of-bags lifestyle is that you often forget things. You think you put gym clothes in the bag last time but you really didn't. You forgot to bring socks. You didn't pack a bra. Your shirt actually has a stain on it.

I often ended up going to school wearing ugly, mismatched, incomplete outfits. It made me feel horrible. Mortified. It wasn't just school, either. Sometimes my stepmom's family would come over for a family get-together and I'd have nothing to wear. Or we'd have people at the house and everyone was swimming and I didn't have a suit. Or I had a suit that was either way too big or way too small. Or we went to a school carnival on a Saturday afternoon and I was in trouble for not having the right kind of shoes, but who the fuck told me to pack for a carnival?

When this would happen, when I was stuck wearing a big T-shirt from my dad or sandals to an event that required tennis shoes, I would often get a feeling that at the time I couldn't label; in my mind I referred to it as The Nothing Feeling. I could never tell when The Nothing Feeling was going to happen; it was hard to predict. But it often happened around clothes and changing. As I grew up, I realized that the feeling was shame, akin to the body dysmorphia

* One time Lena and I mentioned being embarrassed by this, and my father, who grew up so poor that he didn't have a bedroom and slept on the porch in good enough weather, was rightfully apoplectic.

I would later feel. A shame so deep it felt disorienting. A shame so deep it became impossible to perceive myself as anything other than BAD. It felt like arriving at school naked times eight hundred.

You know when you're talking on the phone and it starts to play back what you're saying and you can't keep talking because it's *so* distracting? That's how The Nothing Feeling felt. I felt like everyone was looking at me and could see too much of my body and they knew it was all wrong and they hated it. It also felt like somehow *I* couldn't see my body, that I couldn't even get a glimpse of what they were so disgusted with in order to fix it. I got that feeling a lot living out of bags between parents' houses.

Perhaps part of my deep discomfort in not having the right clothes was because of how much I loved "fashion." Look, I do not think it's fair to you or to myself to call what I wore in eighth grade fashion without quotation marks around it. I liked getting dressed; I *loved* shopping—or at least I loved buying things.* This might seem unusual for a fat person, but every time I went shopping I felt that I was going to somehow purchase *just the thing* to make me look entirely different. I read article after article about what was flattering, as if you can somehow hide two hundred pounds under vertical stripes, or as if hiding two hundred pounds is a good thing to do.

I loved clothes, shoes, and purses. If anyone would have taught me about makeup, I would have loved that. I couldn't dress like other kids who wore short skirts and jean shorts and basic white T-shirts. All of those things, I had been told, looked "bad" on fat people. They don't, of course, but I also didn't know how to find versions of them that made me feel good about myself, so I avoided them.

Since I couldn't dress like my peers, I veered wildly, recklessly, *embarrassingly*, into: dressing like an adult. I'm sure this is common for kids with body types that are not traditionally childlike, but it

---

* My mom buying things for me with *her* money!!

was heightened for me because I read a lot of fashion magazines and I wanted desperately to emulate what I saw. It's hard enough for a size 0 adult in the suburbs of St. Louis to copy what she sees in *Vogue* without looking like a clown; it's downright discomfiting to see a fat twelve-year-old try to do it. I strong-armed my mom into letting me buy these chunky mule heels that would probably be cool now because everything that is ugly as sin is cool now. I would clop down the tiled halls of my elementary school—where technically heels were not allowed—feeling like I was in *Glamour* and looking like an anamorph of Danny DeVito turning into a Clydesdale. I didn't yet understand the power of flying under the radar as a fat kid. Luckily for me, very few photos of me at this age survive. I, like many middle schoolers, occasionally thought I looked *really* cool; now it makes me want to hurl myself off the roof of a Ross Dress for Less to think about what I wore back then.

Another key component of the nightmare of being overweight was, of course, gym class. I'm not entirely sure they should be teaching gym as a required class at school. First of all, not everyone is able-bodied, so it seems exclusionary at best, and the fact that you can get graded and scored on what your body can do is . . . dicey.* Everyone who has ever had a body that did not cooperate with what they wanted it to do in gym class: I see you. This book is for *you*. I know I said it was for my parents in the dedication, but that's so they don't get sensitive about it.

In elementary school we had two gym teachers: Ms. Williams and Mr. B. I can't remember Mr. B's full last name, but I do remember all the girls had crushes on him. He was very Midwest-teacher attractive. He was the kind of blond-buzz-cut white guy who thinks that

---

* Of course, this is also the case for the rest of the school system as well, because it's not like being smart or good at school is inherently good or makes you a more worthwhile human. Anyway, our institutions fail people at every turn!

putting on khakis is dressing up. But everyone loved him because he was the "fun" gym teacher. Poor Ms. Williams was a much more serious gym teacher, probably because she had to be. She was also the single mom of a student who was in my class, which was always a weird dynamic to watch. That poor kid.

Anyway, Mr. B and Ms. Williams did not seem to get along, despite being the only two teachers in their department. The one thing they could agree on was me. I was a gym-class villian for them. Not only was I overweight (a sin) and gaining more weight (double sin), but I *often* forgot and sometimes "forgot" to bring gym clothes to school. Part of it, of course, was because of going back and forth between houses; I frequently reminded them that I had divorced parents, something rare enough at my school to earn me a pass semi-regularly. However, you can only cast yourself as a child of divorce so many times before the institution of physical education comes for you. Ms. Williams and Mr. B eventually caught on that I was trying to avoid run-walking a mile at half the pace of my classmates and they started sending notes home with me that I could *not* wear heels to gym class. That I *had* to wear actual gym clothes and participate. They made me—and none of the other kids—bring a bag of gym clothes to school and keep it on my little hook in my classroom so that I had no excuse for evading the pull-up bar.*

There's no way to avoid shame as a fat kid. I'm sure there is no easy way to avoid shame as a kid altogether, but in my experience shame usually centered around my body. What my body couldn't do, what my body did that I didn't want it to do, what my body looked like, what my body told other people. I think adults forget sometimes how much shame young kids can feel. I think it's very easy to imagine children as resilient because it's somewhat horrific

---

* Seriously, why the fuck on earth do kids need to learn to do pull-ups?? Why?

to operate otherwise. It's a bit horrific to imagine all the ways children can get hurt by little things like running a mile slower than everyone else and having to wear an ugly sweater and forgetting to pack a bra for their dad's house. Here's what I know: I know that my parents not being married didn't have nearly the lasting effects on me that wearing weird clothes and sucking at the PACER test did. At least my parents' divorce occasionally got me out of gym.

"I'm Difficult." —Sally Albright
(but Really Nora Ephron)*

For my fifth birthday I got the best gift that anyone can ever give another human being: the *Grease* soundtrack on CD. I was in a California Pizza Kitchen—my restaurant of choice in kindergarten—and I got the gift from my stepmom's parents. *Grease* was my absolute favorite movie at that age, much to the chagrin of my mother, who did not think that it was age-appropriate to watch a movie that included assault, a condom breaking, teenage pregnancy scares, and the raw hotness of a young John Travolta. I'm kidding about the last part; no one is immune to young Travolta's charms.

My father let us watch somewhat risqué movies on occasion when we were really young because young kids are idiots. For example, I watched the (problematic, transphobic) movie *Ace Ventura: Pet Detective* as a young child and there's a scene where Jim Carrey gets sucked off in return for bringing a woman's dog back to her. He's

---

* I've always thought it was weird to give actors or characters credit for movie quotes, when a writer wrote them.

holding on to the top of a doorframe making funny (orgasm) faces. As a child, I thought he was doing the monkey bars. I did not get *why* he was doing the monkey bars inside someone's house in this scene, but I was little and I only understood about 24 percent of any movie I was watching anyway. As we grew to be more impressionable and more likely to understand what a blow job is, we would suspiciously stop watching certain movies at my dad's. *Grease* stopped at some point—maybe because of appropriateness, maybe because I'd forced everyone to watch it 742 times and if anyone in my family heard "Summer Nights" one more time, they'd die.

Eventually, though, when I was about sixteen, I watched *Grease* again and hoooolllly hell. There's a lot in that film that needs to be examined. I don't have time to fix classic cinema, so let me just address one thing: the lesson of the movie *Grease* is ostensibly that you should change—and start smoking!—for the person you love.

I feel that I should hate the ending of *Grease*. Sandy is like, "You almost killed yourself racing. I'm going to change everything about myself so that I finally have some power in this relationship outside of withholding sex." This is, on its face, a terrible ending both narratively and, of course, morally. However, who can deny the raw power of Sandy Olsson showing up to the school fair *sewn into* that black outfit with heels on? And then Danny's voice cracks and he's like, "Sandy?" in the most horny, desperate way. And she then says the best line of all time with the best delivery of all time as she puts out her cigarette,* "Tell me about it, stud."

Just thinking about it gives me chills!

He just says her *name* and she's like, "Tell me about it!" kjas;lkd-fjalsakdjf;akjd! The power! Yes, she's changed for the male gaze. Yes, she has basically adopted the same aesthetic as the Pink Ladies!

---

* Remember the girls' sleepover when she used to suck at smoking? NOT ANY-MORE!!! Now, *that's* a character arc!

Yes, she's going to get lung cancer! But by fuck she's cool. And she's finally in control. You can give Sandy shit for trying to be something she's "not," but it should be noted that Danny *also* tries to show up to the end-of-year carnival with a letterman sweater on—a half-assed attempt to be more of the jock that he thinks she wants *him* to be. After a recent rewatch, in fact, I would argue that a woman becoming even *more* cool and bad and then singing a song that insists "You better shape up" is not as bad a moral-of-the-story as it's made out to be. She gets power! She stops being a Goody Two-shoes! She gets what she *wants*! And she looks fucking hot on the last day of school! I wish I would have followed more closely in Sandy Olsson's red-stilettoed footsteps.

I took a long, hard look at some of the rom-coms that shaped my childhood, or at least rom-coms that I watched over and over again.* I left many out. Frankly, I can't believe that *The Wedding Planner*, *The Proposal*, and *13 Going on 30* didn't end up making the final cut, but I wanted to talk about the protagonists who really stood out to me, who had a lesson to teach, potentially. And then I wanted to see if that lesson was good, because rom-coms get a lot of shit for "setting unrealistic expectations" for women, as if anything that happens in the *Transformers* franchise is somehow more likely to happen than dating a less-shitty-than-the-last-guy guy. Some rom-com leads, like Sandy Olsson, helped shape my idea of what a grown-up

---

* This list is, unfortunately, dominated by white women. That's true for a lot of reasons. One, they make way more rom-coms with white leads than they do for any other race. Two, I grew up watching a lot of movies starring white people. Now, I didn't necessarily have control of that as a young child, when I first watched some of these movies, but I definitely could have done better as I got older to watch movies that don't just star white people. I make more effort now to watch movies that aren't just about the same thin, able-bodied, cis, straight, rich white women, and I *sincerely* hope that more and more movies get made that do not center on them. Especially rom-coms, since that's what I really want to watch, let's be honest.

woman was and, more important, could be. Some . . . not so much. I rated each protagonist based on whether I thought their character was a helpful or harmful depiction of adult womanhood.

Mary Hatch Bailey, *It's a Wonderful Life.* The earliest memory I have of any movie is the "Buffalo Gals" scene in *It's a Wonderful Life.* It's one of the most romantic scenes of all time, and if you just take the scene itself, it's a perfect miniature replication of the themes of the movie—George (Jimmy Stewart) almost getting what he wants, and then being called away by duty. Anyway! The real star of that movie, I have to say, is Mary Bailey, née Hatch (Donna Reed), would-be spinster librarian in the alternate universe where her husband was never born. Mary is, ever so coolly, *the* driving force of the romance of this movie. She makes every move. In 1946! She's the seducer! In fact, she drives most of the non-romance action of the movie, too. She's the one who initially likes George, who wants to dance with him, who wants to marry him, who suggests giving up their honeymoon money to save the Building & Loan, who (spoiler) gets everyone in town to come help her husband raise enough money to avoid prison. She also has some of the best lines of the movie, including when she whispers in George's deaf ear when they're both kids, "George Bailey, I'll love you till the day I die." And boy oh boy does she! Clarence's dedication to George should have read, "Remember, no man is a failure who has a bomb-ass wife like Mary." **VERDICT:** Helpful depiction, although some have suggested that she was better off in the alternate universe where she was a spinster librarian. I reject that; her ultimate life goal is marrying George and having children, and that's valid. However, I do think George could have been a better spouse.

Kathleen Kelly, *You've Got Mail.* Kathleen Kelly (Meg Ryan) is trying to run the children's bookstore she inherited from her mother while dating the world's most boring man alive when she starts up an internet flirtationship with Joe Fox (Tom Hanks). Just Call Me Joe is a very New York piece of shit who owns a book "superstore." Remember Borders? Unbeknownst to Joe and Kathleen, they're rivals in real life even as they're falling in love online! Can you believe it? I can! The writing is, as per usual in an Ephron vehicle, flawless, but Kathleen is a bit of a sweet dope. Perhaps the best part of her character is that Joe Fox brings out the *worst* in her instead of the best, which is very fun to watch, if problematic in real life. Of course, as they spend more time together, Joe becomes a better, kinder person (the journey seemingly every single cis straight man ever must go on because they all suck before a woman helps them realize they need to not suck) and Kathleen stops having to be biting and mean; she submits to the grief of losing her business and tries to make a full life for herself, which weirdly includes a friendship with Joe before she finds out that she's been cyber-dating him. **VERDICT:** Surprisingly, harmful??? A lot has been said about this—much of it by my boyfriend every time I try to watch this lovely, perfect film—but Joe Fox is less than ideal. He's a multimillionaire, first of all, and a dick to her. Plus, this movie gave me the idea that you could viably own a bookstore in New York and afford to live. She should have ended up with Patricia Eden. Or just living single with Birdie.

Emma Thompson, *Love Actually*. *Love Actually* was the first R-rated film I ever saw. My mom took my sister Lena and me to the movies to see it and then let us skip school the next day and I don't give a shit about what you're supposed to do as a parent because that's one of my favorite memories of all time. Plus it was the first time I saw two fully naked people on-screen. I was . . . titillated, to say the least. Anyway, of all the romances in this movie, Emma Thompson and Alan Rickman's is the best. Don't care about their characters' names, frankly—probably like Nigel and Gemma, knowing British people. Emma Thompson has the most poignant arc of *any* character in that film, hands down, and if you don't feel something when she uses the word *absent* as a verb and goes to her room and cries because she realizes—on Christmas Eve!—that her husband is cheating on her, you're a monster. Honestly, though, for me, her greatest moment comes right after that when she dries her tears and has to come out of the bedroom and get her kids ready for their recital and be a jazz hands! excited mom, even though she wants to cry. *That* is some real shit right there. That's one of the hardest micro-moments* on film for me to watch, but it's probably also exactly what it's like to be a mom. At least, I always saw my mom in that scene, and all the times she probably was having her heart broken but had to still show up and be a mom because you don't have a choice. **VERDICT:** HELPFUL! WE LOVE EMMA THOMPSON AND MOMS.

Anna Scott, *Notting Hill.* This movie was groundbreaking because it featured an unlikable female lead! In a rom-com! I have multiple friends who love rom-coms, but who don't like this movie because Anna Scott (Julia Roberts) is kind of a bitch and I'm like . . . that is the point of this movie!!! Do you know how many unlikable male leads there have been? Come on. This woman gets to mess up *and* be powerful *and* be harmful *and* grovel *and* end up with a bangin'-

---

* Another one, since *you* asked, is in *Shrek*—STICK WITH ME!—when Shrek has just rescued Princess Fiona and they're outside the castle, away from the dragon, and she insists that he take off his helmet so that she can see the face of her rescuer, and he's like, "Uhhh, I'm just here to bring you to this other guy. Trust me, you don't want me," because he's insecure and self-hating (due to people being cruel to him). Anyway, she is persistent enough, so he takes his helmet off to reveal himself and for this tiny, tiny, tiny moment he has a little sheepish smile like there's a kernel of hope that just *maybe* this smokin'-hot princess is going to want to marry and sleep with him. And then she doesn't and he's like, "Oh yeah, why'd I think anyone would choose me?" It's HEART-WRENCHING.

hot bookstore owner who lives in Notting Hill? Are you joking me? This is what feminism fought for!*

VERDICT: I want to say helpful because I'm in love with a movie having an unlikable lead woman, but ultimately this was harmful because I am not a famous actress, I am not porking 1999 Hugh Grant, and I am not getting to be a little bit of a bitch about it. Unrealistic expectations: set.

Julianne Potter, *My Best Friend's Wedding.* Look, this movie is absurd. Two friends have a semi-serious pact to marry one another if they're still single at age twenty-eight. Twenty. Eight. Right before that happens, hunky hunky Michael (Dermot Mulroney) tells Julianne (Julia Roberts) that he's actually about to marry a twenty-year-old named Kimberly (Cameron Diaz) who is going to drop out of college for him so that he can be a sportswriter. Okay. There are nine hundred things wrong with this plot, obviously, not the least of which is that if my twenty-eight-year-old guy friend called to tell me he was marrying a twenty-year-old, I would go to his house and beat him up. With a baseball bat. That said, almost nothing has ever made me cry as hard as I did when I first watched this movie as an adult,† and it's all because of Julianne. She's a disaster and a half! She's desperately, disastrously in love with her best friend—something I had been *many, many* times in my life, although I never actually *did* anything about it, because I'm not out of control. I know that Julianne is reckless, harmful, and irrational. I know she's "fighting" to win over a guy who was fine with his new twenty-year-old wife dropping out of college, arguably not a man worth having. But I also loved watching female longing. Do you know how few depictions there are of a woman who can't get the guy she wants? NONE. Okay, well there's

---

* No, it's not. Sorry.
† Okay, I was eighteen. Which is not really an adult, but kind of.

this one. Usually the only time women don't get the guy they want in movies is if they're "ugly." Certainly, the main character—and most especially 1990s Julia Roberts—doesn't end up alone! And actually, in this movie, she doesn't! She ends up with George (Rupert Everett), one of the best friends of all time. And I think she and Michael likely remain friends. **VERDICT:** Helpful depiction of female longing and how you often use friends to get over heartbreaks that feel gutting at the time but that ultimately don't kill you. Harmful in the sense that she is incredibly selfish with her love.

Kenya McQueen, *Something New.* I remember which movie theater I saw this in; I think I was skipping hockey practice with Lena and we went to the movie theater in the mall instead of the ice rink. Immediately I wanted to watch it again because it was one of the most erotic movies I've ever seen, but also because it was just *so* good. Modern romances are difficult to write well because most of the obstacles that keep people apart these days are "I don't like him" or "I'm not satisfied with our relationship" instead of things like "Our houses are at war" or "I'm a maid in his household and he's the duke" or "He left for the army years ago, we thought he died, I married his brother, and now he's back." (You know, the classic shit.) But this movie actually has a couple struggling with a real issue that isn't just: "He leaves wet towels on the bed." Kenya McQueen (Sanaa Lathan) is Black and Brian Kelly (Simon Baker) is white. He's a chill guy with a jeep and a landscaping business and she's a high-strung CPA. Of course, she *has* to be on top of her shit because she's a Black woman who is constantly questioned, condescended to, and overlooked at her job because of her race. Kenya has to this point only dated Black men, and she's interested in getting married, so meeting a white guy that she's into is a curveball for her. But, while being a bumbling idiot on occasion (and *super* insensitive at one point), Brian helps Kenya loosen up a bit in her personal life. There's a really hot scene with nail polish. Anyway, this was a formative film for me about letting go of perfectionism a bit and opening yourself up to people.* **VERDICT:** Helpful depiction! Kenya practices vulnerability and also balances societal expectations of being an independent career-driven woman with what she actually wants, which is a partner. Chef's kiss!

Elle Woods, *Legally Blonde.* This script is, with a few minor exceptions, practically perfect. They could, and perhaps should, teach this script in film school. Firstly, there are *so few* over-the-top female characters who exist in normal worlds. The same is not true for men. Men get to be characters all the time—think Ace Ventura, Buddy the Elf, Inspector Clouseau. Often, too, those men end up with beautiful, competent women who seem to not notice anything off about them, or who appreciate their quirkiness. Women do not get roles like this; Elle Woods was this role. The most inspired part of the film, however, is its celebration of femininity. Elle Woods (Reese Witherspoon) is one of the first female characters I saw who was not just unafraid of being feminine, but who used it as a power. At no point in the film does she change herself, despite the derision of nearly everyone around her. She is smart enough and hardworking enough to get into Harvard Law School ("What, like it's hard?") and yet kind enough and empathetic enough to make friends everywhere and to protect the people she cares about. And she does it without sacrificing an ounce of femininity (to steal a line from *The Spy Who Dumped Me*). At no point does her power come from being more like a man; at no point does the film suggest that she is weaker or dumber for her womanhood. **VERDICT:** Perhaps the most helpful character on this list? Hard to say!

---

* I'd like to open myself up to anyone who looks like Simon Baker, if you know what I mean.

Grace Hart, *Miss Congeniality*. Grace Hart (Sandra Bullock) is the *opposite* of Elle Woods. She's bought into the common idea that masculinity is strong and protective and that femininity is weak and pathetic. Due to . . . terrorism? . . . and there being no other hot women in the FBI, she has to go undercover in the Miss United States Pageant, where she learns that actually women are good and that being feminine doesn't make you lesser. Who knew! **VERDICT:** A helpful lesson in someone learning to reject the conditioning of society that says that masculinity is power. Harmful because she's ultimately still a cop.

Jesminder Bhamra, *Bend It Like Beckham*. This movie is, to me, flawless. First of all, there's a love triangle that isn't about two men competing over a woman. In fact, the real love story here is between Jules (Keira Knightley) and Jess (Parminder Nagra), rather than Jess and her hot hot hot Irish soccer coach, Joe (Jonathan Rhys Meyers). (Why do all their names start with *J*???) Or perhaps the love story is between Jess and her family or, if I'm *really* being corny, which I usually am, I could say it's between her and soccer. But the point is that the movie recognizes that Jess loves and cares about things other than just how horny her coach makes her. It's wonderful. Here's a female lead who attracts *and* gets the guy and it isn't the most important thing in her life, even though it's lovely and sweet. *Bend It Like Beckham*, much like *My Big Fat Greek Wedding*, always spoke to me as a teenager because they both dealt with familial and community expectations, which a lot of mainstream American white-led rom-coms ignore. **VERDICT:** Helpful as hell! Here's a woman who isn't weaker because she's in love with someone, but also isn't shaping her whole life around a man. She has things to do! She has soccer to play! She ends up with her best friend in a way. Classic. Beautiful.

Sally Albright, *When Harry Met Sally*. JLo says that this is her favorite rom-com and that she's watched it fifteen thousand times and guess what? JLo is *never* wrong. This is obviously the big daddy of rom-coms; the apotheosis. And it could never get made today. Why? Well, because it's mostly a movie of people sitting around talking. Very little "happens" in the way that Hollywood people want things to "happen." (As if sleeping with your best friend is not a thing happening). Regardless, the movie is perfect; there are some lines that are so brilliant they make me want to scoop out my eyes with a grapefruit spoon.* Anyway, this film brought to the mainstream the question of whether straight women and straight men can be friends. Most people think that the answer the movie gives is no, straight men and straight women can't be friends, because sex always gets in the way (as it eventually, delightfully did for Harry [Billy Crystal] and Sally [Meg Ryan]). This is nonsense! The two *are* friends for *years*. They are excellent friends to one another. Anyway, one of the most key moments of Sally's character is when she's crying about an ex, Joe, whom she thought she was over, and she cry-yells, "I'm difficult!" It's hilarious and raw and real and every woman I know can relate to feeling like you're simply too much work to love. **VERDICT:** Sally Albright is a gem. Helpful depiction of a "difficult" woman being loved. Although if you think Sally Albright is difficult, God help you.

Ultimately, do I think movie characters *shaped* me as a human? No, not entirely. That honor belongs to my parents and siblings and teachers and Mary Oliver poems. But I do think that what we see on-screen shows us possibilities. Movies give us the lessons of what life might look like if you were like someone, if you acted as they did.

---

* Someone is staring at you in Personal Growth; Baby fish mouth; Harry's entire exchange about Helen going to a Big 10 school. There are twenty million moments in this film that are crafted as intricately and soundly as a wedding cake. It's like a cathedral of a movie.

When I first rewatched *My Best Friend's Wedding* as a college-age adult and not a nine-year-old who thought kissing was gross to witness, I remember thinking, *Holy shit. That's me. If I'm not careful, I will be Julianne.* These characters didn't make me who I am per se, but they certainly gave me a glimpse into adulthood and what I could be like. In often subtle ways, these movies let me know that it wasn't bad or lesser to be a woman, to be feminine, and to want love—even if you have to get sewn into leather pants for it.

The Tyranny of Great Expectations

I remember the day that my dad was the most disappointed in me: March 18, 2005. (Truthfully, it lasted a few days). It's easy to remember because it's the day my youngest sister was born. I had gotten back a progress report—not the actual report *card*—and I had gotten Bs in all four of the main subjects: English, math, science, social studies. I planned intentionally to tell my father this at the hospital where his daughter had just been born because I felt that he'd be riding off the high of having a new child and might be a little more lenient. Perhaps he was; I have no idea how it would have gone on a normal day.

I told him in the elevator on the way up from the hospital parking garage. I laughed nervously and made a joke about it. My father was *not* having it. "This isn't funny, Sophia." My dad thinks *everything* is a joke, so that was not good. Plus, no one who knows me personally calls me Sophia unless I'm in *trouble*. It's always Soph. We went to meet my sister Giovana, but my father made it clear that we would pick this up later.

And we did! Lo and behold, three days later my father, while driving me somewhere (School? Hockey practice?) had a *long* conversation with me about where my life was going. Because of four Bs. On a progress report. I remember so clearly being like, "Bs are above average!" And he was like, "Not for you they're not." He asked me what I wanted to be when I grew up and I gave him a few answers that included actress and lawyer, and I only said lawyer because I'd seen actresses do it on film. He gave me a lecture about how hard I would have to work if I wanted either of those jobs to happen. He was disappointed in me, because he knew I *could* have gotten As, but that I simply wasn't doing the work, which was true. I was always losing or forgetting to do homework because homework sucks ass. My dad was clear, though: Bs were not allowed.

My mother was softer: she made it clear Bs were okay with her . . . *if* that's the grade I had earned after turning in every piece of home-work and trying my best. If I wasn't doing the work, *that* wasn't acceptable.

I never got another B again.*

My friends thought this was . . . a bit much.

My parents had high expectations for just about every facet of our lives; we were expected to do *a lot* of things that we didn't nec-essarily want to do or like. Because Lena and I were living between two houses, we had chores at *both* places. Because we had younger siblings, we were expected (not asked) to provide care for them. Because we didn't get full time with either parent, they both wanted a lot of (enforced) Quality Family Time.

For both my mother and father, we could *never* be at either of their houses enough, and that was made clear. It wasn't meant to be communicated to us as a failure of ours, but there was always a film of blame: you're not here enough. At one point, my stepmom

---

* Until I got to college and realized I wasn't planning on going to grad school (because I was going to become an actress) and that college was hard as balls and no one gets all As unless they're willing to not get laid.

started keeping a calendar of what *time* we arrived at their house and what excuses we gave if we were late. Often, it was a game of deciding which of three parents to disappoint. Since my stepmom and dad rarely communicated with one another, one might be asking for us to pick up a kid from school and the other might be wanting to go on a grocery store run with us while we had a hockey practice to go to and skates that had been left at the other parent's house. Meanwhile, rarely was anyone asking us, "Hey, do you *want* to do this thing? Do *you* have homework to do? Would you like to just relax a bit?" Or if they did, it was very clear that they would be hurt if you turned them down. That was the real punishment in all of this: hurting your parents. It was the worst thing Lena and I could imagine and yet we did it all the time, simply by being at the other person's house.

Holidays turned into wars over whose house we stayed at and until what time. And what time had we stayed until last year? I love Christmas; it's my favorite holiday of all time despite me having no personal relationship with religion generally or Jesus in particular. I'm at a 10 about Christmas, which is astounding when you consider that it was also almost always the worst, most stressful day of the entire year to have divorced parents. My family did five Christmases. One with my mom at her house, one with my dad at his house (Santa went to both; he can do anything), one with my mom's extended family, one with my dad's extended family, and one with my stepmom's extended family. And they were all supposed to happen between December 24 at 1 p.m. and December 25 at about 9 p.m. Every year it was a mad dash to get Lena and me to all the right events at the right time, to say enough thankyous to people before we got hauled to the next place. Everyone involved *hated* it. Everyone was bitter that their family's event didn't get the largest slice of our time and gratitude. I still remember standing at different landline phones, my heart racing, calling the other parent to ask them to come a little later please, or to tell them that we were finally ready to go, hoping the parent whose house I was at didn't hear.

My mom and dad were entirely—at least I believe—acting from a place of simply wanting to see us more. I don't want to sound ungrateful for being loved so much, but their tug-of-war meant that so much of our childhood ended up with Lena and me in the middle. And because of this, we rarely got time for ourselves. We didn't have whole days or weekends with nothing to do—ever. Everything was on a calendar; one of the cardinal sins in my family was to change plans. You want to go to the football game on Friday night when it's Papa's weekend? Okay. Well, which weekend are you going to trade for? The weekend with the school play? You can't do that because that would mean him having to drive you to and from each rehearsal. And now every weekend with this parent is a weekend when you're doing *fun* stuff with friends instead of seeing them. *Why do you always do the stuff with friends on my weekends? Why can't this person drive you? Why do you want to be outside the house ever at age fifteen when you could sit at home and talk to your parents?* Rarely were any of my parents low-key or relaxed about schedule changes. Everything needed to be planned and approved, and every parent (my mom, dad, and stepmom) had competing interests, something that Lena and I were expected to navigate and excel at. If my mom wanted us back over at 5 p.m. on a Sunday and my stepmom wanted us to go pick up one of my siblings at their friend's house at 4:30 p.m. and my dad didn't want us to leave his house to go pick anyone up because that would mean less time with him, what were we supposed to do? The answer: figure out which parent would be the least mad or least hurt, and hurt them. If you hurt them earlier in the month, hurt the other parent. If they were in a bad mood, pick someone else. Do you want to be yelled at or cried to?

I remember, in one of my most vulnerable conversations with my stepmother, she explained how difficult it was for her to not know what days we were coming over and for her to have to explain to her children when to expect to see us. And I finally said something that to me felt incredibly emancipatory. I was like, "You know what? No adult here has *ever* acknowledged how much it sucks to be Lena and me."

My mom tried a lot, I will give her a ton of credit. She acknowledged that it was hard. She tried to be flexible and chill about scheduling. And I absolutely see where my father was coming from in terms of the fact that he did have less time with us in the custody schedule. But ultimately, all the adults were competing and also they didn't speak to one another, so most of their pain and sadness got filtered down to pressure on Lena and me to perform. To make each weekend *fun*. To make each weeknight dinner conversation *engaging*. To make every holiday *the best*.

It became clear that the easiest way to take pressure off, or at least to not add to our parents' stress, was to be Good Kids. And so we were. I don't think it ever occurred to either Lena or me to rebel in any way. We didn't want to make our mom sad or our dad disappointed or our stepmom angry. Our childhood was tap-dancing on eggshells.

I'm sure my parents aren't going to like reading this. I apologize to them, because so much of the pressure came from love and necessity. I think my mom and dad did their best and I love the shit out of them. I cry if I even think about them. They're both still alive, I just miss them so much because we live far apart and I see them only a few times each year! I cried writing this because I don't want to hurt them again; it's my biggest fear of all time. But I also look back at my childhood and think, *My fucking God, those kids*—Lena and I—*needed a break*.

I talked to my little sister Olivia once about how at Papa's house— where she lived full-time—there was no such thing as sitting on the couch. If you sat on the couch, it was to watch a family movie. If someone caught you just sitting around, you were asked to do something. Chores or childcare were the most common order, sometimes homework. Occasionally, there was an order to go outside and do something active, but even that had the tinge of compulsion. For example, in the summer my stepmom used to open the pool, which was shaded and did not have a heater, making it frigid. She would then harangue us all into going swimming so that she got her money's worth out of the pool opening, which was not logically sound at all, since the pool opening was already paid for and therefore a sunk cost. In my family, you did not expect your weekends or summers or breaks to be relaxing.

My mom's own upbringing in many ways mirrored this, with chores and responsibility being core aspects of being a good family member, with misbehavior out of the question. You behaved *or else*. I think my youth provided a whole lot more warmth than hers, and tons more love, but I still think that the concept of family for me in many ways centered around obligation. The ideas of duty and love became tidally locked for me. You love these people so you do things for them, even—especially—when you don't want to.

It's not that I thought I would get in trouble if I didn't oblige, but I never tested the theory. Lena and I never snuck out or got grounded or broke curfew or anything. The only rule we broke with any regularity was when our mom would tape a to-do list on the TV in the summer and we had to do everything on the list before we watched anything. (There was *always* a list, because God forbid we not "be productive.") We just moved the list and watched TV and then hurried to do the chores in the last hour before she got home. And once or twice we skipped hockey practice. But we were good; we were always, always good. It wasn't because we were going to get in trouble, or be grounded, or lose our parents' love or anything. The major incentive for behaving was simply to make our parents' lives easier.

I think Lena and I both recognized the obvious hard work and love our parents put into raising us, and to misbehave or to do something "foolish" or financially unsound was to dishonor that. It's what kept me in a "practical" college major, it's what made me not study abroad, it's what made me not want to try cocaine ever because what if it's laced with fentanyl or you have an unruptured brain aneurysm and you try coke once and die and then someone has to call your parents and be like, "Yeah, your idiot child did coke once and died." I did as much as possible to keep them from having to worry about me any more than they already were. My cousin had also died when I was in high school, and my mom repeatedly made it clear that we *couldn't* die, which is obviously not how the world works, but there was *a lot* of pressure to stay safe. We were good because it was easy for them, and because it was expected of us. We were good because it was what you did.

I put in *a lot* of effort to be a good kid who didn't require work from them because they were both already overworked as it was— my mom as a single mom of two with a full-time job, and my dad as a father of five who owned his own business and worked eighty-plus-hour weeks. Lena and I knew that family meant pitching in. It meant packing your own lunch and calling your own doctors. It meant babysitting and laundry and dishes and cleaning bathrooms and grocery shopping. But it also meant giving each parent a lot of quality time, being home for dinners, doing your homework without being asked, not being late to check in with them on a night out, being generally responsible for your own shit so they didn't have to take on more. I do not want to suggest that we did all of this perfectly all the time. We were children! We messed up a lot! The expectations, however, were *sky-fucking-high*.

I don't know that I resent this per se; *resent* doesn't seem like the right word at all to me. It's too blunt and one-sided. It's about anger and bitterness, which are not what I feel when I think about my parents. And their impossibly high expectations have helped in many ways. I went to a great school on scholarship, as did my sister.

We both got great grades and did well. Neither of us smoked ever or drank until college. We're both extremely hardworking. I still can't, for example, go a whole day without doing something productive. I give *a lot* to people I am close to. I know I have done well not just from the material goods that my parents gave me, but from their expectations in regard to how I ought to behave. But there is still a bit of . . . soreness . . . I have around the fact that so much was asked of Lena and me so young.

Look, pretty much everything I have I owe to my parents; I *fully* recognize that. But I also recognize *now*—which I didn't recognize until the age of about twenty-two, when it hit me like a lightning bolt—that if they can be disappointed in *me*, I can also be disappointed in *them*. And sometimes, I am!

This revelation gave me a little more distance from them. It allowed me to do things like decide to never move back to St. Louis. It allowed me to take nonpractical trips to Europe with my best friend that my mother didn't think were fiscally responsible.* It allowed me to choose a career that my father (jokingly??) hates but which I adore. Of course, in a broad sense they support me no matter what, and I know that they want me to be happy most of all. My mom makes that very clear, and my dad occasionally lets it slip that that's his real goal for his kids. But they also have always had high expectations as well, which meant I always knew it was possible—easy, even—to disappoint them. And until I was farther away, I didn't understand that the door could swing both ways.

This realization bubbled up again recently when the pandemic hit. Both of my parents logically understood the virus; neither of them thought it was a hoax or manufactured in a lab or anything. But both of them—in their mid- to late sixties—took risks that I thought were foolish. They invited friends over or played hockey

---

* I often got asked, "How will this help your career?"

or had people in their house who weren't wearing masks or went to work like usual, and that's just what I heard about over the phone. Now, of course, they're adults and they can do what they want to do. There's also a limit on how good any of us can be at keeping a deadly virus at bay through personal action. Safety is relative and often a false feeling, and I get that. My mother frequently pointed out the things that *I* was doing that were similar,* despite the fact that with thirty-eight years on me, she was at much higher risk. My dad just full-on did normal-life activities, despite my nagging him.

I kept wanting to scream at them, "I DIDN'T DO COCAINE IN COLLEGE SO YOU TWO WOULDN'T WORRY!!" Or, "REMEMBER WHEN YOU DIDN'T 'GET' WHY I WANTED TO SEE FRIENDS, PAPA? AND YOU MADE ME STAY HOME INSTEAD AND HAVE FAMILY TIME??? WHERE IS THAT INTROVERT ENERGY NOW? STAY HOME!!!" I felt the full imbalance of power, perhaps of respect. I had tried *so hard* to be good so they wouldn't worry, and I felt they were sometimes only trying a medium amount. At times my parents simply didn't seem as concerned as I was that they might die. And there was nothing I could do about it, other than nag them.

Maybe I self-policed too much as a teenager; maybe they didn't intend for Lena and me to take them so seriously; maybe they didn't realize how high their expectations were. Maybe *I* always put too much importance on what they wanted out of me. Maybe I had some room to rebel more, mess up more. And they would have loved me anyway, just as I love them anyway now. I have to let go of the idea that they're living their life for me, just as I let go of the

---

* For example, I had one friend who was on lockdown (not leaving her house except for groceries) from the same exact date that my boyfriend and I were, so we all decided to basically make a pod together from the get-go because she lived alone. She came over once a week.

idea that I was living my life for them. It's all part of the untangling of the apron strings, not in one single moment but many of them. Eventually you have to become your own person and not live for your mother's approval or your father's approval or even your daughter's approval.

Although, based on their pandemic response, I feel like I should have done a whole lot more sneaking out.

What I Wouldn't Give to
Be a Teen in a Coke Ad

The way I thought youth would go is incredibly similar to a certain Coca-Cola commercial that used to play before the movies. Actually, I may be combining about six different Coke commercials, because frankly, they're all pretty similar, but the way I remember this one is that a beautiful girl with gorgeous, shiny, perfect hair and a Polly Pocket–size body goes to a carnival and meets a "hot" teenage guy* and one of them is on a Ferris wheel and they're both drinking fountain Cokes. There are no parents in the ad, no acne, no homework; I think the guy comes to the carnival with friends but I can't be sure. There is very little if any talking. It's horny but in a supremely tame, manageable way. The vibe is you long for the hot girl in your honors algebra class and then you two hold hands on the Tilt-A-Whirl and then three days later you kiss in the field that used to be a drive-in movie theater. The youth this Coke commercial was selling was one where you live in an area that has fireflies and ice

---

* It feels gross to say that about a teenager but he's supposed to be hot for a teenager in the commercial. I don't know!!!

cream trucks in the summer, but no racism or poverty at any time of year.

That's what I think of when I think of youth. Not that I thought life would be *exactly* like that—who walks around drinking a fountain Coke? But the commercial upholds two of the tenets of youth, the things that all American teenagers are apparently promised as part of the teen experience: attractiveness and irresponsibility.

By *attractiveness*, I don't mean base-level hotness, I mean being desired by others. I mean quite literally being attract*ive*—attracting the wanting of others, people yearning for you in sexual ways. These two crazy Coke-drinking kids are horny for each other, and they honestly probably had a lot of other options at their school as far as whom to meet at the carnival. By *irresponsibility*, I don't mean the abdication of responsibility, but rather the sheer *lack* of it. No one in the commercial is *working* at the carnival. No one is a teen parent. No one even has SAT prep classes the next morning at 9 a.m. The world of the Coke commercial, like my platonic ideal of youth, is carefree and romantic.

Of course, so few of us get either attractiveness or irresponsibility, let alone both of those things, out of our childhoods. For pretty much everyone who is not rich *and* white, you're unlikely to be able to relish those particular benefits of being young. Certainly gender plays a huge factor, as does being cis. If you're a girl, for example, you're more likely to have an expectation of attractiveness, and if you're a boy, you're more likely to have an expectation of being irresponsible. But the expectations of both attractiveness and irresponsibility apply to everyone to some extent, to be sure. We also expect that, for the most part, young men are in their "sexual prime"* and that young women aren't yet taking on the role of caretaker. I don't think most people actually had the experience of being desired and having nothing to

---

* Gross gross, sorry to use that phrase.

worry about, but I *do* think that's what we all feel like we were promised out of youth.

I experienced neither.

Perhaps even more than being overweight, what kept me from feeling like I could experience *true* youth was that I helped raise my siblings who are seven, nine, and twelve years younger than I am.*

I changed hundreds of diapers. I was thrown up on more times than I can count. I helped kids with homework, I made their dinner, I packed lunches, I took them to skating practice before school and picked them up afterward. I was involved in, although not solely responsible for, things like driving lessons, college move-in, and college move-out. Off the top of my head, I know what age kids usually start crawling, eating solid foods, talking, walking, and texting their crushes. I know about teething necklaces, snaps versus zippers on onesies, PSAT registration, and dorm mini fridges. I know about cradle cap and Apgar scores. I had a car seat in my car all throughout high school. The first week of college someone made fun of me for pushing glasses away from the edge of the dining hall tables so that they didn't get knocked over. I was so used to living with toddlers that it did not occur to me that this was a weird thing to do. While I was not a parent, I did a lot of parent*ing.*

For a lot of reasons, many obvious, this eroded my youth. I remember mentioning to a therapist that I started doing my own laundry at one house at age seven. She stopped me and said in that grating tone that therapists sometimes use when they think they're being gentle with you, "You were forced to hypermature. Do you get that?" After

---

* I never know how to word how I helped with my siblings' care. There's likely no way to describe my role in a way that is fair to all parties involved. My stepmother and father will likely downplay what my older sister Lena and I did. I will probably (accidentally) exaggerate it. This is what it felt like to *me*—because I am the protagonist of this book and my father and stepmother are more than welcome to write their own books about my childhood years, should they choose.

that session, I stopped going to her as a therapist because I was like, "Yeah, no fucking shit."* When you're asked to care for yourself at too young of an age, you're forced to become a responsible party, and when you're asked to care for *others*, well, you're simply not going to make it out of childhood irresponsible in almost any way.

I'm not sure which came first: being responsible or not being invited to do fun things. I *think* I was pretty much always a good kid, so the responsibility probably came first. But I'm sure that my friends expected me to on some level grow out of it, to relax my rigidity on living up to parental expectations. Most of my friends grew from good kids to a-bit-less-good teenagers in the classic ways. I did not. When it became clear that I wasn't going to do the teenage version of "growing up"—becoming insubordinate—it became easier for my friends to exclude me.

I already worried about being left out because of my weight. Unlike my average-weight friends, I didn't attract anyone; an under-talked-about truth is that most friend groups past the age of like twelve revolve around people being attracted to one another. One girl likes this guy, who has a crush on this girl, who used to date that guy who is currently dating this girl and on and on. The motivation around *a lot* of youthful hangouts is simply the chance to be around your crush. I was *not* part of that. No one in the group of guys we hung out with was hoping that I would show up. I was a distraction at best and a detraction at worst. There was no *need* for me to be somewhere, especially if the goal of the night was to get drunk and hook up. I wasn't going to do either, because I was responsible and fat, and so it became easy—natural, even—to exclude me from things. If you lose the opportunity to be irresponsible and attractive, it only further reinforces that you aren't those things.

---

* This was our fifth session and she had just come to the conclusion that I maybe grew up too fast? Yeah, I know. Let's keep it moving, Lisa. (All therapists are named Lisa.)

When I *was* invited to things, I was anxious, a worrier. I wanted to follow the rules and do the right thing. If someone's mom said don't go on the roof at the beginning of the night, I was the person three hours later reminding everyone, "Hey, Mrs. Ford said not to get on the roof." I had been quasi-parenting for so long that I simply didn't know how to turn responsibility off. I started watching my siblings when I was about eleven; I was a nervous wreck. I had no idea what I was doing, and often I was left alone with them for longer periods of time than intended. Sometimes there was no adult around to relieve me. It was mostly okay—no one died or got seriously injured ever—and I often had help from Lena, who was three years older. But when you're responsible for kids for hours at a time, you learn to be on the lookout for everything; it becomes intrinsic to who you are. Like a drop of food coloring in water, it marks every part of you. All of a sudden, you're the kind of person who *is* responsible, rather than just the person who happens to be in charge at the moment. A large part of watching kids is worrying, vigilance. You have to make sure they don't choke on things or hit their head or jump in the pool without floaties on or pull the dog's tail while she's eating. The world becomes about safety when you're in charge of children, and good safety comes from never letting your guard down.

A similar thing happens when you're overweight. It seeps into every part of your life, into all your daily interactions; you have to be on constant alert in order to mitigate your fatness for others. People watch you eat, people watch you sit down, people watch you stand up, people watch you walk, run, shop, bike, drive. There is no escaping being overweight, and as the overweight party you're often asked to manage the situation: fill in the words that other people should call you, check to make sure the activity can accommodate fat people, make sure you'll fit in the seat, make sure you won't break the bench, make sure you won't slow the group down. You have to be fourteen steps ahead of the game, and should you for any reason encounter a situation where you being fat makes anyone else feel uncomfortable, you've also got to smooth things over and soothe everyone until they feel okay again. Despite all of that vigilance, all the responsibility foisted on fat people to make others feel comfortable, fat people are constantly infantilized. I can't tell you how many doctors tried to tell me that I was overeating because of my parents' divorce. Or how many adults felt certain that if they just *informed* me about healthy choices and calorie counting, I would figure out how to be thin. Strangers would comment when I got *Diet* Coke from a soda fountain at the movies. (No one even asks you if you actually *want* to be thin, by the way; *they* want you to be thin because it would be easier on them.) At the same time as I was making dinner for my siblings, no one trusted me to make dinner for myself.

I had much less control over watching my siblings than I did over my weight. If anyone wanted to take the reins on something in my life, I wish it would have been childcare rather than my diet. When Lena and I cared for our younger siblings, we weren't really asked. Not in a way that we could actually opt out of. If someone needed us to watch the kids, we watched the kids. It's not like you could say, "I don't feel like this, I'd rather stay up in my room playing *Sims: Livin' Large*, making my Sims fuck and die." That wasn't an option. If you got out of childcare it was due to something else taking precedent, like the SAT on a Saturday morning.

I often wonder what would have happened if Lena and I were boys. I know my brother goes into the basement to play video games for hours on end and is left mostly alone; we were so rarely left alone to do things for pure fun. I think that had Lena and I been male we would have been left with almost no caretaking duties. I think we would have been asked to do other things—lawn care, pool care, moving furniture, cleaning out the attic. But I don't think responsibility becomes a core tenet of your personality when you're asked to mow a lawn. There's a difference between making sure the grass looks good and keeping a human baby alive. Childcare and general care for others overwhelmingly falls on women; that isn't a secret. The gap in chores and household tasks starts early and continues into adulthood. Even in straight couples where the wife makes more money than the husband, mothers tend to do more work while men have more leisure time. The world expects women to clean up other peoples' messes, help other people process their emotions, know when everyone's birthday is, plan the vacations, look into care homes for aging parents, actually care for said aging parents, sign permission slips, take off work to bring a kid to the hospital to get a cast, find a physical therapist to help the kid after the cast comes off, call the vet to see if the dog has worms, notice when an adult sibling seems to be depressed, check in on the neighbor who just got divorced. And you're supposed to be socially adroit while handling all of this. That kind of care for and ease with other people is expected—not asked—of women in ways it will never be expected *or* asked of men.

Gender differences in the brain have been vastly overstated and reported on, so I'm not trying to sell you on the idea that Lady Brains somehow are better at caring or planning than men are. I'm saying this stuff is taught implicitly and explicitly from birth and it comes from seeing thousands of representations of women as caretakers and social virtuosos from a very young age. It's cyclical. The more you see women carrying conversations, holding babies, going to doctor's appointments, the more messaging women get that this is the norm, and the more they're required to be good at it.

One time in college, one of my guy friends got sick. Not like go-to-the-hospital sick or anything, just like a run-of-the-mill flu kind of sick. His mother drove three hours up to Los Angeles from San Diego to take care of him. I almost lost my mind. All my guy friends thought I was being rude, that clearly his mother wanted to do this, wanted to go to the store and buy Gatorade for her son (who lived a block away from said grocery store). Which is probably true. She probably did want to help her son out, but how on earth do you raise a child who asks their mom to come up from another city hours away when you have a cold? All the guys—all of them—thought this was reasonable and normal. None of the women I knew did.

Of course it was his mother coming up to take care of him. There's a reason it's rare for someone to have their father as an emergency contact. Men aren't trained to be caregivers, women are. And it's fucking exhausting. When I was younger, I used to say that I'd have kids if I got to be a dad. I was mostly being trite, but there's a veneer of truth to it as well. The amount of work women have to do—most of it unpaid—in the service of others, and the expectation that they simply will play along with no questions asked, is infuriating.

I also wonder what would have happened if I'd been a fat guy. There is a lot of stigma for anyone overweight, so I'm not trying to take away or diminish anyone's pain. I do, however, think that the emphasis that society puts on women's bodies is overwhelming for even the most conventionally attractive women, and to not fit the standard—for whatever reason, not just being overweight—is painful. I think we allow men, and especially white men, a lot more grace for perceived flaws. We let overweight men be funny and rich and powerful, or at least a friendly guy. We let them have narratives that aren't just "Here is a fat man." We *rarely* let overweight women do that. Being an overweight girl is a transgression. The agreement when you're a young woman is that you'll be consumable, attractive, enticing. It's a sick, bad system. But being overweight and unwanted in that system is excruciating. The area your value supposedly lies in—the body—is said to be worthless, less than worthless: actively bad. Now, none of that is true. And of course, there are plenty of people who are attracted to people who happen to be fat. But that is not the story you get told when you're young and fat. And that's especially not the story you get told if you're a young fat woman.

To put it simply, I think I would have gotten more youth if I had been born male. I think I would have had both beds and excuses made *for* me by the women around me. I think I would have learned to do laundry later (or never). I think I wouldn't have gotten a big talk about how my grades were slipping when I got a few Bs on a progress report, because people would have assumed I was doing my best. I don't *wish* by any means that I had been born male; I think I wouldn't have had the emotional support to deal with certain parts of my childhood if I were male. I think I would have been angrier and less likely to reach out for help. I think my emotional and mental health would have suffered. But there's one thing I believe very deeply: I think I would have gotten more youth.

Instead, I feel deeply the lacunae of my childhood. I think most people do. I think that when you don't get the adolescence you think you were owed—not that any of us is actually owed anything—you start to chafe when you reach adulthood. The shameful stamp of being a late bloomer lingers. It's what so often leads people to abandon good things for fun things, like cheating on a partner or leaving a family or quitting a salaried job to open a jungle-themed bar in Amarillo. If you didn't get the youth you feel you deserved, you often spend your life chasing it, looking for chances to make harmful, irresponsible decisions or basing your actions around people who find you attractive.

But you can't go back. You can't re-create true youth, where someone will care for you and clean up your messes, where people will come to your birthday, where a hot stranger will beg you to have sex in the bar bathroom.* I mean *some*times some of those things happen for a moment, but they aren't promised, and they usually don't come around often. You can spend your life chasing

---

* Unless, of course, you're extremely wealthy. Or extremely hot. Or an average white guy.

youth if you want. I know some adults like that. Frankly, to lay myself perfectly bare to you—the point of this book, some would say—*I* am like that. I have spent a surprising* amount of time and energy longing for, trying to re-create, raging against my lost youth. But I don't think it really works. The adults I know who are like this—those who are convinced their better years are not just behind them but never happened—well, they're lost. The best tactic I've found, and maybe I'm wrong—I'm wrong about a lot of things—is to mourn. Allow yourself to get really, deeply, unimaginably sad about the fact that you had to work two jobs in high school or that you didn't go to prom or that your parents were too busy to teach you how to drive or that you didn't have money for a car or that no one kissed you until you were twenty-seven. All of those things are sad and fucked! They aren't the worst thing in the world, but you don't get to mourn only one sad thing in your life. You get an unlimited amount of mourning.

Of course, mourning isn't *just* about sadness, and it's certainly not just about death. At least not the literal death of another human being. Mourning is about loss and ritual. It's about relearning how you relate to the world. It's about finding small moments where you accept what happened, even if that thing is sad and fucked. It's about learning how to *sometimes* embrace that you're an adult now and that you've kissed only two people and you're never going to be a world-traveling slut like you expected. I'm not saying you're not going to be bitter that you never got to study abroad or go to your dream school. I'm not saying you should move on and let go and ignore the loss. I'm saying you should confront it. Confront it head-on before you let your lost youth shape too much of your adulthood. If you're not careful, everything in life becomes about how you didn't get sucked off in a movie theater when you were

---

* Embarrassing.

fourteen, and that's not the way to spend your one wild and precious life.

What I get now—not that I always accept it—is that I'm never going to stop being responsible. And while I've lost some weight, I still have parts of my youth that I missed out on because of my size. I'm not painting over anything, or pretending like everything was beautiful and nothing hurt. I'm just trying to remember that no one got exactly the youth they wanted, that almost everyone was lost and in pain and felt unpopular and unloved and weird. Almost everyone would have done it differently if they were in charge. I didn't get to be wild and free, but I also possibly didn't get hurt as much, or at least not in the same ways. I became funny and smart and I read a lot and I got good grades and I got into a college I might not have if I had more to do on the weekends. And after years of childcare, I'm totally unfazed by people throwing up on me. So it wasn't all bad. But I still often wish I'd gotten to study abroad or sneak out of the house or make out in someone's parents' basement on a beanbag.

Instead of believing that I was owed a certain amount of irresponsible fun and sluttiness, instead of trying to go out and chase those things in reckless and potentially unhealthy or harmful ways, I just try to be aware. I try to remember why I'm sad, I try to mourn it. I try to find things in my life that feel exciting and fulfilling and carefree that aren't about being wild. I've worked hard to try to find the value of being steady, of doing the right thing again and again, of behaving. In a lot of ways, I was ready for adulthood before it came. While everyone else was giving hand jobs in Jettas, I was calling doctors' offices and arranging college admissions interviews and fish-hooking choking hazards out of kids' mouths. So I'm ready now. I'm less fun than a lot of people my age, but I'm pretty good at taking care of things and people. I'm good at showing up. I've been doing this shit for a while.

Things I Want My Little Sisters to Know, Which I Will Write Here Since They Aren't Texting Me Back Right Now

1. If the person you're sleeping with *always* makes you come over to their house and never wants to come to yours, that's a red flag. It means they don't want to put in effort, and as a woman, you will almost always naturally put in more effort than the situation requires, so find someone who also puts in more than the bare minimum.

2. Deodorant also works great under your boobs.

3. You're going to make a ton of bad choices just because you have a crush on someone. Embrace it. The two most luxurious things in the world are having your bed made for you when you stay at a hotel and doing stupid shit for the sake of a crush. Nothing in the world feels as youthful or carefree as making a medium-size dumb choice for a hot person.

4. Speaking of which, the only thing worse than having a crush on someone is not having a crush on anyone. Always maintain a crush. It's a motivator. Horniness will get you to an 8 a.m. class better than coffee.

5. Don't buy the books for your college classes until at least the second week, if at all. You can usually fake having read them.

6. For the love of God, pay more to get a gel manicure. There's no point in getting a regular manicure. You've just paid fifteen dollars to smudge your nail polish within seconds of leaving the salon.

7. Spend as little time as possible in your Chill Girl phase. It's like driving through Kansas; you might have to do it to get to your destination, but don't linger.

8. Keep deodorant in the car, but the spray-on kind. The regular sticks melt. I would also recommend keeping a set of tweezers in the car. We're Italian; they only get more useful as we age.

9. Always wake up early enough to get free breakfast at the hotel. Even if you need to scuttle downstairs and grab a waffle and bring it back up to your room and fall asleep. Life presents so few opportunities like that, you have to take advantage of those rare ones.

10. Detail clean your car before you even consider selling it. It will make you feel like you have a new car for about $100.

11. Sweaters and jackets are some of the easiest things to buy second-hand because the sizing is somewhat imprecise. You almost never need to buy a new sweater.

12. If you roast almost any vegetable with salt and pepper and olive oil, people are going to think you're a real adult. If it's squash or sweet potatoes, add a pinch of brown sugar.

13. Don't worry about fighting aging; you're going to get old. Accept it.

14. Learn to be good at lying to people whenever you need to. Especially if it's to creepy men trying to get you to sleep with them. Everyone lies.

15. At some point, you will realize how UnFun you are, perhaps when you skip a party to get in bed by 10 p.m. because you have to finish an essay and twenty pages of reading tomorrow. This is a realization most women in our family face. It will sting, but eventually you will embrace it. Being unfun is ultimately freeing.

16. Remember that you do not need to be friends with your roommates. You need to be roommates with them. The two are distinct! It's not always better to live with a friend. Sometimes at the end of a long day you just want to come home to tacit silence.

17. You can find ways to be okay with just about any partner. I know that's not what other people tell you, but it's true. Pick someone you like being around. A lot.

18. Take thirty minutes out of your life and go buy good bobby pins (the kind that are rounded instead of flat). Just buy a metric ass-ton of bobby pins. Put them everywhere in your house. Think you have enough? Buy more.

19. Adulthood often means choosing between two really shitty options. Or two really good but mutually exclusive options. Remember, if there were one really good choice and one really bad one, you would have already made your decision. Imagine yourself at eighty years old (if climate change doesn't kill us by then) looking back on your life. What will future you have wanted current you to do?

20. Do work first. Take care of what you have to do first and then relax later. Work as hard as you can without hurting your mental health when you're young.

21. Send every single scary text.

22. The secret to finding a good partner is to look for someone else who also did all the work in group projects.

23. Every time you have a problem with your partner or with your boss or with your friend, you are probably being *much* more reasonable than you think. You're probably *under*reacting. Hold the line; do not move your boundaries.

24. Write things down about your parents so that you have those memories. Take videos. Take notes. Make voice recordings. Our parents are old as shit, sorry.

25. Learn how to make three signature dishes. A side, a dessert, and a showstopper that really impresses. My three go-tos are (1) Papa's arugula salad, which is *always* a banger, (2) gooey butter cake because it's easy and no one outside of St. Louis knows what it is, so it kills, and (3) bagna càuda, because again, no one knows what the fuck it is, so you virtually can't mess it

up and *everyone* likes butter and garlic. Plus, because it involves cooking, it *seems* like you're really doing something.

26. If someone breaks up with you they suck and you should call your best friend so you guys can talk about how much they suck. They will remind you of all your ex's flaws, like when they thought Al Jazeera was a city.

27. If you haven't heard back after an interview, follow up, even if you think you're bothering them. Who cares if you're bothering a company?

28. Take ibuprofen and chug water as soon as you start crying or drinking. It will help the next morning.

29. Buy baby wipes. Have them on hand at all times. You'll find all kinds of uses for them. Real adults own baby wipes. And the realest adults realize there is no such thing as a flushable baby wipe. You're going to be paying for a new septic tank if you pull that.

30. When you reach your emotional limit, take a hot shower. When you're exhausted, take a cold one.

31. Text your crush back right away if you want to. Who gives a shit? Anyone who gives a shit is weird and has no business dating you.

32. Learn how to apologize sincerely—listen to how you harmed someone; don't defend yourself; take responsibility. Even more important, learn how to apologize when you didn't *intend* to do anything wrong.

33. Voice your expectations. Do not wait on anyone to guess them. Do not get upset with people for not guessing them.

34. Sometimes you need to quit when things get hard. Don't do shit you dread if you can avoid it. Don't stick with things just because you made a commitment if it's making you miserable. Get out. Life is short. Sure, there's light at the end of the tunnel, but there's also light everywhere if you get out of the damn tunnel.

The Idea Is to Look Like an Idiot

M y father has a rule. He actually has loads of them: Never lean your seat back on an airplane, never stand up during a sporting event or concert, never use your horn unless it is the *only* way to prevent an accident. Another rule he has is that he will not dance with any of his daughters at their weddings; my sister got married last year and they did not have a father-daughter dance. He himself has been married four times and to my knowledge he danced at none of the weddings. In fact, I have never seen him dance, period.

I grew up, therefore, with the understanding that dancing was an embarrassing thing to do with your body, unless, of course, you were one of the titular seven brothers in the wood-chopping scene of *Seven Brides for Seven Brothers*, or you were in *West Side Story* as a horny, dancing, gang-affiliated teen, or perhaps if you were Cha Cha DiGregorio. In the movie musicals of my youth, of which I watched many, dancing was not just without shame, but celebrated. I mean, have you *seen* Vera-Ellen's toe taps in *White Christmas*? But I understood that normal, everyday people were not to dance.

Especially if you had anything less than a perfect body.

Being a good dancer takes a whole lot of things: rhythm, practice, innate musicality. It does not take having a thin body. That is not a requirement. There are many, many phenomenal dancers who are not thin. But that is not something I was aware of growing up. The most I had seen of a fat person dancing was Chris Farley as a Chippendales stripper on *Saturday Night Live* in the '90s. I recently rewatched the sketch out of curiosity and realized that Chris Farley is an *excellent* dancer. He's keeping up with fucking Patrick Swayze. And still, the joke is: Ha-ha-ha, what if fat people were good at dancing and people took them seriously?

Growing up, I just knew that dancing, like many things, was something I was not supposed to do with my fat body. For fuck's sake, some of my *thin* friends got made fun of when they danced. I was certainly not supposed to.

The thing about dancing circa middle school is that the environment in which it occurs sets you up to feel awful. No actually fun dancing is happening at 7 p.m. in a school gym under the watchful gaze of a vice principal. School dances are both heaven and hell. Movies and TV will tell you that they're a place to hang your dreams. They're a night for declarations of love and decampments of virginity. Supposedly.

In my experience, the school dance itself is rarely the site of any excitement. The only thing I ever remember "happening" at a school dance was in sixth grade, in the half darkness of the Nipher Middle School gym when Mrs. Miller pulled Lexi K. (who was "new," in that she'd moved to the district three years prior) out into the fluorescent-lit hallway to admonish her for grinding on two eighth graders. Frankly, I didn't even see it happen. I can't even be sure that she was guilty of this infamous middle school crime. But I found out within minutes via the strong school-dance whisper network. After that, nothing exciting ever happened at a dance that I recall. And there were multiple dances a year! In high school, we had The Hatchet Hop (ostensibly a Sadie Hawkins dance, although that was loosely followed), prom for juniors and seniors and the various people they were dating, and then the Friendship Dance, a dance we shared with our crosstown football rivals before The Big Game. At Friendship my freshman year, I met Karlie Kloss, who was still attending high school at the time in between being an international model. She said nothing to me and talked to my friends for half a minute while I ogled her tiny clavicle. So, I guess that happened at a school dance.

Really, any and all intrigue happened either before or after the actual event. Beforehand, for weeks, you had to worry and wonder about getting asked to the dance. I, of course, did not. But some people did. Getting asked to a dance is a major *thing*. On the one hand, I can't imagine anything else so benign as a promposal that I wish to eradicate from the earth with such fervor. On the other, I wonder if my outsize response to them is in some small way a case of sour grapes. I don't think that had I been asked to a school dance I would all of a sudden find elaborate promposals sweet and not the deranged behavior of popular teenagers with too much time and money on their hands. But I do wonder if I would be less miffed. And then afterward comes the drugs and sex and alcohol. I presume.

The only thing I ever did at a school dance was stand on the side-lines and watch my friends engage in normal behavior. My most generous, patient friends tried to get me to join in, but I had *no idea* what I was doing since I'd never danced before—and in front of literally everyone I knew outside of my family seemed like a bad place to start. I used to mostly make fun of people for having a good time and take photos for my friends who weren't deeply ashamed of their appearance. One entire school dance I spent in the girls' bathroom comforting my friend Abbey about a boyfriend debacle. He was Mormon and therefore unwilling/unable to dance with her, which she was sad about. I remember standing outside of the stall, talking to her, hoping that she would be filled with gratitude for me spending the night with her when I could have been dancing. Although I think we both knew that the reason I was in the bathroom with her to begin with was that I was not really going to dance. Certainly not with anyone other than female friends in small, semiprivate bursts where I felt no one would see me.

The idea of dancing with a guy I went to school with seemed as likely as Tony Shalhoub walking into the school gym and doing a striptease. I think the first time I *ever* danced with a guy at all, I was eighteen years old and it was part of a school play. One reason I'm still so hung up on this is that it's a rite of passage, I feel, to grind on a person. Should it be? Debatable. But dance is pretty intrinsic to human connection, if not human romancing. Even bigger than my grievance over not being a part of a Classic Youth Moment, however, is that it turns out that I fucking *love* dancing.

I know. I was as shocked as you are.

One of my biggest fears about getting older is how much less socially appropriate it is to go out dancing with your friends. People always push back against this and are like, "You don't have to let that stop you!" But who wants to be the weird forty-seven-year-old in a bar for twentysomethings? Not me. And I'm not going to get into line dancing or square dancing or some other shit that older white people love. I'm not doing it. I do not want to learn choreography. I want to drink two to four glasses of wine and be a little dance-floor slut while "What the Hell" by Avril Lavigne plays.

I do not have any desire to do a bunch of drugs or go actually clubbing like a cool, interesting young person. I do not want to go to anything that has a line out the door. I want to go to a bar where I know all the words to all the songs and I want to dance with my friends and *only* my friends. I do not want people (men) to come up and talk to me or even dance with me. Yes, I've evolved! Dancing with men no longer is of interest to me; men are, on average, shy and stiff about the whole ordeal, and almost never more enthusiastic or fun than my friends and I are. They seem mostly to be either uncomfortable or aggressive; I sympathize with the former—I was you! I was uncomfortable with this!—and I have no patience for the latter.

Not that I'm getting many offers to be danced with or anything. I go out dancing *a lot*. I try to go out almost every weekend, and very rarely am I in any way approached, be it to dance or to talk. (This may be in part because I mostly go to bars that straight cis men don't frequent, more fools they.) I think this is somewhat true everywhere, but I've traveled to other cities and haven't found men as chary as in Los Angeles. The men of Los Angeles stand in groups with the friends they already have, and the normal, kind, regular guys pretty much leave everyone alone. And then you'll have one or two dickish ones who will follow someone around for the whole night, purposely ignoring any hints of disinterest.

And now I *love* it. I love being left alone. I love not being asked to dance by anyone. I love being able to dance like a complete fool and have not a care in a world whether it impresses, disgusts, or interests any man in the vicinity. I love that I get to do something with my body that I thoroughly enjoy doing that's for me and no one else. I love dancing and I wish I would have let myself do it during all of those school dances with friends where I knew the words to every song and men left me alone.

Of course, it's much easier to say that now that I have the help of vodka.

How to Hate Yourself Enough That Men Will Like You (but Not So Much That They'll Be Turned Off)

I grew up in houses dominated by women. Not just headed by women, but numerically imbalanced in favor of women. At my mom's, before we left for college, it was just her, Lena, and me.* And at my dad's there was my stepmom and sisters Lena and Olivia and Giovana and me, outnumbering my dad and brother Angelo. Also, my dad is not exactly the traditional hypermasculine American dad; he is much more interested in fashion than in football. He likes philosophy and hair products in about equal measure. Like all good Italians, he wears a lot of jewelry and cries easily. We talk often about death and how hot Raquel Welch was in the '60s. None of my friends' dads or brothers were like this. I say this because it took me a while to understand how American straight cis men, as a gen-

---

* Except for one year when my mom remarried and then divorced a guy. But we won't count that. Now she's married to someone wonderful, my stepdad, Jim, and we absolutely will count that.

eral group, behaved. This meant I came late to the universal truth that the chiller you are the more (straight cis) guys like you. For a while, I was blissfully unaware of the near-universal veneration of the low-maintenance girl.

Everyone in my family talked *all the time*.* We talked quickly, we talked constantly, we talked over each other in collaborative, rather than competitive, ways.† Perhaps the most illustrative example of this is that Lena and my mom and I used to watch *Gilmore Girls* and *none* of us realized that the characters spoke really, *really* fast. It might not *seem* like talking is connected to being low-maintenance or chill, but I promise you, how much you talk as a woman and how fast matters. As soon as we're around men, women are expected to match *their* conversation style. It's not like men become more excitable or ask more questions or hedge their statements when they're around women. Instead, we're expected to speak more assuredly although less frequently; we're expected to adapt to the communication patterns more commonly preferred by men.

Outside of my parents' houses, I was friends almost exclusively with other girls. While I was boy-crazy from the age of about four, I wasn't about to go as far as *talking* to guys, which left me with a dearth of knowledge of what they were like and what they liked. I occupied a weird space in my high school because I was fat but also really good at school *and* a theater kid *and* the class clown.‡ This led me, bizarrely, to be friends with fairly popular girls. Not the pierced-belly-button, sleeping-with-guys-who-drove-jeeps popular girls, but like the straight-As and JV-field-hockey-team popular

---

* We still do!

† A hallmark of female conversation.

‡ The phrase *class clown* gives me hives. Why isn't there a better way to describe this?

girls. I was hitting above my weight* when it came to friends. I was the one who very clearly stuck out in the friend group.

When we entered high school at fourteen, my friends—like me—weren't doing drugs or drinking or having sex. We were all getting good grades together. The first year of high school, I wasn't excluded from much other than clothing-related events—formal dress swaps, group Halloween costumes, borrowing pajamas for impromptu sleepovers—because the shit we were doing at that point was, frankly, too tame not to include me. We were all getting driven around in our moms' minivans to play Wii tennis in someone's basement. My friends were buying denim miniskirts and North Face jackets while I shopped in the adult section of Old Navy and Target for more modest and sophisticated (cringeworthy) clothing to try to hide how fat I was. We were having rapid-fire conversations that consisted of about 85 percent laughter and inside jokes. We were loud and no doubt "annoying"† and incredibly *free*.

As soon as guys got folded into the herd, though, my position within the friend group became precarious. I was more of a liability. All of a sudden my jokes went "too far," my voice was "too loud," I was "too much." See, once you're around men, you're *supposed* to modify your behavior. You're supposed to give them the floor, to tone your shit down. All my friends knew this, and I guess in a way I did too. But while they were willing to demur, I couldn't figure out how to modulate myself for very long. I wasn't good at being quiet, at deferring. And I was *not* hot enough to get away with being annoying. When you start scaring off or bothering men, you become a problem.

Sophomore year, I was still mostly doing okay in the friend group. I was still funny and therefore sort of fun; we were all still in the same classes, too. More and more, my friends grew out of want-

---

* Not a pun, but kind of.
† A word that people *love* to throw at young women.

ing to hang out with just girls; every Friday and Saturday became about doing what the guys wanted to do. No one wanted to hang out and play *Sims* in someone's unfinished basement anymore. Now we could be drinking Smirnoff Ices and sitting on guys' laps in someone's unfinished basement. You know who you *don't* need in the second scenario? Your loud fat friend who is making fun of the whole situation and pointing out (loudly—did I say loudly??) how stupid this all is, how juvenile. Vying to be the center of attention worked just fine in a group of all girls going for walks in the small downtown area of my hometown. It was great for when we were building fire-pits in someone's backyard and I was making fun of myself, or when we were sitting in the back of Mr. Warren's social studies class and I was going on a comedic rant about our dreaded science teacher Mr. Muckerman. It was decidedly less desirable when that group of girls was trying to impress a group of boys.

Around the guys, I had nothing to do other than to make fun of other people for trying to get male attention because I was *not* getting male attention. Honestly, even tacit male acceptance would have been cool with me. But I was, for a myriad of complex reasons,* not even getting that. The more left out I was, the louder I got. The louder I got, the more left out I was. On top of it, I was convinced that the guys didn't like me because I was overweight— which probably had a kernel of truth to it. When I was hanging out with all girls, I didn't fixate on my weight so much, but now every single hangout felt loaded. I was either in a corner, seething about my station in life, talking shit to whoever was generous enough to hang out with me, *or* I was doing some obnoxious attention-seeking shit in the hopes that some guy would overlook literally every single thing I was laying out on the table and all of a sudden find me hot, fun, and fuckable. It quickly became apparent that no guy was going

---

* My looks and personality.

to do this, and I started to become bitter and resentful of all my friends who were giving hand jobs during movies and exchanging cheap plush toys for Valentine's Day or whatever it is teenagers do.

Other women don't ask you to be chill, as a general rule, unless they're in the presence of men. That under-the-table kick of "Be cool. We want them to like us" always felt like a betrayal to me in high school. I resented it. I resented that *we* were always the ones changing our behavior to fit the guys. I resented and I resisted at times, and it always backfired—most people want to fit in more than they want to make a statement. In high school, I wasn't even necessarily trying to make a Big Feminist Statement as much as I was confused as to why we had to talk more slowly, more quietly, more deferentially when guys came around. I got the rules, but I didn't get *why* they were the rules, and I wanted everyone else to question it too. Why couldn't guys simply learn how to keep up with us? To talk over one another, but not interrupt? To weave stories together and collaborate instead of compete in conversation? Why were *we* always adapting?

By the end of sophomore year of high school, most of my friends had pretty much stopped telling me about their lives. By the end of junior year, they stopped inviting me places. It was pretty easy for them because all they had to do was say, "Oh, I thought you were at your dad's that weekend," because my dad didn't really let me see friends. Because he got less time with Lena and me due to split custody, he *always* wanted us to be home during his days, so if we wanted to do anything with our friends, they had to come to his house, which is understandable, but he didn't live in the school district—he lived fifteen minutes away, which is a lot to ask teenagers who live down the block from one another. Additionally, there were always young children at my dad's house, so you had to be quiet, which meant that really only one or two people were allowed to come at a time. *Plus* if you ever invited anyone over, my stepmom would insist the *entire* house get both picked up and deep-cleaned, and because you were the one to invite people over, you had to do it. (Keep in mind that Lena and I owned about six items each in the entire house, *none* of which were in the common areas.) So I would have to clean an entire house of other people's shit (mostly baby toys) to ask one person to skip going to an event with twenty friends and instead come over to my dad's house farther away to eat a staid family dinner.

This created a built-in excuse for my friends to exclude me. I specifically remember calling one friend and crying and being like, "You *knew* I wasn't at my dad's. And if you didn't, you could still invite me." They assured me it was oversight and not exclusion that kept me from getting party invites, and I was hopeful enough to believe them. I always thought the invite would come *next* weekend. Looking back, it is very obvious to all of us (me and you) that they didn't want me around. I don't blame any of my then friends for their reaction to my oft-atrocious behavior in large (and occasionally small) groups. We were all The Worst.

Partially because of this repeated friend-rejection and partially because I wanted to have money to buy more of Target's affordable fashions, I got a job as soon as I legally could in Missouri at Cold Stone Creamery. I was the *only* one of my friends who had a job outside of babysitting, further drawing me away from that group, just as a matter of scheduling. At sixteen—the same time I got the job—I lost sixty pounds. I now had something to do on weekends (work a minimum-wage job) and I was, in my opinion, more appealing to guys. I was ready. Ready for *something*.*

Turns out that something was getting fired from Cold Stone by a woman named Karen who called me "sunshine" *while* firing me.

---

* This part of the book is thematically parallel to when Tony sings "Something's Coming" in *West Side Story*, except, unlike Tony, I don't get shot.

She also offered to let me keep my apron and hat, even though the cost had been deducted from my first paycheck, which meant that I *owned* those items. I got fired for reading a magazine while I was left to run the store alone because there was bad weather and the manager couldn't make it in. Yes, fired for not doing enough at an ice cream shop during a snowstorm. I'm still *extremely* bitter about this firing despite that leaving Cold Stone was a boon for me.

Because it was almost Christmas, my dad's company—an ice hockey equipment business—needed more box makers in the warehouse. If you're unfamiliar with warehouses, as I was, the job is literally just being told what size box to grab and then making it into a box and taping it up. This job offer from my father *terrified* me. I kept insisting that I could not do this job. I had never been inside a warehouse (privileged) or worked a job that wasn't designed for young, friendly teenage girls (privileged) and the unknown scared the shit out of me. I couldn't even *imagine* what the warehouse was like, who worked there, what the hierarchy was. I didn't feel protected by my dad being the boss (even though I *obviously* was), because my dad made it extremely clear that I'd have to work the hardest of anyone or he'd fire me.

But as my grandfather told my mother and my mother told me, "No job is above you and no job is beneath you," so I took the job. On the first day my dad came in and introduced me to a guy named Ben and said loudly, "If she does *anything* wrong, let me know; I'll fire her." He checked on this regularly, too. Once, he saw me eating lunch in the break room and took me aside to tell me not to because it looked lazy.

The hockey warehouse was a . . . magical place. Two of the first people I met were named Fudge and Nugget; most of the people working there had lost at least one tooth to hockey, and one guy simply stopped replacing his because they got knocked out too often. I was the only girl in the warehouse—I was younger than everyone else by at least five years, which, when you're seventeen, feels like twelve years—and I was coming after school to help out at what was most people's full-time job. I was silent for the first two weeks because I was so intimidated. Because of my dad being who he was, my coworkers tried for a few days not to cuss in front of me. They acted as if I was going back to him with tallies of who took the longest bathroom breaks and who kept falling asleep on piles of hockey bags.*

The two weeks of nervous silence bought me time to do something I had never done before: become a chill girl. This, a hockey equipment warehouse in the middle of the Christmas rush, was my first real exposure to men. I had actually *never before* been in a male-dominated group.† Unlike everyone at my high school, who had known me since first grade, none of the guys in the warehouse knew I'd been fat. None of them knew me as a know-it-all, straight-A kid. I mean, they probably got that vibe because I looked like a fucking horse girl, but they didn't have to sit with me in classes. They didn't see my hand shoot up for every single question. I had a chance—purchased with two weeks of staying silent out of fear of messing up—to start over and talk to guys. To be someone who guys wanted to talk to—someone chill. And to me, these guys were low-stakes risks in terms of talking to. I didn't know them outside of work, I was around them a few hours a week, they were older, we were clearly *not* going to date, I was leaving for college in a few months. This was my time to change everything that my last friend group had hated about me—not that I even had good insight on what that was, just various insecurities and presumptions.

---

* It was Fisher, I remember this clearly. He also broke two iPads and crashed the forklift.

† I played hockey for years on an all-girl team and had the option to play on my high school team but I was too nervous to try out because . . . men.

I figured—and I'm not exaggerating to say that I actually *thought* about this—that I could try on a new personality before college and by the time I left eight months later, I would be different. I would be an approachable, kind, upbeat girl who didn't talk too much. The kind of girl I had finally realized straight cis guys wanted.* Step one: Stay quiet. I learned to add to the joke rather than to be the one to make it; I learned either to ask questions or leave men alone, to not talk about myself, and to be happy but not in a giddy, grating kind of way; above all, I learned to not bother anyone else and to not let *anything* bother me. "Oh, it's no big deal!" was my motto. I worked almost as hard at being chill as I did at the actual job.

Within a month or so of working (and being a chill girl) in the hockey warehouse, I got asked out by a guy working there. Let's call him, out of an abundance of creativity, Hockey Warehouse Guy. He was not missing any teeth from hockey and he was vaguely hot and was very nice to me, even if he was constantly getting in disagreements at work (red flag!) and threatening to quit to his manager and anyone else who would listen (red flag!). When he asked me out, he was also twenty-three to my very legally convenient eighteen years and twelve days.

For our first date, he took me to his family's pizza restaurant and then a Blues game—yes, the Midwest is romantic. It was New Year's Eve and we didn't kiss, which was good because I'd never kissed anyone before. I couldn't eat because I was shaking the whole time—like actually shaking with adrenaline because I was on a *date*—and he thought I was cold, which I also was, because it was December and a hockey arena. Everyone at his family-owned pizza place stopped by our table and told me he was the best guy and that I had to treat him

---

* I know not all straight cis men literally want this. Or they say they don't. But when I was eighteen, the men I was meeting certainly did.

well, which I apparently took to heart because I kept dating him for almost two years after that.

Dating him felt like when you're on a road trip and you skip a rest stop because you don't *really* have to go but then you find out that was the last rest stop for miles and miles and there are not any obvious exit ramps. I had very few female friends that I was close to at this point, none whom I felt were going to be low-key about me dating some old guy, something I was deeply embarrassed about, so I had no one to ask questions like, "Is this normal?" or, "Do I even like him?" or, "What do I do if I don't like him?" I kept conflating the excitement of dating *someone* with excitement from dating *him*. I hadn't even kissed a guy before and this was so clearly my fucking shot.

He had dropped out of college after a couple of semesters about four years back, and did not intend—and could not afford—to go back. He lived with his mother and grandmother in a part of St. Louis I'd quite literally never even driven through before we met. His family was conservative, religious, and racist. He was a little bit of all three, and wouldn't admit to any of them. He liked country music and getting drunk at his family's farm. Other hobbies: me watching him play video games and me watching him and his one friend play video games. I lost my virginity to him with *Storage Wars* on in the background, turned up extra loud so that his grandmother wouldn't know he was having sex—despite the fact that I was spending the night in his room. Sex was another opportunity I had to be chill around him. I was the one, of the two of us, who wanted to have sex—he was mostly indifferent—and in that lay a lot of his power. The less he cared about having sex with me, the more I became desperate for sexual validation from him. But of course the *last* thing I wanted to show him was desperation.

He, naturally, was virulently anti-choice. He said once that if he ever had a girlfriend who got an abortion—not me, *necessarily*—he'd want to kill her. For a while, he stopped watching NHL games—

one of his only pastimes—because they were sponsored by Susan G. Komen, which funded abortions, according to him.*

I was chill about this.

Being anti-choice is one (terrible) thing. But he was also not that into protection. He refused to wear or buy condoms and I had no idea what I was doing buying them—or if he would wear them if I did. I had not even sat on a guy's lap before! How was I supposed to know which condoms to buy? Instead, I went and got on birth control. Paid for by my mother and remembered by *me*. A key part of being a chill girl is letting a guy not have to take any responsibility ever for his own behavior.

If you haven't taken birth control pills before, you have to wait a week before it starts working. During that week, he tried many times to put his dick just a little inside me. Without a condom on. Because who cares if I get pregnant? Not him. Unless I were to end said pregnancy, in which case he might want to kill me. Hypothetically.

I was chill about this.

My biggest opportunity to be chill came when his entire extended family was going up to his family's farmhouse—a very Missouri thing to do—and he invited me to come along. I hated his extended family because they were racist and awful, but of course I went along with it because That's What You Do, I thought. He and I had been to this farmhouse before with his friends, where I usually made food for everyone and cleaned up. When we stayed there with friends, we stayed in his grandmother's room, which was the "best" room of the house. The thing is, though, that he refused to have sex while we were there because it was his grandmother's room. Understandable! But also, why not pick another room so you can have sex with your girlfriend on "vacation"?†

---

* First of all, they did not fund abortions, and even if they did, good.
† Is going to a farmhouse that you own a vacation? Unknown!

This time, however, we were lower-priority guests, so we stayed in another room. I figured we still weren't going to have sex because his whole family was in the house and if you don't want to have sex in Grandma's room when she's not there, why would you want to have it in another room when she *is*? Regardless, I knew the drill at this point: we had sex when he wanted to because I was pretty much always up for it and he never was.

That night, we ended up in the living room watching a baseball game with his mom and someone else, whom I don't remember; all I know is that the guy fell asleep. Hockey Warehouse Guy and I were sharing a couch and his mom was sitting on another couch right next to us. He was drunk—*very* drunk. And he was finally ready to have sex. Under a throw blanket. With his mother in the room. A foot away from me. Fully awake.

I remember being embarrassed more than anything. I didn't want her to think I was the type of person to have sex in someone else's living room in front of their mother. IN FRONT OF THEIR MOTHER! I mean, what?! I told him no, and to stop a couple of times, and tried to pretend he was just being flirty and annoying rather than *actively trying to have sex with me*. I hoped his mother would say something, even something jokey along the lines of, "Hey, cut it out, you two."

But she didn't, and my noes had no effect, and he had sex with me on a couch with his mother a foot or two away and I didn't break up with him or even demand that we go home immediately or anything.

I was chill about this.

In some way, I felt like I had *asked* him to be more demonstrative of sexual interest in me and there it was! Exactly the thing I'd been asking for. It took me a decade to admit that what happened could qualify as rape. I *desperately* don't want to use that word—and in fact, outside of this book, I never have—because to me, at the time, it did not feel like what I had been taught rape would feel like (as if there is a certain monolithic experience of being violated). At the time, I didn't believe I would have stayed with someone who raped me, and since I stayed, it must not have been a big deal. I certainly didn't feel like I could wake up the next day after something like that and just keep going on with my life like usual. And I definitely didn't think I'd be the type of person to explain away similar things happening over and over just for the sake of feeling like he wanted me.

What I know now is that brains are extraordinarily good at normalizing mistreatment. We're really good at explaining to ourselves that bad sex is common and harmless and that sex you didn't want is the same as sex you simply didn't enjoy all that much, but those things aren't true.

I feel two ways about this situation now. On the one hand, I feel embarrassed that I didn't realize until ten years later with *a lot* of messaging about sexual assault that what happened to me could qualify as rape. On the other hand, I still don't want to call it that. I still *don't* call it that. I still say I've never been raped and I still don't think of myself as someone who has been. I feel like I didn't claim it soon enough, or it wasn't bad enough, or I can't remember enough of the details of what I said afterward and if something *that* bad happened to me, surely I'd remember all the details of the whole night. I feel like I wasn't harmed enough.

But that's not how it works.

The depressing truth is that my story is common, that so many people I know have similar experiences and feel like there's an excuse for why they happened, or an explanation for why it wasn't that bad. But that doesn't make what the other person did not assault. Or not rape. It doesn't change what happened.

I *get* why I didn't leave after that, or any of the other times we had questionable sexual encounters.* You don't leave because this is

---

* "Questionable sexual encounters" feels like it *really* lets him off the hook. I don't know. I don't know.

so pervasive as to seem normal, and what if you misunderstood, or what if you weren't being clear enough, and isn't sex kind of bad for women anyway?* I didn't leave because it was my first time dealing with not being listened to, with a man being in control of what happened between us, and because I had no practice doing anything else other than smoothing things over for men, then making sure *they* didn't feel bad when they hurt me.†

In addition to all this shit, which came up just rarely enough to not be a deal breaker, his life had almost nothing in common with mine other than we worked at the same place. I'm not sure what the hell I was thinking other than he had abs and wanted to date me and occasionally wanted to sleep with me, and I had no idea what the hell else a boyfriend was supposed to be, but I had some idea things weren't right. Hockey Warehouse Guy and I didn't say *I love you* for a year and a half. Me because I didn't love him, and him probably because he was waiting to say it when he proposed or finally got me pregnant or something corny. I finally said it because my older sister Lena thought it was weird that we hadn't professed our love and I was trying to prove to everyone that I was not an idiot for dating

---

* NO, IT'S NOT!

† Also, I was eighteen and he was twenty-three, remember? When people talk about the problems with age-gap relationships, what they really are wary of is the power and experience imbalance between the older and younger parties. This is especially true when you have an older party with more macro power, too, like being a man versus being a woman. Someone being five years older doesn't matter much when one person is forty-two and the other is forty-seven; the amounts of power and experience they have are likely similar. But when older people target eighteen-to-twenty-four-year-olds—which seems to be the sweet spot for problematic but technically legal age-gap relationships—they usually have outsize control and influence. They're usually able to say, "Hey, this is normal. Trust me, I'm older." Or they make more money. Or they live away from their parents or from roommates and can isolate you more easily. For me, I didn't know how to say no in relationships yet. I had no practice in drawing lines. And he knew that.

this guy who had nothing—NOTHING—in common with me. Looking back, I realize she was trying to make a point about how my relationship was not working, but at the time I was embarrassed and ashamed and it was easier to just be angry with her for not "getting" our relationship. Though, of course, she *got* it.

But I got it, too. When you're in a bad relationship and everyone thinks you're in denial, often you really aren't. You aren't obtuse or unaware of how This Is Not Working. At least *I* wasn't. I would drive home from his house and park in my high school parking lot and cry a bit before getting home so no one saw (dramatic, I know). We had awful sex that I basically had to beg him to be interested in. He insisted that men in their twenties normally had low sex drives; only later did I realize that he was probably depressed. We didn't go out on dates because he couldn't afford it—which was totally fine with me—but he also wouldn't let me pay for us to go out because "chivalry." Look, he didn't go down on me the entire two years we were dating, despite me asking. It's not like I wasn't privy to how bad shit was.

He very rarely listened to me, even when I was incredibly, unmistakably clear. I told him multiple times to *never* buy me jewelry as a gift. First, at the time, I didn't *wear* jewelry at all, and most jewelry picked out by straight guys is ugly as sin. It's not like I was uncommunicative or cloying about what I wanted either. I told him specifically what I'd like for my birthday—a dinner date. I got an ass-ugly heart-shaped necklace.*

I was chill about this.

I wore that ass-ugly heart-shaped necklace often. I would plan entire outfits around how to make it look the *least* bad. Sometimes, I

---

* If you are reading this and thinking about giving your partner a heart-shaped piece of jewelry, PLEASE reconsider. If this is the only thing you take out of this book, I will die glowing with the pride of someone who has saved a relationship.

would leave school and drive to his house (thirty-five minutes away; he never drove to my house, of course!) and then put the necklace on when I got outside. I wore it almost every single time we saw his friends because I figured he'd be all weird and prideful about that. My saving grace in getting the necklace was that he asked my sister Lena to help him pick it out and she warned me ahead of time that I was not going to like it; she was like, "I tried to steer him in a better direction; I'm sorry." God bless Lena for that.

Here's the thing: everyone's first partner sucks. Sucks. (For the exactly 492 people reading this who married their first partner, just ignore me and roll your eyes at yet another Enemy of Your Love.) First loves are terrible. It's like getting the chicken pox. You have to do it once just so you don't have it again later, when you're an adult and it's worse. Unlike chicken pox, we have not figured out a vaccine or workaround. Nor do they let you out of school if you suffer from it. So, in that way, being in love or dating someone for the first time is even *worse* than a viral infection.

Hockey Warehouse Guy and I had been together for eight months when I was leaving for college. I tried to talk to him about breaking up. Or at least not having such an ironclad exclusivity agreement. Or at least about how my living two thousand miles away might change our relationship. He got upset that I even brought it up. Was I planning on *leaving* him? *Cheating* on him? I assured him I was not because how can you say, "Yeah, well, I'm certainly not as jazzed about this relationship as you are, and college would be a clean break." You can't be eighteen years old and say that. At least, I could not.

So I entered college as I'd *sworn* I never would: with a boyfriend. More prepared than ever to be chill.

The hockey warehouse and then Hockey Warehouse Guy himself had taught me—trained me—how to garner male attention and approval. I knew how to always let him pick the music and the movie and the date. I knew how to let him and his friends be the stars of the show. I knew exactly what to do, and more often what *not* to do, in order to be liked. I learned how to be quieter.

I took *all* of that knowledge to college. *Plus* I had the added benefit of having a long-distance boyfriend. You can easily become invisible to men when you're dating someone else because really, upsettingly, most straight cis eighteen-year-old guys are not all that interested in female friendship. They're also simply not very good at it—they've been taught to relate to women as sex/dating objects and when that's off the table, they're not sure what to do. This is true in the reverse as well. A lot of young people have no idea how to untangle attraction and friendship with certain people. Being eighteen is all about being a horny, hormonal dipshit.

Even though I already had a boyfriend, I was not ready to cede to anonymity. I wasn't ready to disappear. Frankly, I didn't even *like* my boyfriend that much, and college often felt like being free of him, but he did give me a bit of a gift: if you play your cards right, you can make being in a relationship a facet of your chillness. The mere existence of a boyfriend gave me license to be a whole lot more relaxed around straight guys, a group that had historically made me *extremely* nervous. The answer to "Do you like me?" was suddenly unimportant, as was the very question itself. I was liked by some guy (my older boyfriend) somewhere (Missouri), and if someone on the fifth floor of the Birnkrant honors dorm didn't want to fuck me, well, tough shit; I wasn't free to fuck anyway. I made friends with women, too, to be sure. My roommate Shelby and I were the closest roommates on our entire floor, probably. We were obsessed with each other; we kept each other up almost every night just laughing. But for the first time in my entire life, most of my friends were guys.

By the end of freshman year, I'd made enough male friends and gotten enough male attention that breaking up with Hockey Warehouse Guy didn't seem like a loss, but a gain. Despite my conviction that it was the right thing to do, it remains possibly the hardest thing I've done. Hurting someone who doesn't know the hurt is coming is *the worst*. I was stupid about it, too. First, I broke up with him during the summer after freshman year.

It started when he asked me to marry him. Well, more specifically, it started because he asked me via text if he should ask my dad's permission for my hand in marriage. He literally said "hand in marriage" in the year of our Lord 2012. I mean, please. Please. He had never outright proposed to me before, but he talked about it *a lot*. He talked about how it would be the best day of his life when he proposed, and how he believed all men felt the same. He talked about us honeymooning in Ireland. When his uncle got married, he insisted we go along to the engagement photo shoot to get our own pictures taken and I worried he was going to propose there, while someone was photographing my reaction. Which would have been one of horror, by the way. I had told him from the beginning that I was *not* into marriage, which was true at the time because I thought marriage and weddings were feminine and therefore pathetic but also because I did not like *him* and the thought of a lifetime with him quite literally made my heart race. In a bad way. But he was never any good at listening to me, so he asked me what I thought about him getting my dad's blessing for us to wed and that was the final straw. I knew I needed to break up with him because I was never going to want to marry him.

He was away on a work trip—keep in mind he worked for my dad's company, which was a complicating factor. I think I realized while he was gone how much nicer my summer back home was when he wasn't around, when I could see friends and family and not spend my time coddling him and walking him through all his bad days at work. I don't really remember much about the first breakup because I was so scared. I panicked, called him, broke up, hung up, and then sat around in my living room with my mom and my sister and I made a bunch of jokes about it. I remember thinking, *This is the funniest I've ever been*, even though I don't remember any of what I said. I just know I was elated. Weightless. Giddy. I was so excited to be single. I was so glad I wasn't going to have to marry him.

But the next day I woke up feeling the worst brand of horror: guilt. He called me and texted me about how sad he was and how he was thinking about leaving the work trip early to fly home, which I knew *would not* look good for him as an employee, especially because he was vying for a promotion. He was very into rash decision-making and my role was usually to talk him down. This time, my role was to agree to get back together. I kept telling him over and over during this call that I didn't want to waste his time because he wanted to get married and I didn't. Again, I was nineteen! He insisted that if I thought there was *any* chance that we might get married in the future, it wouldn't be a waste of time. I, being the nineteen-year-old that I was, wanting the pain of the breakup to stop, told him, mostly honestly, that I didn't think we'd ever get married, but of course there was *some* chance. And that was enough for him. He stayed on the work trip. A month later he got the promotion and I went back to USC.

I paid for him to fly out in September. He had never been on a plane before and he hated it, which probably set the tone for the entire trip. He was thrilled to see me and I was indifferent. It felt like my grandparents had just shown up to a night out. I couldn't stand him being around my friends because the person I was with him was *not* the person I was with my friends. With him, I was more meek, I was less fun, I listened to country music and let him open car doors for me. At college I was still deferential to men, but it played out differently. I laughed at their stories, I went along with their dumb ideas, I took every dare.

As soon as he left at the end of his weeklong visit, I felt pure relief. I was noticeably happier; my friends commented on it. My roommate Shelby urged me to break up with him. October 2 was a Tuesday and I had decided that I needed to do it once and for all. I needed to break up with him, and I had to do it over the phone again, this time because we were long distance and not because I was a coward. I made a plan to wait until Friday of that week because I felt like I should give him the weekend to process it before he had to go into work and see my fucking dad—his boss. Also, I had asked him two days earlier to do me a favor and buy flowers for my mom and leave them at her house because it was her birthday and I couldn't figure out how to send flowers to her from LA that weren't eighty-nine dollars. So I knew I couldn't break up with him while he was doing that errand for me.

When we got on the phone for our daily phone call I panicked (a theme for me) and adrenaline surged through me and I broke up with him. I don't know how I said it. I mean, I know I said some version of "This isn't working and I don't want to marry you." I know he asked me repeatedly where this was coming from and I had no answer to give because I couldn't be like, "The entire relationship." He asked if we could keep talking, as friends, which I said yes to because I felt evil and would have done pretty much anything to feel less cruel. Breaking up with him was probably the least chill thing I did in our entire relationship; maybe the only not-chill thing I ever did.

So the next two days we had our normal daily phone call and he texted me throughout the day and I knew, I just *knew*, that this was his way of trying to keep us together, but the thing was I had no desire to even be friends with him. I didn't like him as a person *at all*. If I had met him in college, I wouldn't have spoken to him after the first time. He was boring and conservative and traditional and he didn't actually give a shit about me and I didn't give a shit about him. I wanted a fuck buddy and he wanted a wife and neither of us cared to find out who the other person was until it was way too late.

I don't know that he ever did find out who I was. I worked up more adrenaline and told him we had to stop talking. He was distraught. He told me he had been planning to fly out to LA to surprise me and talk me into getting back together. I can't think of anything that would have made things worse than that plan. I told him in no uncertain terms to *not* do that. And then we hung up and I never talked to him again.

I felt consumed by guilt. I felt certain that I was responsible for messing up this guy's whole life. How will a guy who works in a hockey warehouse with all men find another girlfriend, a future wife—his *only* goal? I felt guilty because I *knew* I hated commitment and exclusivity. Why the hell had I even agreed to date anyone? I swore to never date anyone seriously *ever* again, lest I ever wanted to leave someone. Here I had ruined Hockey Warehouse Guy's life, when I only ever wanted to make men happy.* After a couple of days of self-flagellation, I took a nice long bath and in the bath I farted and bubbles came up and it made me laugh so hard that I remember *knowing*, "Sophia, you'll be just fine."

---

* After we broke up, he started dating a new woman and changed his Facebook relationship status (lololol) *on our anniversary* and then posted some almost-cryptic thing about "Everything happens for a reason; thank God I only wasted two years of my life." And my friends got drunk and took my phone and liked his status, which is *very* funny now and was not as funny then. Anyway, he married that woman eventually, so I think things turned out fine. He did, however, unfriend me on Facebook after they got married, which is bullshit because if I've sucked your dick, you don't get to hide your social media from me.

SECTION TWO,

in which I try really hard to impress shitty men,
discover Skinnygirl piña colada mix,
and learn how to do eye makeup.*

---

* Kinda.

One Time I Listened to the Sara Bareilles Song "Brave" to Work Up the Courage to Ask a Guy Out (I'm Embarrassed for Me Too)

Once I broke up with Hockey Warehouse Guy, some part of me half assumed/half expected that I would be getting dicked down on the regular. It wasn't that I thought I was hot. This expectation was a function of the number of times I had heard some version—mostly explicitly stated, occasionally hinted at—of "You're a woman; you can get laid anytime you want." Straight cis men are *convinced* of this "truth," which is not a truth at all. Straight cis men say this *a lot*. It's the stupidest fucking thing I've ever heard and I worked with improv actors for years; I've heard stupid things.* Sex being available for any and all women practically on demand is

---

* I myself have not done improv. Please do not let this impugn your heretofore pristine opinion of me.

105

perhaps the only myth more omnipresent than the myth that sex with straight men is rewarding or worthwhile.*

I can't be sure of why precisely I failed to find casual sex partners as often as I would've liked, but I have my suspicions. I'm stabbing in the dark here but I would guess that it was a heady combination of (1) the times my "too-much" (actual) personality would break through the chillness, (2) the scent of desperation lingering around my person, (3) the abundance of *other* more chill and more hot casual sex options, and—perhaps the biggest issue of all—(4) none of us knowing what the fuck we were doing or how to initiate casual sex.

I had the idea in my head that everyone else magically knew how to hook up with one another. That they'd gotten a head start in high school that I hadn't. I knew for a damned fact that I had never even texted a guy not-about-homework before I was eighteen, and I felt sure that every other person had already perfected the art of casual but flirty, chill but encouraging messages. In reality, I think all of us were kind of stumbling around in the dark, hoping to hook up with people, praying for no one to get hurt by or disappointed in us.

If you want to know my deepest, darkest, most shameful secret, it's that some of the best advice I ever got came from the horrendous film *We Bought a Zoo*. At one point, Matt Damon tells one of his kids, "Sometimes all you need is twenty seconds of insane courage." I could be paraphrasing or misremembering the quote, which is fine with me. I'm not going to rewatch *We Bought a Zoo* just to get this right. But this is excellent advice when it comes to being vulnerable, because there's no way through it but, well, through it. You basically

---

* I'm kidding!!! I've slept with a lot of straight men! But also, the orgasm gap is real and basically it says that women sleeping with men have the fewest orgasms of all. Women who sleep with women have more, men who sleep with men have more, and, of course, men who sleep with women have the most.

just have to accept that opening up to people and getting love and sex requires moments of really dumb courage. This is a speech I've given to multiple friends while very, very drunk and I always cite where I got the advice from because my friends deserve to know that it's from *We Bought a Zoo* before they follow it.

The truth of the matter is that almost everyone in college was horny all the time and many (or at least a handful of) people probably would have been down to bone me; I just didn't understand how to get out of my own way and make it happen. Most of the hookups I *did* have came from myself and another person being *incredibly, excruciatingly* awkward and fighting through that in order to have a chance at sex. One time, for example, I commenced a friends-with-benefits situation because I jokingly said I loved barbecue sauce so much that I would suck it off a dick and a guy was like, "How much are you joking about the barbecue thing?" We had sex, although we never, ever, ever involved barbecue sauce in it, because I was NOT serious. I don't think. Anyway, he and I hooked up on and off for a few years at the end of college, mostly when he got drunk enough not to care that he would feel weird and apologetic about it the next day. I always felt like it was no big deal. What's a blow job in the shower between friends?

But perhaps I thought it was "no big deal" because I was desperate as hell. I had always enjoyed flirting with guys while dating Hockey Warehouse Guy because it had seemed harmless,* and now I was ready to actually do some rumbling. Get ready for cringey shit because I'm about to dump a whole load of it on you. I would walk to class with earphones in and purposefully be really smiley and happy, assuming that people would want to ... I don't know ... stop me on their way to chem lab and ask me to fuck? I was fanatical about wearing perfume.

---

* Yikes for me!

I tanned constantly. I shaved my legs every day.* I worked out daily and hung around my apartment and friends' apartments in vaguely slutty—FOR A MIDWESTERN HORSE GIRL—loungewear that didn't actually look that good on me and just made me seem like I was trying too hard. I went to three football games and got very sunburned and even more bored. I mean, I really *tried*.

More than anything else, I showed up to *everything*. God fucking forbid I miss even one fun night where a guy I'd known for weeks or months or semesters might realize that after all this time it had always been me; he wanted to fuck *me*. Imagine: *You see me—almost as if in slow motion—across the beer-pong table, laughing with my dozens of friends about getting the words to "Just a Friend" by Biz Markie wrong and realize, "Wow. Sophia? How could I have overlooked her?"* I didn't want a guy to actually fall in love with me—that seemed overwhelming and icky—I just wanted someone to be, like . . . very into hanging out and sleeping with me. I wanted late nights in someone else's dorm and walks of shame and hookup disaster stories that I could share with friends. So I showed up *all the time*. But it's very hard to be mysterious or alluring, or to embody any other facet of desirability, when you're around constantly. I'm not saying that it's bad to show up all the time, or that you can hang out with your friends too much. I *am* saying that if you're around people all the time and they haven't tried to fuck you, maybe they don't want to fuck you. And maybe being around people a lot is not the way to convince someone they want you.

Because of my desperation, almost every experience that involved a semi-attractive guy felt laden with meaning. Just bursting full of what *I* thought were opportunities to flirt and what everyone else thought were normal everyday experiences. By my sophomore year I was friends with pretty much exclusively guys, who hung out with

---

* Every three days.

pretty much exclusively guys. Often, I'd go to a friend's apartment to play beer pong with six to eight guys and one of them would have invited another group of friends over and when that new group arrived, it would be made up of six to eight guys with their own Token Chill Girl. That's college, babyyyyy!

Anyway, because I was friends predominantly with men out of desperation for male attention—literally if I had gotten laid sooner after my breakup with Hockey Warehouse Guy, I think I would have made way more female friends in college—I leveled up into a somehow even *chiller* Chill Girl.

Before I continue, I want to clarify that while I was *attempting* constantly to be a chill girl, I was not always succeeding.* Often, I would suppress my thoughts and words and personality for as long as possible, pushing things down like a trash compactor until I would explode at seemingly random times with anger and irritation and anxiety. These explosions became more and more fun when I started drinking late in my sophomore year. And by *fun* I mean mortifying. I would end up in the parking lot of a Panda Express, passive-aggressively ignoring half of my friends for something hurtful they'd done two hours ago, or halfway through a party I'd climb out onto the structurally unsound roof of my apartment to have a panic attack. But day-to-day, and without the influence of Skinnygirl piña colada mix, I was really becoming an expert at chillness.

The key to my leveling up was one of the most classic attention grabs of all time: [confetti trumpet emoji] hating women! I made jokes about women being bad drivers, annoying girlfriends, and emotional wrecks. Yes, outside of being sexist, these are terrible, pedestrian jokes. And while many men loved getting to talk shit about women to a woman, I think a lot of them found it grating,

---

* Yes, lots of people saw through this and found me annoying! I know that now with hindsight!

weird, and annoying. I remember many people hearing my "jokes" and responding with "Jesus Christ." Which I hoped was awe, but which was likely disgust. Probably a few of them even did the simple math and calculated that if I was that loud about hating women, I probably just hated myself.

It's hard for present-me to tell how much I actually disliked women at that point. In places where I was not trying to sleep with anyone—at home with family, with my best friend of eighteen years, when talking to a professor about essays—I certainly didn't hate women. Big Picture, most of the people I liked and felt safe around and looked up to were women. Maybe even *all* the people who fit that description were women. But in the everyday agony of being in a college full of rich size 0 blonde women who joined sororities and felt like they fit in there, it felt easy to hate women, or at least to blame them for what I didn't have but desperately wanted.* If you're told over and over that the most you can offer a man is perky tits, a wet pussy, and no expectations, eventually anyone else who is also potentially providing that becomes competition.

Most of my guy friends came from either my freshman dorm floor or from the stand-up comedy group I was part of. The guys in the stand-up group all congregated at one house that had been dubbed Casablanca, since it was a white house.† Casablanca was a ramshackle off-campus house that had something like fourteen bedrooms, all filled with guys. I hung out there *a lot*. Something was *always* happening at Casablanca and it almost always involved a lot of beer and a moderate amount of property destruction. Casablanca was owned by a crazy landlord, Jerry, who truly *did not care* if you

---

* Nota bene: there were thousands of women at USC who did not fit this description.
† The creativity!

did ANYTHING to the house.* Rumor had it that Casablanca was going to be torn down the next year and thus there was no reason to keep it nice. I would often come over to find two guys drunk in their underwear fighting with balustrades they'd pulled off one of the many staircases. One guy occasionally got drunk, woke up, peed directly onto his carpet, and then went back to bed. This house was vile, a caricature of an abandoned frat house from a bad comedy.

I loved it. After growing up with sisters and a brother who was nine years younger, I had never experienced unruliness like this, such worship of pure pleasure, total hedonism. Even being a spectator felt thrilling. I was off-balance the whole time I was there and, like a younger annoying sister, desperate to keep up.

Casablanca is where I first met Gator.† We hated each other as soon as we met. More accurately, I made fun of him wearing a plaid shirt and figured that if he lived in that house and was that hot, he could take it, but instead he immediately disliked me, which is fair.‡ We both liked being the center of attention too much for us to ever get along amicably without one of us ceding. When I first met him, we were both dating other people long-distance, which I thought would be something we could connect over, but instead, we decided to hate each other. Anyway, about a month after we met, we both broke up with our partners the same week—I did my breakup, his girlfriend did the honors for their relationship—and that left us with

---

* Jerry was later my landlord and I can testify that this man was . . . wild. He offered that if I ever couldn't pay my rent, we could work out a "comfort-girl" situation. In 2012, he claimed that he went to Syria to "sort things out." He once came over to our house at 9 a.m., grabbed a beer out of one of the *six* fridges he kept there, cracked it open, and said, "I found out God isn't real." He also supplied all our toilet paper because he "got a good deal" on it.
† I can't use this guy's real name, so I'm going to call him Gator because at least it's funny to me and if I pick a normal guy's name it will be . . . weird. Anyway.
‡ No, it's not. Grow up.

a perfect patch of soil in which to sow our flirty-hatred shit. It took a little bit of time, actually, before we got to flirting. For the first bit, we just earnestly were kind of mean to each other, but funny, but still kind of mean. The few times we hung out, he would spend the night correcting everything I said, and in retaliation I would try to make fun of him publicly as much as possible, over everything from what he was wearing to what he was drinking to how he lost at beer pong. Anything and everything he did was fair game and anything and everything I said he made clear he thought was stupid.

He was—and probably still is—a hot asshole, and that was, unfortunately, exactly my type. Here's my impression of me in my early twenties: *A hot person who treats other people like shit? Okay, yes!!!! I'm going to build my entire existence around them!* Despite that, I didn't find myself initially attracted to Gator any more than to any other hot mean person.

Things changed course one night when my best, best, best friend in the world, Emilee—whom I have known since I was two years old—was visiting me at college during her school's spring break. This was after months of Gator and I semi-playfully disliking one another. Anyway, that night Emilee and her then boyfriend were hanging out with the boys of Casablanca and me. Gator was sitting near me and kept "bothering" me—trying to take up my space on the couch, flicking condensation from his drink on me, asking for gum and then putting the wrapper in my sweatshirt pocket. You know the way sixth graders flirt? That. Well, I thought he was just being annoying, but I found it lightly pleasant because he was very hot, and hot people's attention feels like wearing clothes right out of the dryer. I did not think it was romantic or even aimed at me because, you know, again, he was hot and he flirted with everyone. Male, female, old, young, single, taken; there were no bounds to his flirtation and almost none of it was done with any seriousness. At the end of the night, when everyone was standing around saying long goodbyes to Emilee because it was her last night and because she's one of those people *everyone* loves pretty immediately, he started playing with the strings of my hoodie.*

You have to get very close to someone to play with the strings of their hoodie. And when a group of about seven people is saying goodbye to Emilee (and a little bit to her boring then boyfriend) and you step out of the receiving line to go mess with someone's hoodie strings, it turns out that everyone notices. EXCEPT ME. ME DID NOT NOTICE.

On the walk home, Emilee was shocked. Shocked that I didn't find the moment noteworthy. Shocked that I dismissed this as "just the way Gator† is." Shocked that I didn't already have a crush on him because, as previously stated, I'm incredibly shallow, and hot asshole is very much my *type*. I remember very, very clearly Emilee saying, "Sophia, he's so into you, holy shit. He was watching you all night." Which is exactly some shit out of a rom-com; like that *exact* line is in so many would-be Meg Ryan–led movies as the proof-flavored pudding that some Byronic guy *loves* our protagonist. I protested, and I *really, really* meant it at the time; I wasn't trying to be demure or modest. I was like, "I think he's just annoying and needs attention." Then Boring Boyfriend chimed in to agree with Emilee: "No guy does that if he's not into you."

I had never, ever, ever, ever been liked by someone I actually thought I might like. I mean, my first boyfriend—Hockey Warehouse Guy—had asked me out and I was like, "Yes, okay, I would like to have sex one (1) time before I die." I didn't admire him or anything; I wasn't even friends with him, really. I was used to one dynamic and one dynamic only with hot men: I want to fuck them

---

* For everyone out there who is a real Chan-Head (Channing Tatum fan), you will recognize this as a scene from *She's the Man*, a flawless film.
† Sorry that I chose this name and did this to all of us.

and they do not know I exist. It was so unusual for me to not be the one trying to flirt with someone, for someone else to—appear to at least—be flirting with *me*. I had no idea what to do with this information. Frankly, as soon as she said that he might like me, I was like, "Ehhhh, that's kind of a turnoff." Anyone showing interest in me was, ironically, a real buzzkill for me. Not that it had happened often. I'm just saying, by any normal measure, I should have had no interest in Gator.

Except for one thing: Gator and I still quasi-hated each other. So *of course* I was hooked. All of a sudden, he had become really, really flirty with me about 30 percent of the time, and the rest of the time he was his regular very rude and very hot self. If you know anything about conditioning, it's best to be unpredictable: that way, the subject never *fully* gets what's happening and when, so they're always on the line. And within a month of Emilee telling me that she thought he liked me, I was in trouble. All of a sudden his rudeness, his *mean*ness, seemed like another type of flirting. You know, *Jane Austen*-y shit where they hate each other but they really like each other? I thought that was happening. I don't know! We hung out almost every single day, as my friend group was his friend group, and if anything was happening, I was *of course* going to show up, because crush logic says hanging out around you a bunch = you falling in love with me.*

Because his rudeness now seemed like flirting to me, I pulled back just a little on my insults, which gave him room to do the same, so now we were hanging out constantly because I had a crush (and assumed he did too), and we were 30 percent nice to each other and 70 percent still pretty mean. Which meant we were *obnoxious* to be around. We had a game when walking down the street of trying to

---

* Please, *please* note—if you take nothing else from this book—that hanging out with someone more will not make them like you, nor will it make them realize that they've always liked you. If your crush wants to date you, they will.

push each other into bushes or trees. We would challenge each other to see how hard we could slap each other. We would compete for any chair or couch seat the other person wanted, always trying to displace one another in a weird two-person game of musical chairs. We made scenes pretty much everywhere we went. From the outside, I'm sure people felt embarrassed to witness our antics.

From the inside, things were confusing, to say the least. If I hadn't written some of this stuff down in a journal,* I would have a hard time remembering or even believing it. I'll start with the stuff that made it seem like things were going in a flirty direction: We fell asleep on the couch a lot. I sat on his lap a lot. I spent the night in his bed at least once. He grabbed my boobs at least once. He would kiss me "as a joke."

But the flip side of this was that he was, well, an abusive friend, and not just to me. He was the most attractive member of the friend group and therefore was the de facto ruler. This seems to happen a lot in friend groups—people just do what the hottest person wants to do. Whatever he said went. If he wasn't feeling like going out, everyone stayed in. If he wanted to go to the rugby party, we went. If he was bored of beer pong, we didn't play. It wasn't explicit that he was in charge or anything—the other guys often *thought* they were weighing in on what might happen that night—but to me, as a Not Guy, it was very obvious. He was one of those people who enjoyed crossing a line, and *nothing* you did or said could make him stop. The word *no* didn't work for Gator. I theorize that it was because he was an *extreme* mama's boy and the youngest child in his family and thus incredibly unused to hearing the word. Anyway, with this suzerainty bestowed upon him, he often chose to rain terror on people who were not as established in the group. Many times, that included me, as the only girl.

---

* I was very emotional at the time; *of course* I had a journal.

The boys once spent a whole evening throwing dried pasta at me; anytime I tried to do something else, they'd follow me out of the room. I stayed in the kitchen and waited for them to finish throwing the entire box of macaroni. They once dragged me into a closet with no lights, just me and Gator (in only his underwear), and he popped balloons to scare me.* They threw rocks at my window, which broke the window and got glass in my bed while I was *in* the bed, and then got upset that I was mad. They spent a whole party throwing things down my cleavage and then inviting strangers to do the same.† They would often lock me out of or into my room. They once used a staircase handrail knob that fell off—we lived in a Jerry house; what can you expect?—to bang holes into my door that you could then see through. And of course, they often looked through. Gator was the instigator, the worst of them. He came up with stupid nicknames for me that he'd then tell to any guy who wasn't him whom I was talking to—Meat Hooks, Badgersnatch, and Sturdy Sophia. He would take his pants off and jokingly "apologize" by thrusting his underwear-clad dick at me; he called it "cockpologizing." One time I tried to share a story about working at an internship and I mentioned how I had to learn basic coding, and he and another guy cut me off midsentence to mock me, saying, "Beep boop beep boop beep beep beep boop," for about *half an hour*. Anytime I tried to talk for the rest of the night, they brought it back. And I couldn't leave because that would be "dramatic." I didn't talk the rest of the night. If there was ever a person willing to take a joke too far, it was Gator.

There's more. There's so much more, and some of it is weirder or worse and some of it is no big deal, or sounds like no big deal. And I let it all happen. Some of it I enjoyed. Some of it I ignored. Some of

---

* Why were there balloons in a closet? I don't know.
† To be fair, I was cool with this, but also . . . why would you do that? What?

it I hated. Some of it I begged them to stop and they wouldn't. Some of it felt like flirting and attention.

Looking back, it is *very* easy to see that this was fucked, fucked, fucked. But I wanted *sooooo* desperately to be chill, to be their friend, to be accepted by them. And every time I made a big deal out of a thing they did that I hated, they punished me for it. At the beginning at least, I felt like I was just in the process of learning how to be more chill. Every time I accepted their mistreatment, I thought I was just being low-maintenance. I thought I was proving myself. I thought that eventually they'd like me and accept me and maybe even care about me as a person. Which retrospectively seems like a really dumb thought to have about people treating you like shit, but which felt like a worthy goal then. Occasionally, I would explode with rage—how long can you deal with harassment before you lose it?—and then they'd call me bitchy or tell me I was overreacting and then I'd feel like shit and beat myself up for not laughing along, for not holding it together longer. On some sick, pathetic level, I was getting male attention and it seemed worth the price.

Anyway, after months of thinking that Gator might actually like me back due to all the "joke" kissing, cuddling, and even *some* of the insane mistreatment that seemed adjacent to flirting, I decided to ask him out sort of. I don't know why I thought I would give him a break and do the work of being rejected; I guess I thought I owed him a lot because he was more attractive than I was? Regardless, the funny part is really that I sat in my car and the song "Brave" by Sara Bareilles came on the radio and like the absolute *corniest* person you've ever heard of, I thought, *This is a sign I should ask him out.* I asked him out and he basically said no, but in a wishy-washy "maybe" kind of way. Of course, I'm not an idiot—if someone says maybe when you ask them out, that's a "FUCK NO."

That was when I knew I needed to move on from him. Of course, I did not do that. Instead, he slept with one of my closest female friends on campus, and I got bitter and angry about that, which made things very weird in the friend group and with said female friend. I cried a lot and she and I wrote each other emotional Facebook Messenger statuses, and I was determined to be "cool" about the whole thing—a chill girl!!! But I was so hurt and pissed off that for about three or four months, every time I would get drunk—which happened a lot in college—I would lash out at him in front of everyone. I would get sad and leave parties early without telling anyone, and someone would have to go find me. One time, while walking home from a party, I decided—and my reasoning here is very unclear to me—that I needed to *run* to McDonald's at full speed. In flip-flops. Also, the McDonald's was a mile and a half away.* It was like I had used up all my chill trying to get him to like me and when he didn't I became an angry little tornado.

So, I distanced myself from that friend group and went and worked on some of the other friendships I had been neglecting while I had been mooning after a total douche. PSYCH! Being the big giant dumbass I was, I thought it would be totally fine to live with Gator and the rest of his friends the very next year after that, which went pretty poorly and made us *actually* dislike one another rather than semi-affectedly hate each other, as we had when we first met. He graduated a semester earlier than I did and we never spoke again after seeing each other almost every day for three and a half years.

Now, I will say, because I'm a magnanimous angel, that my friendships with men in college were not all bad. I had *loads* of fun. Frankly, for the time and place in my life, I got a lot out of it. In

---

* I am *not* by nature a runner. Except while drunk. When drunk, I get superhuman endurance, like how moms are able to lift cars off babies, and then all of a sudden I have not just the urge but the ability to sprint for long distances. I don't know what this is about.

many ways, I got exactly what I had always wanted: male atten-tion. I had social capital in the spaces I wanted to be in, because being liked by men gives you extra points in the world—at least the straight cis male–dominated world of USC and, I imagine, many college campuses. When men like you it signals to other men, men you might be interested in dating, that you are acceptable. That you aren't more trouble than you're worth. That they aren't going to have to tone down their jokes around you.* That you aren't going to "get mad"† at them—the very, very, very worst thing a woman can do to a man.

Not only do you gain male approval, but you also frequently gain some approval, if not friendship, from the other women who are doing what you're doing, who are seeking out acceptance from guys. It's not like everyone is actively conscious of how much they're trying to appeal to straight cis men. We've all just been steeped in this shit from the beginning. We don't even know all the ways in which we're bending to fit the cis straight male gaze. But when you accept that as the preeminent gaze, even subconsciously, you tend to admire (if compete with) other people who *also* believe the same thing, who also hold men in high regard. In many ways, making friends with straight cis guys made me feel, for the very first time in my life . . . normal.

There are material benefits of being a chill girl, a guys' girl, a girl who eschews female company, unfortunately. How could appeal-ing to the dominant group not provide advantage? But you also lose a lot. You lose the magic that is female friendship, although *magic* is too light and too corny a word for the reverence I feel toward female friendship. You lose the ability to separate what is

---

* Not be sexist/racist/homophobic/etc.
† Have a reasonable expectation and be disappointed in them when it is not ful-filled.

right and what is popular. You lose the skill of dissenting in regard to your mistreatment. Mostly, you lose yourself. You become, in ways both large and small, a reflection of what the men around you want. Or, more often, what you think they want, what you've been taught—by TV, by music, by teachers, by movies, by art, by peers, by parents, by culture—to think that the men around you want. It's an anemic version of yourself, a lacuna of personhood.

But my God do you learn a lot about Ben Affleck movies.

Everything I've Ever Done
to Impress Men (and How
Successful Each Was)*

1. Learned to throw a football. (It did not get me any dates.)

2. Got into country music for two years, including buying tickets for a country music concert. (Very successful, sadly.)

3. Took AP calculus instead of AP statistics because more hot guys were taking it. (Incredibly unsuccessful, except that AP calc was where I first created my Twitter, which in a way led to later romantic success, so kind of a long-game situation.)

4. Got really good at beer pong. (Successful: [a] I'm still above average at the game and [b] I slept with at least two people directly after winning at beer pong with them; you do the math.)

---

* Just kidding: this is only a very small selection of the things I've done to impress men.

5. Opened up two bottles of wine with fabric scissors. (Very unsuccessful in every sense of the word.)

6. Had anal sex. (Successful for an extremely short amount of time.)

7. Ate a weed gummy bear that turned out to be 100 mg—which, if you aren't versed in weed, is way too much; 10 mg is like a nice, normal dose for normal folks—had a visual blackout, threw up at a church, and marched—yes, marched—one mile home because I thought the police were watching me and they'd be less suspicious if I was marching. (Not at all successful. One of the worst experiences of my life.)

8. Tried quinoa. (Turns out that the nutty flavor of America's trendiest pseudo-cereal of 2013 is not the way to a guy's heart. At least I got some fiber.)

9. Chopped down a tree. (Successful.)

10. Watched a *Star Wars* movie. (Mixed bag. I found the movie so boring that I blew the guy instead of continuing. So. That probably impressed him.)

11. Learned all the lyrics to a J. Cole album (Successful in that I did learn the words, unsuccessful in that . . . why the fuck would a guy care about that, Sophia?)

12. Purchased the book *All the Shah's Men* as an ebook because a guy I was talking to from Bumble for over a month recommended it to me, but never read it because I find it very difficult to read ebooks. (Unsuccessful. He stood me up on our eventual date to meet in person.)

13. Baked gooey butter cakes and brought them in for the cast of plays I was in in high school.* (Semi-successful. A hot popular senior guy proposed to me. A few years later he came out, so it does not seem like the wedding is going forward.)

14. Jumped fully clothed into the Mediterranean. (Successful. I got my first "kiss," which was really a kiss on the cheek, but I lied and told everyone it was on the mouth.)

15. Worked out every day. (Unsuccessful and I still can't do a single push-up.)

16. Read *Anna Karenina*. (Unsuccessful. Hated the book. Didn't finish. Had to use CliffsNotes for the first time in my life. No one slept with me.)

17. Got into basketball. (Extremely successful for me. I don't even care about men outside of the NBA anymore.)

18. Tried to talk less. (Unsuccessful both in my attempt and it impressing men. It turns out that even when I'm quiet I give off the "Don't *ever* speak to me" vibe. I think it's because I have a really big rib cage, so I seem tough.)

---

* Again, this is a St. Louis thing; they're amazing. Imagine a cake batter–flavored lemon bar.

Cracking Open an Ice-Cold Bud Light

I came to drinking late, like almost everything else in my life. I had my first cigarette at age twenty-seven and I only smoked it to take a picture.* I didn't try weed until I was twenty-one. I didn't even have coffee until I was nineteen, a year after my first kiss. I was behind in every nonacademic department imaginable. Mostly because I was trying very hard to be good and because I think my parents read me too many Boxcar Children books.† For most of my youth, I planned on not drinking basically forever. By the time I was leaving for college, I had made it through high school without taking up Pretty Much the Only Fun Thing to Do in St. Louis, Missouri, and I figured I could survive college sans alcohol as well.

In high school, when I was first glaringly sober, I didn't real-

---

* Since then, I have had one other cigarette at age twenty-seven for another, different picture. And yes, I was reluctant to post said pictures on social media in case anyone thought I was promoting smoking.

† No offense to Henry, Jessie, Violet, and Benny but they are boring as all hell. They're jazzed about doing chores and coming home on time and mending socks or whatever kids in the 1930s did.

ize exactly *why* my teetotaling ass lurking at parties made people chafe so much.* I assured my friends, "I'm fun without alcohol! I don't need it to have a good time! I'm already loud and crazy enough; you don't want to see me after four Smirnoff Ices." I begged them to believe me, but they remained unconvinced, likely because what drunk people do *not* want is a loud, opinionated, kind of judgy sober person. They want a chill friend. Now that I've had a drink (not to brag), I understand that getting drunk is a deeply shameful state where you're willing to be yourself. It's horrific to be yourself, especially as a teenager, and no one sober should be around to witness and therefore remember it.

Naturally, I got invited to fewer and fewer parties (if you can call fourteen teenagers taking bad pictures with digital cameras in someone's basement a party). I genuinely resented all these people for picking tiny things like "being cool" and "getting laid" over their friendship with *me*. I complained about this often to my mom, who would remind me that it was probably a good idea to not drink because of alcoholism on both sides of my family and also, what if I got caught and got in trouble and had my college admissions ruined?† My mother kindly suggested that perhaps I was more of a daytime-hangout person, and that I wasn't necessarily meant to socialize in big groups of people. "Why don't you just invite one or two friends over during the day on Saturday? Or after school?" she would often suggest. *Because, Mom!!! I'm trying to be something I'm not!* Instead of heeding her wisdom, I just kept trying to force it.

---

* I was also sober in middle and elementary, but can you really be sober when no one around you is drinking? Or are you just a kid?
† I'm really not even sure that this happens, now that I think about it. I feel like colleges are aware that most teenagers drink before they arrive on campus.

But my mother also deeply empathized with the feeling of being left out of something. She understood what it was to *want* to fit in, to go along with things to please people. After months of awkward sobriety, heartbreaking loneliness, and an abundance of caution, I again asked her what I should do. Was I supposed to not drink and be uncool forever, just for the sake of being "good"? Was I supposed to stay unfun until the age of forty-seven, when all my peers would catch up to me and be similarly boring on Friday nights? I have no idea how my mother kept a straight face while her seventeen-year-old daughter came to her asking her if she should drink at the next party, to help her weigh the pros and cons of imbibing some stolen store-brand vodka. She calmly asked, "Well, do you *want* to drink?" To which I replied, "No, but I also don't want to not be drinking." My mother reiterated that she understood if I felt like joining in and reminded me for the four thousandth time in my life that I could always call her to pick me up and she would come, no questions asked. Yes, I realize how pathetic it is to announce to your parent that you're going to misbehave.

So the next party I went to (I *had* to be invited to it because it was a post-show party for the winter play I was in, and everyone in the cast and crew got invited), I decided to drink one beer. If I sipped on it all night, I'd have something to do with my hands—the *real* reason to drink—plus I wouldn't have a scarlet *U* emblazoned on my chest for *Unfun*, since for the most part no one cares how little you drink as long as you fucking put some alcohol in your mouth, goddamnit!!! Also, one beer wasn't so much that I couldn't drive home safely. My plan was brilliant. I know.

Unfortunately, even brilliant plans have flaws. Have you ever even seen *Ocean's 8*? Yeah. Things go awry. Even Sandra Bullock makes mistakes. That was the night I found out what beer tastes like. It tastes awful. Specifically, to me, it tastes like if you left piss

out in the sun for a few days and then crushed up wheat and emul-
sified it and then somehow made that piss/wheat mixture sour and
bitter (or maybe that's just from leaving it out in the sun?) and then
you served it to people, like a massive fucking asshole. Whoever first
created beer: okay, I get it, you needed a lot of calories easily and
cheaply, and drinking water wasn't as sanitary as your nasty new
invention. But to whoever first pretended that beer tastes good:
fuck you. You're on my shitlist along with people who don't appreciate JLo's acting career and people who are on their cell phones
while ordering something.

So there I was, with a fucking Bud Light in my hand, and a
sip that I could not, would not, swallow. Luckily, all parties in the
Midwest take place in someone's unfinished basement, so I spat it
on the concrete floor, right into the drain that all basements have.
I don't make the rules; I'm sure some construction regulatory
body does, but all unfinished basements have a drain in the floor,
and it seemed like a good place for my used beer. People laughed
and enjoyed my "first time drinking beer" face, and they all moved
on and I held on to the 99 percent–full can of beer for the rest of
the night and I went on with my life with brand-new knowledge:
beer sucks.

I came home to my mother, marched up to her bedroom, and
immediately shared the new information I had. "How the fuck do
adults drink this? Why is cracking open a beer portrayed as a thing
people do after a long day of work to unwind?" I was incredulous and
she laughed at me, which is probably her best trait, in my opinion—
how often she laughs at me. She and I devised another plan. I have
to give her credit, this was her idea. The next time I got invited to a
party, a few weeks later, I grabbed a beer, had some people witness
me opening it; then I went to the bathroom, poured it down the
sink, rinsed out the can a bit, and then refilled it about halfway up
with water so that it didn't look like I was a weirdo holding an empty

can.* While this "worked," it didn't make me a chill person, which is the actual purpose of beer. People tolerate the rotten beer-piss taste because they need to crawl out of their skin suit for four short hours.† I didn't get that at the time.

I finally gave up and realized, much to my chagrin, that my mother was right: I was a "daytime hangout" person. I was meant to meet up to study at a Starbucks. I was meant to bake cookies with other girls. I was not meant to watch girls named Katie sit in the laps of boys named Justin while I was stuck holding beer water. Did I learn this lesson and carry it with me with grace? Hell no. I just kept forcing the issue via a sort of misguided exposure therapy.

The whole concept of exposure therapy—which I'm almost sure no one reading this is unfamiliar with—is to gaslight your brain into being okay with fear. The premise suggests that if you just keep going to parties and feeling like the Trunchbull in a room full of Miss Honeys, one day that knot of pain in your chest that is telling you to both run and cry will dissipate; in its wake will be a staid comfort with all things social. I don't want to dismiss exposure therapy—it seems to work wonders for people on *My Strange Phobia*—but it's not *ever* going to fix how being sober in a room full of drunk teens feels. It's the most excruciating awareness of just how boring you are, stretched out for hours, set to the tune of "Party in the USA."

And *that* is why I started drinking. The truth of the matter is that I come from a long line of unfun people on both sides of my family. We're high-strung and careful. We're philosophical and judgmental. We are smart, we are hardworking, we are fun*ny*. But we are, by and

* Okay, her plan was just "Why don't you hold a can of beer and not drink it?" The other theatrics were my idea.
† Yes, I've tried IPAs and stouts and sour beers; I even tried a Guinness, which someone had the *audacity* to tell me would taste like chocolate milk! They all taste like piss.

large, not a *fun* group. And that's where alcohol comes in. As my mother so frequently reminded me: we're alcoholics.

Really, the only notable thing about my family members' drinking problems are how tame they are; drinking is the white noise machine in the corner rather than a smoke alarm going off. No one is a fun drunk or an angry drunk, and often, they're not even drunk at all. They're all just drink*ing*. Constantly. (Or they're in the process of cutting back, which is usually much more commendable than successful). They're drinking because their kids don't visit as much. Or because their wife is cruel. Or because they never learned to be fun without alcohol. Or because some part of their brain needs red wine every day around 4 p.m., otherwise it will rattle around their head.

Drinking in my family looks like red wine with dinner, and usually after dinner and often before dinner. It looks like a bottle of wine per person per night, which doctors might describe as "too much." By 9 p.m., everyone makes a little less sense and gets a little more sleepy than the average person, but if a stranger walked in, they probably wouldn't be able to tell right away who was drunk. The drinking is to make it through. The drinking is because it's worse if you don't drink.

Of course, on holidays and during family events, the intake increases. Then—when it's more like one and a half or two bottles per person per night—everyone gets (somehow!) louder and (somehow!) cries even *more* easily than they do while sober. My family is made up of people who are a poetically bad combination of critical and sensitive; Malbecs act as fuel for both. Everyone hurts feelings a little more and gets their feelings hurt a little more and usually someone goes to another room to cry or to do dishes passive-aggressively. If you're doing the math you might be thinking, *Wouldn't it be better to stop drinking, then? Wouldn't it cause fewer hurt feelings and inane arguments?* Yes. Yes it would. But most people in my family are in a little too deep; they love alcohol just a little too much and they haven't done anything *so bad* as to warrant checking into a rehab center in their opinion.*

Every time I go home brings a new method for stopping, or a new soon-to-be-unfollowed rule. No drinking before five. No drinking before noon. No drinking at home (if you knew how agoraphobic my father's side of the family is, this would be even more impressive). No drinking if you haven't worked out that day. No drinking alone. Hard alcohol only (that's how much my family likes wine). One person bought a shock bracelet that he pushed every time he drank to break himself of the habit. It didn't take.

My family doesn't lie about their drinking habits—it's not a secret how much they love alcohol—but neither do they talk about it in ways that might be productive, that might get them help, or that might actually acknowledge what happens when they drink. In my family, alcohol consumption is treated as a personal issue, like having arthritis, rather than something that could—and does—affect others. And as much as a health issue this is, the amount each person drinks is mostly treated as an inevitability, a fateful quirk of the body. The older family members get, the more convinced they become that drinking is just part of who they are, an immutable fact about them like their hair color. Yes, you can cut it or dye it—or buy a shock bracelet, or make a new rule—but the tendency is innate. Pretty much everyone genetically related to me just drinks. All the time.

And for most of my life, I didn't understand why. I had no desire in high school or college to actually consume alcoholic beverages; I just wanted to fit in and get invited and be fun. I was (and still am) a high-strung person in general, which was fine—beneficial, even—in an academic setting, but off-putting in a social one. I was always

---

* Not that most people in my family would actually seek professional help for a problem.

cleaning up before the party was over so there was less to do the next day, offering people refills, asking people kind, thoughtful questions, remembering everyone's name. I approached college parties with the same level of staid professionalism with which most people approach networking events. I just didn't have any idea how to relax. Liquor is very, very good, it turns out, at helping you chill out, and I *needed* to.

Specifically, the reason I started drinking was in hopes of becoming palatable. To men. I know, I know, I know. But, come on, you had to expect this of me at this point. The reason I started drinking was *not* because of how painfully unfun it was for me to nurse a Shirley Temple in a roomful of people on their thirteenth Coors Light—it was because of how unfun it made me *seem*.

Sober men can be brooding and moody and taciturn and it's fine; in fact, sometimes that makes them *more* hot. (I really wish God would fix this; seems like a massive oversight.) Women can't be that. You can't be standoffish, slow to warm up to new people, or even indifferent. You don't get to be in the corner and sip a club soda and have no energy. You have to give everyone your fucking energy all the time or you're a bitch. I was already nervous enough around men due to not talking to them until I was seventeen, and also due to caring *immensely* what they thought of me, and it became clear—after about four college events where I interacted with guys—that being sober wasn't helping.

Just to give you a taste of how bad I was at talking to men, I was once at a party where the Outkast song "Ms. Jackson" came on and I said—loudly, in an effort to seem cool—that it is impossible to apologize a trillion times, since it would take thousands of years.* Which is a scene that *might* pass as awkward-cute in an indie movie delivered by a hauntingly beautiful protagonist but which in real life falls very flat.

---

* Presuming that you can say sorry once per second endlessly, it would take you 31,688 years to apologize a trillion times.

I tried very hard to keep up with my credo that you didn't need to drink to have fun, but frankly I was just so fucking tired of being left out, of not getting to play beer pong because I didn't drink, of not getting flirted with because I was sober, of not getting to retell stupid stories the next day, of not getting male attention, of not having an excuse to be irresponsible. And I figured alcohol would help. I was still somewhat in the throes of an eating disorder, so when I started drinking late in my sophomore year of college, I began with Skinnygirl piña colada* mix combined with Diet Mountain Dew, which was actually not as bad as you're probably thinking. And it worked. Sort of. Kind of. At the very least, it stopped being as weird that I was hanging around drunk people until 2 a.m. For the first time in my whole life, I had both a drug to help me relax *and* a built-in excuse if I was ever "too much," which is something I worried about being constantly.

If you're a woman, alcohol buys you something incredible, something priceless: a break from responsibility, a glimpse of the invincibility cis white men feel all the time, an excuse for being too much. You can—at least *during* the drinking—let go. You can be loud, you can be flirty, you can take risks, you can triple text your ex.

Straight cis men don't need alcohol to let go as much, I don't think. I mean, I'm sure they have anxiety and love the feeling of getting to relax. But they *get* to be reckless so much more often than women do. Even *when drinking*, women have to stay more alert, be more careful. If you tallied up all the times I've been drunk around men, I have done *way* more of the caretaking than any of the guys has. They're allowed to fall apart, to be messy, to steal road signs, to be loud and drunk in line at Jack in the Box. Women aren't given the chance to. We still have to be on the lookout for danger. We have to stay in groups.

---

* My guy friends started calling this Penis A Lotta and I can't think of it any other way.

We have to be careful whom we let be in charge of getting us home. Even just on an emotional level outside of safety, men aren't punished socially for being irresponsible, aggressive, or careless the way women are. Guys can get in a bar fight, steal a fire extinguisher, break onto the roof, and it's funny—it's what boys do. Women don't get as many chances to let our guard down; we're so used to having to be alert that it can be difficult to let go even a little. But tequila can help you.

And when you do give in and live a little, relax a little, drink a little, you become so much more appealing to men. Why? Because your inhibition is lower, which really means you're more likely to put up with shitty behavior. Women who have been drinking are "more fun," yes, but they're also potentially less likely to reject men. Or at least, that seems to be the working theory. The (very reasonable) expectations of a sober woman are simply too much for a lot of straight cis guys to live up to. It's so much easier for them when we're drinking. A woman with two glasses of chardonnay in her system is just so much more approachable. And isn't that the best fucking thing you can be, ladies? Able to be approached by a man?

I certainly thought it was when I started drinking. As soon as I did the math and realized that you can both turn down *and* turn up your personality artificially with a few hard ciders, ooooh, boy, I was off to the races. It wasn't—isn't—of course successful every single time. Sometimes you end up in a bathroom crying about how dogs sometimes die in plane crashes, or you become known for leaving parties without telling anyone because drunk-you needs to *get the fuck home right now, no I can't wait for everyone else to get in this Uber!!!** But a lot of times you're a little more fun or a little more

---

* I Irish goodbye'd so much in college—and so well!!—that I ended up getting a tattoo of the word *goodbye* in Irish. (As a footnote to this footnote for the pedantic Americans: the language is called Irish. I know you've heard it's only called Gaelic, but it's called Irish. Chill out.)

chill, which is worth *a whole lot* if you're a woman. Even if you have to sacrifice some safety (and money and calories and liver health) to get there.

It's not like I started drinking alcohol and it erased all my anxiety—in fact, sometimes being drunk made that even *worse*; I still agonized over whether I was likable enough. And often the next morning, even if I hadn't blacked out the night before, I would wake up panicked that I had done something horrendous that I simply couldn't remember. It turns out that if you're a woman you still have to pay the price the next day for being loud, for being too much, for feeling invincible. Alcohol is certainly not a panacea for experiencing anxiety or sexism. But drinking helps smooth the edges of social situations, and social situations almost always favor men. Alcohol gives you an out, a way to shirk accountability for a short while, which is a lovely vacation if you're a woman and you're used to being responsible *all the fucking time.*

I spent the end of college—when I liked a guy so desperately that I turned to alcohol in hopes of making myself likable—and the rest of my early twenties playing a little bit of catch-up. While a lot of my friends were coming down from the freshman-in-college vigor with which they approached alcohol, I was just getting started. I was like a chemist trying to figure out exactly how much Riesling I could pour into my gullet to become appealing to strangers before I tipped over the edge and became Too Drunk. I haven't ever lost my phone on a night out or woken up in a strange place or even thrown up from drinking too much, so I don't mean to make it sound like I went full-tilt binge drinker. But I certainly approached white wine with a lot of enthusiasm during those years. I have been kicked out of a bar. I have woken up with bruises that I don't remember until friends remind me, "You actually did try to get up on the counter of our Airbnb kitchen island and fix a light bulb." I have drunkenly purchased the Italian-language movie poster for *Harold and Maude.*

I worry a lot these days that I'll get to the point my parents are at. That I'll *want* to drink every single night, that it will become hard *not* to. The alcoholism in my family arrives pretty late. Two of the biggest drinkers in my family didn't start drinking at all until they were in their late twenties. I do not feel yet like I am out of the woods by any means, that I have avoided alcoholism just because I'm not a huge drinker right now. Unlike when I was in high school, becoming reliant on alcohol actually *does* scare me now. I'm still afraid of not having control, of not being well-behaved. I don't want to become dependent on wine to make my evenings bearable. That said, I do love a bottle of champagne on a night with friends. I do find it so much easier to unclench my personality just a little bit and actually enjoy myself.

I've had a whole lot of fun and been a lot of fun with the help of alcohol. I don't drink as often now as I did at the end of college and the year or so after; I imbibe maybe once a week now. I still don't drink alone ever—not because of any personal rule, but because I don't have any desire. I drink now for the same reason I started drinking: to be more palatable around other people. To be less myself and more someone easy to be around. It doesn't always work. But I get why everyone in my family does it. It's hard to be yourself and have to be sober for it.

I'm Not Doing Zumba with You

I do not, under *any* circumstances, want to do Zumba with you. Even in an emergency. Even if there's a fire. I don't want to do a free trial of SoulCycle and I'm not joining you for even beginners' yoga. I'm not learning about Orangetheory or F45. We are distinctly *not* going to work out together.

Workout classes, I'm sorry to say, are the opiate of the already fit, or the already thin, if we're being quite honest with ourselves—which I normally don't recommend, but I'll make an exception. They're designed to make the workout that your hot friend Natalia does social for her. She wants workout buddies; she wants someone to hold her accountable for her 7 a.m. workouts.

I do not under *any* circumstances want to be accountable for a 7 a.m. workout, do you hear me? I am not meant to "squeeze in" workouts on my lunch break or otherwise. I most certainly do not want to pay a monthly membership fee in order to re-create my middle school gym class.

I know. I know I'm allowed to "go at my own pace" in theory. But in practice, you want me to keep up with people who can do that thing where you hold your leg up in the air while standing. The cheerleader thing. You know what I'm talking about. I can't keep up with people who can do that. My hips *do* need to be opened; you're right. I'm not going to go try to solve that crisis in front of twenty-five other people in a mirrored room.

Why the hell would I want to work out with other people? Why would I want an experience where we're all trying to get our bodies to do the same thing? Every friend of mine tells me, "Sophia, it's not competitive—just focus on yourself; no one is looking at you." That's utter bullshit, and we all know it. If I was really focused on me, there wouldn't be mirrors and there wouldn't be other people and there wouldn't be an instructor named Mandi or Tracy at the front of the room with a Britney Spears headset on, shouting inspiration at me. If this were about me, if this were for my well-being, it would be an afternoon nap on my couch. Everyone is checking each other out and you can't convince me otherwise. We're human!!

I took a couple of Zumba classes in college at the urging of my roommate; it was a full-frontal nightmare. Not only was I red, sweaty, and more out of breath than everyone else combined, but I never got the moves. Everyone else looked vaguely musical stomping their left foot on the waxed gym floor; I looked like an oversize toddler having either a tantrum or an exercise-induced asthma attack. I can never tell what I'm supposed to do when the instructor is facing me. Do I reverse her moves and mirror her, or do I match her? Am I supposed to raise my right arm because she's raising *her* right arm or what? What's the plan here?? Can't she just face the fucking mirrors so I can follow along?

I don't mind working out. I'm not going to pretend I love it, that it makes me feel *so good* after I'm done. I get weird headaches when I work out that doctors don't care enough about to figure out (despite their fervent enthusiasm for me losing weight). I have low blood pressure that makes it feel like I'm going to pass out sometimes when I bend over. I passed out one time at a gym and had to lie down on the floor; I got up only to pass out again. I like seated exercises like biking and rowing for this reason. My legs get itchy if I walk too much in one day because my circulation is terrible. Workouts are a necessary part of my life that I do a couple of times a week if I can and if I can't, oh fucking well.

I used to work out every day. Every single day! Can you imagine? I lived in a building with a gym (it was college; remember when your every need was met within a one-mile radius?). This gym had glass walls, which I guess are technically just windows. Anyway, there were huge glass window-walls and the gym was smack in the middle of the lobby of the building. I do not know why you'd put a gym in the middle of a fucking lobby; I think that's violent. The person who designed this apartment complex *so clearly* had 9 percent body fat and didn't feel ashamed to work out in a glass box.

I, of course, like a normal person, felt shitty about it, but I was also in college and trying very hard to get fit. Hence working out every day. I was doing tricep dips, that's how much I wanted it. Tricep dips are desperate. If you want to get fit so much that you're doing tricep dips, I think God should just give in and give you the body you'd like to have.

One time I was using an arm machine; I don't like using any machines other than cardio machines, because the bigger weight machines are dominated by men. Men congregate around them and take up space and watch you and talk to you and that is *not* the experience I want to have. I don't want any man anywhere near my body when I'm trying to make it do a thing it expressly doesn't want to do, like lift thirty-five pounds. There should be gyms where cis men are not allowed; I'm sure this exists, but I need more. Men make going to the gym a living hell; *however*, with a gym that's open 24/7 like the glass box was, you can usually stay up late enough on a Friday or Saturday (*or* get up early enough any other day) that no one is there.

In college if you're awake before 10 a.m., it's as quiet as Christmas morning.

One day, after months of being on a recumbent bike and doing kettle-bell squats, I decided, due to a distinct lack of men around, to try using a weight machine. No one else was in the gym with me. It was silent, still. I had the freedom to look like a dumbass while I tried to contort my body into the right shape for lifting.

I've heard the key is to try the machine first with no weights so that you *get* what you're doing, what the motion is, ideally, so that you don't hurt yourself. I sat down on one of those arm machines where you face the machine. You know when people have sex in movies where one person is sitting on the other person's lap (a good shot to hide titties if you need to because of an actor's contract)? Well, that is what it looks like when you sit on this workout machine. You sit on the machine's lap and then you reach your arms around like a big sex hug. Of course, eventually the idea is to pull your arms back in sort of a rowing motion. I started with zero pounds to make sure I got the vibe. Good to go. And then I upped the weight to ten pounds. And then I upped it again and again. I was feeling myself. I was like, "Wow, Sophia. This is fitness. This is health. Look it up, friends, this is *wellness*." No one was around and I was thriving. I'd made a very simple machine work and no one was laughing at me for doing it wrong.

Until, from behind me, I got a tap on my shoulder.

Friends, Romans, countrymen: NEVER EVER FUCKING TOUCH ANYONE ELSE AT THE GYM.

I managed to not scream bloody murder at being snuck up on. I took my headphones out and turned around. Standing there was the guy from the front desk.

I thought maybe I'd broken a rule. Maybe I was there too late and the gym wasn't actually open 24/7? Maybe a water main broke under the gym and they needed to shut it down and do reconstruction? Maybe there was a fire and all the exits were blocked and he and I were going to die together in the glass box and everyone would remember my commitment to fitness? No such luck. The guy from the front desk *had seen me through the window-walls of the gym* and wanted to come in and tell me that I was actually using the machine incorrectly.

This was my exact Nightmare on Elm Street.

He was like, "You need to keep your shoulder blades down. Pretend that there is a walnut in between them and you're trying to squeeze it." I remember him saying this because I was like, first of all, why the fuck on earth am I trying to *squeeze* a walnut? Do you mean crack a walnut? Why specifically a walnut? Is there something about this workout machine that ties it irrevocably to this specific tree nut? Also why is a walnut sitting between my shoulder blades? Who keeps a walnut there? Is it suspended? Glued on?

My biggest fixation, however, was: Why the hell are you talking to me? Why was it so important to cross over an entire massive lobby and use a key card to get into the gym to make sure that I used proper form while lap-sexing this machine? Was this necessary?

The worst part was, he wanted me to be grateful for his coaching. And I was so stunned that this stranger was correcting me that I let him guide me through a few more reps and then he walked away super-satisfied with himself, his charity work done for the year. No need to go to Lambda Chi Alpha's philanthropy events this semester! You corrected an ignorant gym lady!

And *that* is why I'm never going to join you for an 8 a.m. kickboxing class; I know for a *fact* that everyone is watching my shitty body the way you watch a semitruck go down a steep incline. And I obviously never used an arm machine again.

Good Coffee and Why Pierce Brosnan's Voice in *Mamma Mia!* Is Perfectly Fine

I was once hanging out with a guy I'd had a yearslong crush on. To set the scene, this person is *waaaaay* out of my league in pretty much every way other than I'm not a douche and he kind of was.*

I'm at *my best* when I'm around a crush. I've usually done like four or five sit-ups, I'm wearing clean clothes that I think I look cool in, I have good posture all of a sudden, I have mascara on. Without a crush, what's even the point of taking care of yourself and looking nice, you know?† Anyway, my crush and I are walking along the

---

* Look, everyone wants to pretend that leagues don't exist. Absolutely no one is above you and no one is beneath you as a person, of course. But are there conventional attractiveness levels? Yes. Saying someone is out of your league/you're out of someone's league is a very useful shorthand to describe social situations and nuances, okay? Plus, nothing is set in stone; you can always sleep with/marry/date people out of your league; straight men do it all the time!!!! So, to recap: the concept of "leagues" is harsh, but so is social and romantic interaction.
† I KNOW THIS IS A BAD OPINION AND I'M MOSTLY KIDDING.

street and my friend is there and because this crush is a really, really smart person, I'm trying to Prove Myself. (I feel like I need to take a quick detour here and remind you that at the time I was nineteen [or twenty].) So this guy and I are getting into what are retrospectively *very* banal philosophical debates. It's *exactly* like a rom-com, but it's real life and he is not actually attracted to me and is just an argumentative douche BUT I DON'T SEE THAT, OBVIOUSLY.

We're about to go get coffee when I offhandedly mention that I "can't taste the difference between good and bad coffee." Which is 100 percent true and also fair. Like, grow up, people who think "good coffee" is a thing. He starts telling me about how I could *learn* to like better coffee, or at least learn *about* what makes coffee better or worse. I, of course, laugh in his hot face. "Yeah, but I don't care." Douche Crush is flabbergasted, nigh offended—how could someone *not* want to learn this?

And then he said the sentence that made me lose my crush on him for good:* "Don't you think cultivating good taste is the *point* of life?"

LKDSfja;lskdjflksdjfl; ka

I KNOW.

I know.

You guys.

My poor friend who was standing off to the corner sucked in a deep, exhausted breath, knowing that this was going to send Douche Crush and Me down a real excruciating-to-be-around path. We finally had a real disagreement to hash out and not just nebulous, theoretical ideas to bounce back and forth. I need to send my friend a thank-you card for not ending her relationship with me before I ended my crush on Douche Crush.

---

* I still had sex dreams about him for about two years after this. But I also had a sex dream about the guy from the Dyson commercials, so grain of salt.

I still thought he was out of my league intellectually, so what followed his pronouncement that the *point* of life was cultivating good taste was me getting super flustered attempting to explain to him my position, which was, essentially: Are you fucking joking? I made very few good points, so shocked was I to even have to explain this to someone. I'd have been more ready if he'd told me, "I think we should bomb hurricanes to stop them."

This was also before I'd really gotten into Twitter, feminism, or Being Loud Online. At the tender age of nineteen (or twenty), I avoided making any real points outside of classrooms because I was *terrified* that everyone else would have way more information, be a total ass to me, demand to see studies that I hadn't memorized and cited verbally, and then they'd win. Frankly, I was a white lady who was about as informed as a garden rake, so it's not like I was wrong to avoid loud opinions. There were so many topics I felt that I had no room speaking on (and I was mostly correct about that), but the men around me *never* seemed to have this trepidation. Certainly there were topics I *could* have had an informed opinion on; however, I simply figured other people knew better.

Occasionally, I fantasize about going back in time and just fucking trouncing Douche Crush at his own game (debating people in pompous ways). Eight (or nine) years have passed and I think I could "win" against him now. Mostly because I don't care about him anymore, and it's so much easier to debate people who you don't have a hot and horny crush on. But also because I've thought a lot about taste since then. Here's what I know now that I had no idea about back then: he will *always* have better taste than I. Why? Because taste bends to him as a well-off white guy. Taste is not, despite attitudes to the contrary, delivered divinely from above. Taste is decided by the wealthy, the powerful, the victors. Taste is often more about gatekeeping and upholding division than anything else. It also evolves over time; lobster used to be so abundant that they'd feed it to prisoners. For most of history, the people who have been in charge in the West are wealthy white men, which renders them de facto tastemakers; even when they're going to other cultures to steal ideas, they're still in charge of what is highbrow and what is lowbrow, what is substantial and what is fluff, what is beautiful and what is trashy. Of course, "taste" also bends in my direction as a well-off white woman.* But I can never have taste that's as good as a white man's, because society says that women have bad taste.

Of course, we don't *actually* have bad taste. For the most part, we're not the ones keeping the cargo-shorts industry afloat. I've never had to explain to any of my female friends why something does or doesn't match. When my boyfriend and I moved into a new place, he incorrectly insisted that a rug he owned worked in the room because it was colorful and the room was also colorful. Women have perfectly fine "taste." But our taste is undervalued. A wonderful example of this is how early Beatles fans were women, and their love of the band was derided. They were painted as screaming hysterical teenagers whose love of a stupid boy band could easily be waved away as "mania." And then men started liking the band. Of course, this oversimplified example conveniently starts at the point that young, mostly white women started liking the band's music. Since the Beatles lifted quite a lot of their work from Black and brown artists, it's pretty easy to see how the taste of Black and brown fans was ignored until it was stolen.

This replicates itself constantly where marginalized groups enjoy something that is looked down upon until rich white people, and

---

* In my book (literally), *well-off* is defined as: you're not living paycheck to paycheck. Which I am just barely not doing. But also I have parents I can call, a boyfriend I could borrow money from, etc. I'm well-off. You might be, too! That might seem depressing to consider yourself well-off when you make $47,000 a year, and you're doing complex math to see if you can afford a new TMJ retainer. It *is* depressing!

especially rich white men, are ready to like it. And then they steal it. It happens with food, slang, music, dance, pretty much any culture after Christopher Marlowe.*

It's particularly easy to see how women's taste is overlooked since we make up around half the population. This, of course, is not to say that women like one thing and men like others. Or that all women share the same tastes. Please don't be a cabbagehead! There are stories, movies, shows, and even motifs that appeal especially to women, which are consumed by largely female audiences. We know that. And those things are dumb as shit, at least according to whoever is deciding on taste.

My boyfriend's near-encyclopedic knowledge of every basketball player's stats from wingspan to rebounds never earns him a "Jesus, what a waste of brain space." Meanwhile, my similarly useless memorization of the Kardashians' exes, partners, and children is *often* lambasted by other people. Please keep in mind that he has to keep track of 450 people and how well they share a basketball with their friends and I simply know a twenty-five-person family tree. Arguably there is *a lot* less "brain space" being taken up by me knowing what a daughter is and what that daughter's name is than someone having to learn what a point guard and power forward are. I love b-ball,† but arguably knowing about family ties is more essential to being human than knowing that the Sixers require a deeper bench if they want to make it to the finals.

If I somehow magically make my brain forget all the Kardashians it's not like I'm all of a sudden going to be flooded with the info needed to solve the Birch and Swinnerton-Dyer conjecture. If the Kardashians go, all that's going to fit in that tiny space is more anxiety about climate change. And why is everyone so worried about women's "brain space" anyway? I never hear men get asked about

---

* Jk, he probably stole his ideas from marginalized people too.
† I especially love calling it "b-ball."

their brain space. Never. Meanwhile, the men at my last job believed that pads went on with the sticky side up, stuck to the vagina.* When I reminded them that we had hair there, which would be ripped out with each pad usage, one answered, "Yeah, that's why I thought periods were so bad." Let's worry more about what men's "brain space" is up to, okay? I think I'm doing just fine with enjoying Netflix Christmas movies where Vanessa Hudgens falls for the first guy she sees in whatever snowy locale she's in.

Women's stories, interests, and desires simply aren't taken as seriously as men's. I recently got in trouble online (very common for me) because I pointed out that the top four Oscar-nominated movies of the year (2019 or 2020—I don't know how the Oscars work) had almost *no* speaking roles for women. The movies were *The Irishman*, *1917*, *Once Upon a Time . . . in Hollywood*, and *Joker*. I mean, there is no woman in any of those movies who has a groundbreaking role, or even a central one. You could mute your TV every time women spoke and most of the movies would remain pretty much the same. But more than that, the *taste* of the films—the themes, the shots, the point of view—was designed for men. All of those movies individually are fine—great, even, probably!—but when are we going to value stories by and for women and by and for people of color and by and for trans people and by and for people with disabilities? It's not like they aren't being written. It's that they aren't being *produced*, and when they are, the institutions that help "decide" what is worthy and unworthy don't give them attention.†

---

* Yes, I mean labia. No, you aren't smarter than anyone for correcting my usage since we *all* use the word *vagina* to mean labia all the time. It's the informal word for labia. Get over it, Andreas Vesalius.

† Arguably, if they're still being evaluated by institutions like the Academy, which are full of rich, able-bodied white cis dudes, these movies are never going to be respected or recognized, fully. And of course, this begs the question: Should we even *want* to be recognized by institutions like these?

I went to a talk recently where film producer Lindsay Doran pointed out to the crowd that *Mamma Mia!* and *Mamma Mia! Here We Go Again* together made over $1 billion. In just two films. That's an ass-load of money, in case you didn't know. Still, almost no one (in a room full of industry people) off the top of their head could name who directed either film. I'm not saying that the films are master-pieces,* but it's impossible to think of another billion-dollar movie franchise that the industry cared so little about. I'm sure everyone in the room could have named who directed the *Incredibles* movies, another two-film franchise, which also made about the same amount of money.† *The Proposal* made more money than *Step Brothers* and we got like five thousand more hilarious midlevel comedy films and very few more midlevel, well-written rom-coms. Why? Because no one in Hollywood fucking cares what anyone other than cis white men want to see on-screen. Stoner comedies are no more intellectually rig-orous or prestigious than rom-coms or musicals. But men like those movies and men's taste is taken seriously and therefore movies made by and for them are taken more seriously. Obviously—obviously—the numbers are even more bleak when you look at films made by and for Black people, by and for people with disabilities, by and for any number of marginalized people. It's baked into our institutions, too. Every year the Academy tries to make a public push for more diverse films, but then the mostly old, mostly male, and mostly white voting body votes . . . otherwise. The reviewers, the newspapers they work for, the awards shows? They're all overwhelmingly controlled by rich white men. It's no wonder that taste gets "decided" by them.

Recently, in my office, many of the male executives were com-

---

* Yes, I am.
† And the *Incredibles* sequel was . . . meh, while *Mamma Mia! Here We Go Again* was one of the best theatrical experiences of my life. Pierce Brosnan is a gem and anyone who has anything to say about his voice has no room for joy in their life.

plaining about how in *Hustlers* the women stole from "innocent" men and how the movie glorified that—in their words—"because girl power." Please keep in mind that at the time of their complaints none of them had actually *seen* the film (which does *not* glorify this nearly enough for my tastes, if at all). Please also keep in mind that this is exactly the fucking plot of like *half* of male movies. I would bet every dollar I had that these men thought *The Wolf of Wall Street* was brilliant. What I think was *actually* happening was that these men I worked for, who were rich and also likely patrons of strip clubs, were for perhaps the first time in their lives seeing themselves as the target of a threat in a movie. Any of them could have been one of the people getting hurt and it was uncomfortable—a stripper could possibly drug and steal from one of *them*. Do you know how many times I've watched people who look like me, whose lives are like mine, get hurt on-screen? Get raped and assaulted and slapped and hit and killed on-screen? And even less violently but more commonly: be demeaned, humiliated, treated like an idiot, presented as a caricature, used as set dressing? And it's glorified? God forbid *one time* that cis straight white men (and rich ones at that!) are harmed on film by women. These executives were simply *that* unused to, and therefore uncomfortable with, stories that centered on women.

When we *do* tell stories for women, they're seen as frivolous or dumb. There is *nothing* inherently worse or less worthwhile about *The Bachelor* than there is about watching the NFL. Actually, since fewer people in Bachelor Nation are getting CTE, probably *The Bachelor* is *more* worthwhile. I love sports, please don't cancel me!!! Sports are incredibly fun to watch and highly socially valuable. The point is that *The Bachelor* is, too, and yet women who watch *The Bachelor* get shit on *all the time* for it. No one who watches *The Bachelor* thinks that it's a fucking Ken Burns documentary. For years, I didn't tell people—especially men—about watching *The Bachelor*. Every single time I've ever talked or tweeted about it, I've gotten shit for my enjoyment of the show. Meanwhile, when my boyfriend says that he watches it, and that the show is actually pretty good (WHICH IT IS), *no one*—no one!—ever treats him like a vapid airhead.

For many years, and to some extent still, I had a preoccupation with not seeming stupid. Now I'm much more aware of the ableist issues at play there—the horrid but prevailing idea that people who aren't as intelligent aren't as valuable. And the fact that we manufactured the idea of intelligence around who and what we already valued as a society. But as a former valedictorian and know-it-all who grew up in a house with four other really smart siblings, I was very used to the social dynamic of having to prove yourself. One of the most difficult things for me to handle well to this day is people assuming I don't know something, which, if you've ever been not a white man, happens *all the time.* There is something profoundly offensive to me about being treated like I need things explained to me—especially obvious facts, or subjects I know a lot about. It makes my skin get hot and itchy.

It is this fear of being seen as stupid or foolish—and therefore dismissed—that led me to hiding my romance novels *behind* the other books on my shelf. I love romance novels. Each year I read fifty books at least. Last year I read 109. I released a list of the books I read in the year, and I included only forty-one because I didn't want people to know how many romance novels I read, or the content of them. I don't even like checking the physical books out from the library for fear that I will seem like a big airhead for reading books about love, books whose target demographic is . . . women. And I'm not alone in my embarrassment in reading these books; the ebook market for romance novels is off the charts, because despite them being one of the bestselling genres, people don't want to be seen reading them in public. No dad is concerned about someone seeing him read a Jack Reacher book on a plane!

It took me a lot to get over the idea that everything needs to be proof that I was—that *I am*—smart and capable. Intelligent women constantly have to prove themselves, and that of course, like every-thing, is compounded by other marginalized identities a person might have, which makes it hard to want to cop to reading frivo-lous books or knowing all the names of the royals or loving *Dancing with the Stars*. If you're a smart woman, you're under pressure to not ever slip up, lest the boulder you're pushing up the hill each day roll back down even farther. You feel like you always have to be on the lookout for the thing that's going to get you dismissed as not seri-ous. I used to hate UGGs—loathe them—because I thought they were basic. I had been assured they were the shoe of the brainless Midwestern housewife and her four hair-bow-matching daughters. To some extent, yes, I'm sure the shoe appeals to busy moms living in Kansas City. But guess what I found out this year when I stopped giving a fuck and asked for a pair for my birthday? They're just really comfortable, warm shoes. That's all. Shocking! They have changed nothing about me other than how quickly I'm ready to take my dog out to shit.

The lesson smart women get is that if they want to be taken seri-ously intellectually, they need to cultivate their taste meticulously, and ultimately—completely by coincidence, I'm sure—align their preferences with cis white men's. To like the things men like is syn-onymous with refinement, virtue, intelligence. To enjoy something feminine is to admit weakness. Women's taste simply will never be good like that; it will never be dominant. It will always be vapid and juvenile. It won't be Oscar- or center-of-the-bookshelf–worthy. The books we like will be beach reads and the shows we watch will be trashy and the movies predictable.

And *that*, my friends, is why I'll never care about liking good cof-fee. I'll never have good taste and I'm fine with—proud, even—of that.

I'm Pretty Sure My Insatiable Capacity for Desire Stems from the Scholastic Book Fair

I was reading a magazine recently and there was an article on sustainable beauty brands. Great news for me because I love buying things and hate climate change and this lets me pretend those two things aren't at odds. One of the brands was selling a vagina oil, a pink serum in a beautiful clear vial. If you saw the graphic design on this bottle—the font!—you'd want it too. It was perfectly imagined to light up all the circuits in the brain of a woman like me.

I ripped the page out of the magazine and put it to the side, something I do quite often as I read magazines. Later in the week, when I was culling my many magazine rip-outs like a neurotic decoupage enthusiast, I saw the vagina oil and I went right to the website to get some. They actually had two products—a cleanser and the oil. I read reviews and calculated the price if I were to buy them as a bundle. I put them in my cart and then took the cleanser out. *I just need the vagina oil*, I thought.

And here is where you may be asking: *What on God's green earth do you need vagina oil for? What does it . . . do? Do vaginas need oiling like the Tin Man?* No, not that I'm aware of! All of a sudden, I realized that I could not articulate to you what problem I was even addressing with the vagina oil. I was about to spend FORTY-SIX DOLLARS plus shipping and handling (money I do not have to spend on vagina oil), for a problem I didn't even understand, let alone experience.

Per the website, their oil "smooths, brightens, and moisturizes vulva and labial skin." Is my labia not bright enough? What does that mean? Is my vulva meant to shine like a bat signal in the night? Am I supposed to have a smoother vulva than what I've got? The magazine, via its glossy trickster pages, had presented me with both the problem and the solution simultaneously. *Burdened with dull, dry labia? This is a game changer!* And I'd believed. I had believed that I had a bad, un-oiled vagina. That the good vaginas of this world were oiled up and that I was failing to put my best labia forward.

We are the targets of this conscripted envy, wherein the only possible solution is consumption, even as we're derided for it. Selling things is all about making people feel like they're lacking, and women make especially easy prey for this. For instance, rumor has it that the reason women shave their armpits is because marketers at Gillette wanted to sell more razors. No one was even asking for hairless armpits, but if you make a woman feel bad about a body part and then present her with a product as a solution, voilà! You've got sales, baby. While certain commercials for men use similar tactics, often ads for men assume they're *already* powerful and beloved and that the product being sold will only aid in them maintaining manliness. Ads aimed at women present a problem to be solved or an image to be managed, while men are told they're already doing amazing. And then when we *do* consume, we're ridiculed for it. See: every single straight cis man ever picking up an eyelash curler and being like, "What does this even do?" Dude, read one book and find out!*

One of the most iconic catchphrases in terms of making fun of women is the *Nutty Professor* line "Women be shoppin'." Of course, the line was intentionally written to be an oversimplification of gendered stereotypes, and it is not literal. But people *do* look down on women for their consumption, while also presenting consumption as the solution to the many problems inherent to being a woman. In how many movies and TV shows has a straight cis guy gone into a woman's bathroom and made fun of all the beauty products she has? How many guys have complained about having to go to stores with their partners? One of the clearest examples of our disdain for the female consumer is in shoe purchasing. While it's certainly an outdated joke, women used to get a lot of shit for buying and owning so many pairs of shoes. Guess what? There are men who stand in line for *hours* for sneakers. I'm not saying male sneakerheads are entirely free from scorn, but rather that there is a space for them in the pantheon of coolness that is not there for women who buy non-sneaker shoes. Women's material desires—like their hobbies, like their ambitions, like their boundaries—are simply not taken as seriously as men's, even as women have been *set up* to be desirous, to be competitive, even as we sell women on the idea of scarcity. There are only a few spots for women: you better show up with your eyelashes *curled*.

Consumption is about wanting material items, but ultimately, it's really about wanting another life. And I'm an expert at that. The more I gained weight as a kid, the more I wanted to remain inside

---

* Good news, you're reading the right book: it curls eyelashes upward so that a person's eyes look bigger and therefore the person ostensibly looks younger. Because of course that's the goal.

my own head, inside a pretend land where I lived another life. And when youth turned to adolescence and I was *actually* left out of things because of my size, my envy fully blossomed. I believed most ardently that I would one day live a life better than my peers; I had a full imaginary other existence, one that was going to happen one day, but that was also, in a way, happening for me internally. In my head, I imagined that I would lose weight, my acne would clear up, I'd look good wearing sweaterdresses, I would date more people, make more money, have a cooler job. I would be beloved.

I wanted. I wanted, I wanted, I *wanted*. I'm very good at wanting things, at wanting lives. I still often find myself wanting to make up for all the time I felt like I missed out, all the parties I didn't go to because I was scared everyone didn't really want me and all the parties I didn't go to because people really *didn't* want me. I want to make up for all the sex I didn't have, the fun I missed, the cities I didn't get to live in.

I know that virtually no one is living the exact life they always dreamed of. I also know that when I find myself flush with bitterness, I am usually envious of only a small *part* of another person's life: their most recent career achievement, how thick their hair is, that they can afford a house. Envy is easy if you take someone's life piecemeal and covet the brightest, shiniest parts. If you forget about their arthritis, their shitty husband, that time they got fired. Regardless of logically knowing this, I still often *want*.

Truly almost all the most thrilling moments in my life have involved wanting something. Very few have involved actually receiving what I wanted. The very act of wanting has become the reward for me; I think I got so used to cycles of unfulfilled desire as a child that I didn't learn how to be content. My favorite night of the entire year is Christmas Eve. If I could re-create one day of my life to live again, it would be Christmas Eve from anytime when I was under, say, eight years old. Anytime when the magic was still real, when, in the parlance of *The Polar Express*, the bell still rang for me. The night is all about desire, anticipation, longing. It's an entire night devoted to what comes next. Christmas morning can *never* match Christmas Eve. Because as soon as you get something—presents, your Amazon order, a new haircut—you find something else to want. Inevitably, getting something doesn't *make* you fit in, doesn't make you happy, doesn't change your personality. I desperately wanted to own Nike Shox in fifth grade, because *everyone* was getting them. I *begged* my mother for them, but I already had tennis shoes and I did not need more in her estimation. Finally, after months and months of begging, she relented and I got a pair. And they . . . were fine, but they didn't make me fit in with the kids who had popularized them at our school. They didn't change *me*, which was ultimately my dream. The fantasy I'd had while wanting them had been so much more fruitful than the reality. Also, by the time I got them, the excitement of the fad had worn off.

For me as a kid, one of the best days of the year was when the American Girl catalog, square and glossy, arrived in the mail. I would sit at the desk in the "computer room" and circle every single thing I wanted even a little bit—Josephina's party dress, a skating outfit for Samantha, Felicity's horse—and then I would add up their cost. The first round through, mirroring my buffet strategy, I didn't limit myself. Anything that I thought that might make my life better went on the list. When I got to the back of the magazine, I'd take out my mom's calculator, which came in a fancy wooden box with her outdated still-married-to-my-dad initials engraved on the cover, and I'd add up everything I wanted. The total was somewhere around thirteen hundred dollars (American Girl dolls are insanely expensive). I would start over from the front, slowly eliminating items I didn't want *as much*, going over and over my list until I got down to a reasonable price, which usually was zero dollars. Which is not to say that I didn't still *long* for all the things I'd circled the first time. If you asked me at age eight what my dream was, it would be to be rich enough to buy everything in the American Girl catalog without thinking twice. But I didn't care about getting the things in the catalog so much as I cared about *wanting* them.

Every time I flip through a magazine or shop online or look up hair inspiration, I become convinced that I've found something to make me seem hotter, thinner, more in touch, generally cooler. I'm always so sure that *this* will be the thing to change my life, if only I am allowed to purchase it. My father has the same issue. Frankly, most people who are American consumers with any level of disposable income have this issue. My dad, who owned a hockey equipment business when I was growing up, who plays hockey multiple times a week, used to have an entire room in our unfinished basement devoted to his gear. He had *everything*! Partially this was to try it out; hockey equipment was his business, after all. One time, though, he said to me, "I always buy new stuff with the hope that *this* will be the thing to make me skate faster. It's never worked." That's the dream of capitalism: if you just buy this one last product, all the pieces of your life will fall into place. Yes, you need a food processer *and* a blender *and* a KitchenAid mixer in a fun color. Yes, you need retinol and vitamin C serums and peptides. You need a night cream and a day cream and a four-hundred-dollar Dyson hair dryer and place mats and decorative baskets and a Nintendo Switch and a new pair of hockey skates. With each purchase I make comes the hope of a new life—the life of the people I envy. The people whose articles get shared online more than mine, the people who have famous friends, the people who own expensive West Elm furniture, the people who sell movie scripts and vacation in Fiji.

I'm full of envy all the time, full of the feeling that people around me are doing better than I am. Part of it, as I've explained, is my childhood, my genes; it's baked into my very being. Part of it also, I believe, is that I'm in an industry (and a world) where the narrative is that there are few spots in general, fewer spots for women (even fewer for other marginalized groups, and even fewer if you're at the intersection of any of those groups), and a very short timeline in which to succeed. Everyone else's successes *feel* as if they're chipping away at yours. Every sold screenplay, every best seller, every stand-up special *could have been yours.**

I'm sure that's crass to admit. We're supposed to say things like, "I love writing for the sake of writing and I don't care how successful or beloved my work is." We're supposed to feel gracious when peers succeed. And I *do* feel that way a lot of the time. I feel real, actual joy when friends of mine do well. I *love* writing for the sake of writing and have done it unpaid and underpaid for years. But I don't think it's evil to want. I don't think it ought to be shameful to cop to our own most fervent, quixotic dreams, or to our moments of pettiness.

When I first started dating my current boyfriend, one of my biggest fears was cheating. Not him, me. I was terrified that a few years down the line, when we'd become bored of each other, restless, when sex wasn't good and conversation was worse, I'd find someone shiny and new and I'd see the possibility of a new life right there before my eyes. I was worried that my being built on desire, being forged by longing, was going to bode poorly for us. After all, I'm the kind of person who can see a new life with a bottle of vagina oil! What about when a person flirts back? How do I avoid buying into the conceit of cheating, which is: here's a better, fresher, more exciting life! How do I, a person who feels like she missed out on youth, on adventure, conceivably walk away from that?

The answer, for me, is a mixture of self-esteem, discipline, and

---

* Of course, that's false math. There is space for a lot of people to create things. And given that I'm a white woman, my odds are fine.

philosophy. I think often of Sylvia Plath and her fig tree.* Like her, I'm desperate to eat *all* the figs and commit to none. But, as Plath says, "I saw myself sitting in the crotch of this fig tree, starving to death, just because I couldn't make up my mind which of the figs I would choose." If you spend your life wanting, paralyzed by the loss that comes with choice, you—ironically—don't get things; I know that. But I also know now that getting things that you want almost always feels like a letdown, at least at first. I know now that the wanting itself is sweet, but that you don't want it to get overripe. A whole life filled only with desire and never with fulfillment becomes bitter in its own way.

I try to remind myself that most new things are like a haircut. Haircuts go like this, for me: I want, perhaps, to do something different with my hair. Eventually I start noticing other people's hair. The cuts, the colors, the styles they've chosen. I start reading articles about what is popular to do right now with hair. I start gathering inspirational photos. I think on it. I imagine my life with this new hair, how people will treat me, how it will look with the clothes I wear, the style I currently have. I wait until I'm positively *desperate* to get a haircut. I am nervous when I finally make the appointment; I feel often like I need to get approval, permission from someone somewhere (usually my mother and four or five close friends) to make the change. I get the haircut, and for a moment in the chair I'm in such shock that I did it—I actually *did* it!—that I feel detached from myself. And then I get to my car and I start to worry. I go home and take pictures of myself and I nervously concede that I love it. I think. Friends and family try to bolster my opinion of the new cut. And then the next morning, I wake up and I hate it. I hate it, hate

---

* Sylvia Plath wrote this whole section in *The Bell Jar* about life branching out before her like a fig tree, where she can't decide which juicy fig to eat and so she sits there and starves as the figs rot.

it, hate it. What have I *done*? Which "friends" of mine allowed—nay, encouraged—this? How have I failed so spectacularly at getting something as simple as a haircut? Yes, it will grow out, but until June of next year I'm meant to soldier on looking like *this*?

And then in a week it's normal and it's just how my hair looks and I move on.

This is what I remind myself when I think about my potential for future cheating, which I don't actually think of much at all anymore.* If you live like this—if you let this insatiable desire guide you—you get something you want and then, pretty soon, it's normal and boring and you're all itchy and dissatisfied again. I'm much better now at simultaneously wanting things and accepting that I will not get them. I'm better at knowing that getting them will not *make* me happy, and maybe not even happier. I've purchased enough shit online on a whim to know that most things aren't as great as advertised. That once you own something, or date someone, or move somewhere, eventually life starts up again. *Your* life. The life you were living before. Unfortunately, wherever you go, there you are, even if you arrive with a shiny vagina.

---

* I should make it clear, for both you and my boyfriend, that there isn't anyone who has actually made me want to cheat. It's more the abstract idea of myself in the future, being a little tart.

Everyone I've Ever Wanted
to Like Me

1. The guy who works at the liquor store on the corner who watches *Grey's Anatomy* reruns all day and compliments my nails every time I get them done.

2. My brother's new girlfriend, whom I haven't even met.

3. The Apple Genius Bar employee who replaced the malfunctioning *e* key on my computer the first time.

4. Lindsey Leeker, a popular girl from my high school.

5. The Apple Genius Bar employee who replaced the malfunctioning *e* key on my computer the second time.

6. Actually, pretty much all the popular girls from my high school except for two of them who were straight-up unkind and the ones who seemed Republican.

7. The Apple Genius Bar employee who told me that they could no longer fix the *e* key on my computer and that it would take two weeks for them to replace the entire keyboard.

8. Every hairstylist who has ever cut or colored or even washed my hair.

9. My dental hygienist, whose aunt used to live in the apartment I currently live in.

10. Sophia Bush, especially after I once stole her coffee at the Starbucks on Melrose and Stanley because they called the name Sophia and she was very politely like, "Oh, that's mine I think . . ." and I was like, "Oh, I'm Sophia." And she had to be like, "Me too."

11. Every single English teacher I ever had.

12. Just kidding! Every single teacher I ever had, period. Including substitutes.

13. My landlord, even though being a landlord is unethical.

14. The guy who detail-cleaned my car.

15. My literary agent.

16. My editor.

17. About 90 percent of the interns who have ever worked at a place where I'm employed. Sometimes you get weird vibes

from the beginning and you know things aren't going to be simpatico and those people . . . you just have to let go of.

18. I don't want to say *every* coworker, because I have certainly disliked some coworkers, but in all honesty, I thought about it, and yeah, I would like for literally every coworker to have liked me. Even the ones I didn't like. So, yeah, every coworker I've ever had going all the way back to Cold Stone Creamery.

19. The couple who own the coffee shop I go to.

20. The woman who own the *other* coffee shop I go to, who always asks me how she should get her hair done.

21. Every woman I follow on Twitter.

22. Every nonbinary or gender-nonconforming person I follow on Twitter.

23. A couple of the men I follow on Twitter.

24. The women who work at the front desk of the doctor's office where I go to get tested for UTIs.

25. The hot bartender at Davey Wayne's.

26. The rich couple I used to babysit for.

27. The children I used to babysit for whose parents are rich.

28. My sexist, racist, piece-of-shit ex-boss.

29. My other sexist, racist, piece-of-shit ex-boss.

30. Most of the guys I met in college, with very few exceptions.

31. Especially this one guy on my freshman dorm floor who ended up leaving school the next year to serve in the Korean army; I *think* he had a crush on me. Fucked-up that I was dating someone else at the time. Anyway, I really wanted him to like me.

32. Every single person I've ever met in a bar bathroom, especially if I talked to them, but even if I didn't. You look great, babe! I'm your biggest fan!

33. Mary, the woman who used to do my nails when I was in college and didn't drink and had nothing better to spend my money on.

34. The entire cast of *Mamma Mia!* I really think I could have fit in on set.

35. This cool fifty-year-old British woman I met at a wedding once who bragged about not having any cellulite (problematic) and then proceeded to lift up her dress and show me (hysterical).

36. Gabrielle Union, because she seems like just the best person. We haven't met and I wouldn't subject her to me, obviously, but if she had to meet me, I would hope she liked me.

37. Nora Ephron, even though she's dead.

38. Trick-or-treaters who come to my house, even the ones who take handfuls and handfuls of candy, which I think is kind of selfish. But also, it's Halloween! Go nuts!

39. The car mechanic I take my car to, who didn't charge me when I *towed* my car to him because it was making a weird sound, which turned out to be a plastic bag wrapped around the axle.

40. David Spade's personal assistant. Don't ask.

41. My little siblings.

42. Sherman Jackson, my professor for Intro to Islam, who was way too brilliant to be teaching undergrads, who always wore impeccable suits with expensive sunglasses, and who knew everyone's name—in a 150-person lecture class—the second week. God, I wanted him to like me so badly.

43. Any animal that I've ever even seen a photo of.

44. My neighbor whose dog attacked my dog, but she's actually a *really* good dog owner and it was a total freak accident and also she's the coolest person and she makes chairs by hand. Who can do that? Just building stuff?? At your house?

45. My other neighbor who is a writer and who can grow plants like you wouldn't believe. He has this one plant that is the span of his whole kitchen. He's very smart and kind and outdoorsy and calm. I'm trying really hard to make friends with both of them.

46. All my friends' parents, especially their moms.

47. The vet tech who is *super* chill about my dog not wanting to come into the lobby, even when I am freaking out about how scared my dog is.

48. The theater girls who were seniors when I was a sophomore in high school; they were all great friends and hot as hell and they got the big roles and they all dated/slept with/hooked up with John Lodato. I couldn't sing, so I just made the costumes for them.

49. My parents.

50. Jane Fonda.

The Greatest Joy on Earth Is
Getting Ready to Go Out

I used to work at an improv theater, which doesn't even break the top ten most embarrassing things about me. I want to reiterate, as I have earlier in this book, that I did not actually *do* improv. I liked working there, though, because I generally got along with my coworkers, and since I was uninterested in improv or sketch comedy, I felt little to no competition with the people around me, which in the entertainment industry is pretty rare.* Most of the time, when you work with and especially *for* people who are doing the job you want to have, you feel like total shit every minute of the day, because that could be *you*, but it simply is not. But I did not want to do improv, so I was safe from becoming an embittered front-desk crone.

At the improv theater job, one of my frequent tasks was training

---

* I genuinely cannot think of a non-douchey way to say "the entertainment industry." I think ranked from worst to best the options are: showbiz, show business, The Industry, Hollywood, entertainment (as in "I'm in entertainment"), and the entertainment industry.

interns/giving them an orientation of sorts. I'd worked there longer than most other people at my level (shout out to flexible hours, a casual dress policy, and snacks) and I'd done pretty much every job at every part of the organization. Plus I enjoyed training people because it required talking and I love talking. I had always wanted to be a campus tour guide, and this was basically that.*

One of the interns I was tasked with training was Kelsey. Here's what you need to know about Kelsey. She's hot, she's blonde, she's an actor, and she's from Utah. At least, that's what *I* knew about Kelsey when I met her. I was immediately like, "This is not a match." Being hot is one thing (and one which I take personally), but she was also younger than me? And, again, blonde. I felt in my bones that this was not a person who was aligned with my values, which were: being mediocre-looking and the low-level hair maintenance popular in the Midwest. I've watched a lot of kids' movies and they never make the hot young lady who is trying to marry your dad a brunette, okay?? I want to be very clear that I wasn't rude to her or anything, but I also wasn't planning on being friends. Some interns you love, some you mostly ignore, some you give little errands to all day so that they stay away from you because they're kind of creepy. And *some* make you seethe with envy.

Kelsey was new to LA, and so other, more tolerant people at my workplace were always trying to invite her to go out with them and get drinks. Mostly this was because she was hot, and not out of a great interest in actually getting to know her. (Sorry to beat this dead horse, but I'm really wanting you to get the picture here!!! She's gorg!) Unfortunately for all my thirsty coworkers, *I* was—surprisingly—the present authority on Fun Times for Young Ladies in LA, which meant that *I* alone had good suggestions of

---

* I interviewed three times to be a tour guide at USC and didn't ever get the job. They say they have a 4 percent acceptance rate or something, but I'm still miffed.

places she should go and bars she should try. Which got me a little tangled up into hanging out with Kelsey, because she needed
someone fun to go with, and while I'm not fun per se, I can be
fun-adjacent. And also I wasn't trying to sleep with her, so I wasn't
a weirdo creep.

At that time in my life, I'd recently stopped living with two girls
my own age to move in with my boyfriend, who was over thirty
and therefore not a fan of loud bars. Most of my friends were either
too old to want to go out and have *FUN*, or they lived too far away,
or their vibe was more "Let's watch a bad John Travolta movie and
make fun of it," which absolutely has its time and place. I'd also
recently stopped being friends with someone who made me feel
like shit constantly (hell yeah, I'm Boundaries Barbie) and another
close friend had started grad school that required about seventy
hours a week of work and another twenty hours of socializing
with people who were also in the grad program. My best, best, best
friend on earth had never lived in LA with me, but she had recently
up and moved a whole lot farther away, to Ireland. In other words,
I needed a new friend, and if someone wanted to get drunk at a
popular bar with me, then by fuck I was going to take them up on
it, even if they were blonde. And younger. And hot. So I agreed to
take Kelsey out.

Accidentally, we ended up having the time of our *lives*. We got
to the bar very early because it usually has a line after 9 p.m.; we
ended up standing inside a mostly empty room, nursing glasses of
white wine, which turned into talking, which eventually turned
into dancing once other people eventually showed up. Any anxiety I had that I could not keep up with her socially evaporated. We
were both driven and ambitious, dramatic and engaging, political
and outraged. We both had no interest in speaking to men. We were
perfect together. It turns out I was an ass and Kelsey was an excellent, worldly, brilliant person who just happened to be an actor and

blonde and from Utah. It turns out her first impression of me was also less than stellar.*

The first night out was enough fun that we had a second. And then a third. We usually ended up standing still in the middle of a crowded dance floor, wearing absurdly high heels and ridiculously short skirts, and yelling over the music about things like what kind of porn we actually watched and how we got caught masturbating as kids. One Halloween, a holiday we both hate, we tried really hard to go out and Be Fun and we ended up spending the whole night in the bar bathroom, drunkenly complimenting every woman who came in. After a few months of going out together and terrorizing the city of Los Angeles with our drunken antics, we decided due to work schedules that it would be easier for us to meet up at my apartment after work every Friday and get ready (and drunk) before going out. This also ostensibly saved us money on drinks once we got to the bar, as we were both . . . less than wealthy.

Those Friday nights became some of the favorite nights of my life, not to be incredibly dramatic. We would start planning a week or two in advance, trying to settle on a "vibe" for the evening. (I'm so sorry about using the word *vibe*. I started doing so ironically, but now I'm doing it for real.) We'd scour Pinterest and Instagram for inspiration. Target and secondhand stores for outfits. Our houses for props. If we were going out at 10 p.m.—everything in Los Angeles closes at 2 a.m.; you have to get out there early—we would start the night at five or six to make time for drinks, hair curling, outfit changes, a meltdown about false eyelashes, and then at least an hour of photos. We are no longer casual about getting ready and taking photos. We have a ring light we've named Louise to illuminate us. We purchase disposable cameras to get a different look for our pictures. All of this is ridiculous, we are well aware, and yet we are having *the most fun*.

---

* In Kelsey's words, "You seemed really intense."

Kelsey and I have a *firm* and beautiful policy of telling each other the truth. If you feel like something is wrong with your appearance (and all of us feel like that a lot of the time), in this space you can simply ask, "What should I change? I feel like I look like a big cheese stick with legs." Or "Help me!!!!! I look like a news anchor in Cincinnati right now! What do I do?" And the other person will give gentle but incredibly specific feedback like, "I think your eye shadow is too much" or "That lipstick is way too bright with that outfit. You look like a lawn flamingo." Not that looking like a lawn flamingo is bad, but time and place.

Getting ready to go out beats the actual event (almost) every time. Where else can you scream-laugh, "My vagina is going to come OUT tonight, I swear to God!"? Where else are you going to have someone brush down your flyaway hairs for you with hairspray and a mascara wand? Where else are you going to find someone who will lie down on the ground to get the best camera angle? Where else can you be so loudly yourself, so gaudy, so conspicuous, so wanton? Getting ready to go out is all about the promise of what's to come—even if the main attraction can never hold a candle to the pregame. It says: The night has just begun and look how much fun you're already having.

I never really got ready with people before Kelsey. I didn't wear makeup until college, I didn't know how to do my hair until even later. The extent of my preparing to go somewhere until I was about eighteen was me shaving my legs. The problem was that I felt like nothing was actually made for me. I mean, you can put on mascara, but it doesn't make you not a fat kid. And so instead of trying to do smaller things that might help me look better, I was angry at the entire process, and therefore not a very inviting person to have around at an event centered on beauty. But also, I think having a fat person around during events about clothing often makes people uncomfortable. None of my other friends were wearing Spanx to the homecoming dance. Additionally, by the end of high school, most of my friends had actual dates for dances, dates who would pick them up and take them out to dinner before we all met up for pictures, so we weren't getting ready together.

At some point growing up, I had been told wearing makeup was for adults; I stringently followed that vague guideline that my parents had probably said when I was *five* so that I didn't eat lipstick or something. It's not like my parents were actively stopping me from wearing makeup, but they also weren't supporting me wearing it, either. No one was teaching me how to look better, even if my mom offered to help me get ready for big events. I just didn't know shit and I felt left out and overwhelmed by it. It felt like drinking or sex in a way: things I was desperate to hold myself above and yet things I wanted to partake in with equal desire.

Perhaps because I was an outsider, in my younger mind, getting ready together was about being empty and vapid; it was a time of gossip and vanity. (Which was a really wild thing for me to look down on, since I happen to dearly *love* vapidity, gossip, and vanity.)

For so many reasons, until I was in my twenties, I hadn't ever experienced the ecstasy of simply pregaming with female friends. I had made myself so left out in high school, mostly because of my belief that other people didn't want a fat person around them while getting ready, but really because *I* was uncomfortable. I eschewed the company of women in college, a time when I very easily *could* have enjoyed getting ready to go out. I held myself both apart from and above beauty products. Until I moved in with two female roommates at age twenty-two, I simply didn't know the bliss of having a space where you talk about things like thongs sticking too far up your ass or how your drink got spiked two years ago and you're really worried about it happening again.

Slowly, as I stopped looking down on the process and actually opened up, the women in my life introduced me to all the things

I hadn't let myself be involved in before. Kelsey taught me how to contour, my little sister Olivia helped me get the right foundation,* my older sister Lena taught me how to curl my hair with a curling iron before her rehearsal dinner ("You're twenty-six. How do you not know this?"), and Jordyn always let me borrow her tops. Little by little, women around me helped me figure out how to do all the stuff I had never felt allowed to, that I had been too embarrassed or too righteous to ask about before. Eventually the nights at my apartment with Kelsey turned into nights with Kelsey and scores of other people, who arrived when they could, brought bottles of wine, taught each other contour tricks. Friends of mine from high school and college joined in. My younger sister started coming along. Anytime someone came in from out of town, we folded them into our liturgy.

I know now that there is nothing close to the euphoria of getting a couple of friends together in a room with only two mirrors, blasting early aughts music, drinking champagne and energy drinks, and borrowing each other's eyeliner, even though I think that's supposed to make you go blind or something. The vibe—and again, I do apologize for using the word *vibe*—is extreme friendship and support. It's safety and joy and making sure everyone is having fun and feeling good (tipsy). There's no one to impress, no one to cater or defer to. The male gaze is absent. We're here solely to please ourselves.

This is ritual and ritual is vital. Rituals are normally for facing uncertainty or danger, for creating safety and security. We stay in small groups at bars we know, we don't talk to anyone, we watch our drinks,

---

* One time, years ago, Olivia visited me, took one look at my makeup, and pointed out that I was wearing powder instead of foundation. She was like, "That's powder. It goes on after foundation." And I was like, "I don't think so; this is foundation. I swear." But she was right. Do you know how humiliating it is for a seventeen-year-old to come into your own home and have to teach you basic things? Yeah. Within two years I became a skincare expert so that no one could dunk on me like that ever again.

we don't get too drunk (or if we do, only one of us is that drunk at a time). The risk is relatively low—by careful design. The most dangerous part of the evening is probably the Lyft ride there and back. But the ritual of getting ready eases the more general, existential anxiety of being a woman in a public space. Similar to how the ritual of a bar or bat mitzvah addresses the unknown of adulthood, or that a wedding addresses the unknown of marriage, getting ready to go out protects against the unknown of going out, of socializing as a woman in public.

I wish I had found the joy of getting ready in middle or high school. I wish I'd felt comfortable enough among friends to let them help me with my social anxieties via flat irons and setting powder. I wish I had made friends who could teach me the soap-eyebrow trick and how to put hair spray on the bottom of my new heels so I didn't slide all over the place. There is little else so rejuvenating as going into a room with your friends and asking embarrassing questions and complaining about people at work whom you hate and showing photos of the new guy your brother is dating and building each other up and labeling what the vibe is for the evening (e.g., "the vibe tonight is goth cowgirl slut") and talking each other down from a freak-out when fake eyelashes *aren't* working and then—when you've taken as many photos as you can possibly take and Air-Dropped the good ones to each other—going out into the world a little tipsy and as vulnerable as ever. Together.

Adventures at a Lesser Marriott

There are some moments in life where you're just inexplicably lucky. You take the cookies out of the oven at the right time even though you forgot to set a timer. You avoid getting a ticket even though you were parked on the wrong side of the road for street cleaning. You don't get pregnant even though the condom broke. You made it home before you shit your pants. Life hands you these tiny moments trying to make up for things like seasonal allergies and capitalism. One of *my* shining moments, where the heavens opened up and fortune smiled upon me, was being invited to beta-test a then-new dating app called Bumble.

Bumble, at the time I joined, was available only to college students on a few campuses. I already had Tinder at the time, like most people who were horny and technologically literate, although I had never actually met up with anyone. Tinder in college was about as useful to me as the Stocks app, which is to say not at all. College tindering is not like real-adult-life tindering where you actually hope to meet people. College tindering, at least for me, involved getting a little drunk with a few friends and passing your phone around so other people could swipe for you. This was especially fun* if the person whose phone you were holding was interested in people of your gender, so you could see what you were "up against."

Bumble came out during my senior year. I'd already finished college a semester early, so technically I don't think I was supposed to get access to the test app. But no one knows anything, so the engineers over at Bumble (or whoever is in charge) gave me an account that was chockablock full of *filthy-hot* men. I mean, just disrespectfully attractive options, like if you were trying to cast people for a spring-break trip on a CW show.

If you've never used Bumble, (or if your daughter lent you this book and you're trying to "connect" with her and you haven't understood what half of the shit I've said so far means): Bumble is a dating app where, if a man and a woman trying to be part of a hetero couple both match with each other, the woman must be the one to send the first message. If she doesn't message first within twenty-four hours, the match disappears and if he doesn't respond to her missive within twenty-four hours, the match also disappears.†

The concept is very branded Feminism: if we simply have women message first, this will cut down on the harassment and unsolicited dick pics, which, okay sure. Bumble's whole thing is trying to keep their app positive and healthy or some shit. Which is a nice mission, I suppose, for an app where you're trying to find someone to rail you.

Unlike Tinder at the time, which had been around for a few years and which had been flooded with blurry photos of guys next to expensive cars they weren't even allowed inside of, brand-

---

* Depressing, obviously.
† If you're wondering, rightfully, about the experience for LGBTQIA+ people on this clearly heteronormative-as-hell app, for non-hetero matches, either person can message first.

new Bumble was drowning in hot men who were somehow taking high-quality photos, most likely for their LinkedIns, but *who cares*?

I do not believe straight cis men have *any* idea just how far high-quality photos will take them on a dating app. Straight cis guys are addicted to using photos that look like the album cover to *Blonde on Blonde*. Please, straight cis men, I beg you, pay your friend with the most followers on Instagram two hundred dollars and ask them to help you do a natural, candid photo shoot with good lighting in a bunch of different outfits. Maybe even pay one or two *more* friends to come to a biergarten or something with you and pretend to be hanging out. Yes, two hundred dollars seems like a lot, but when you're getting laid every day of the week and twice on Sunday, you're gonna be like, "Okay, Sophia's right." Which is what I want straight cis men to get out of this book. Straight cis men have somehow gotten the idea that having high-quality photographs of themselves is—like yogurt and recycling—feminine and therefore beneath them, God only knows why.

Anyway, because Bumble was new, and I was freshly out of college and therefore suffering from a dearth of dick,* I spent *a lot* of time swiping.

And when I wasn't swiping, I was messaging. On Tinder, no one really messaged anyone—or no one really messaged *me*—which is fair. Is it even worth it to meet up with a stranger? Like not just on the I-could-be-murdered front but on the I-could-do-so-many-things-on-a-Thursday-night-that-aren't-talking-to-a-stranger-about-how-they-grew-up-in-Albuquerque front. But on Bumble, with the twenty-four-hour *Jeopardy!*-style countdown clock, people got down to the business of actually talking to one another.

---

* Perhaps *suffering* is not the right word for there being few men around.

Of all the things I offered on dating apps, my photos were *not* the main event. To be clear, while I spent a lot of time curating them and filtering them and making them as good as possible, I just knew that, firstly, my photos didn't stack up with the photos of other hot singles in the area, and secondly, my real strength was messaging. The strategy for my own personal dick-hunting operation was to get people to like the pictures *just enough* to match with me, and then I'd send them fun opening messages like, "How many movies with nuns in them have you seen?" or "What's the best Sheryl Crow song?" The key was to make the questions zippy enough that someone could answer them while catching up on *Better Call Saul* or whatever show hot people were watching in 2015. I was good at messaging men. (I still am; I do it for friends all the time.) You have to be a straight-up 8+ to message someone and just say, "Hi." I was realistic about what I was working with, and I was good at flirty-but-also-slightly-teasing messaging. It didn't work on everyone, of course. *A lot* of people were turned off by my brashness; many stopped responding—perhaps because they died, which is what you simply must assume when someone stops talking to you on a dating app. Many never answered my prompts to begin with. Many didn't even match with me at all to get to the point of being turned off by my quirky salvos. If you add up all the people you've met in the past five years, that's still probably a lower number of people than the number of people who encountered my Bumble profile and were like, "No thank you to whatever *that* was." But hooking up with people from a dating app, unlike dating someone or actually falling in love, often resembles a numbers game.

On top of the sheer number of good potential matches Bumble was laying at my feet, the thing I had going for me in that moment was some absolutely newfound . . . confidence. I don't think *confidence* is the correct word, and I know I'm the writer of this book, so I'm the one who's supposed to be coming up with the correct word. My bad; sometimes writing is tough. What I had wasn't necessarily assuredness that what I was offering to others was good; it's not like I deeply loved myself and everything I was about. It's more that I didn't care so much if other people weren't into me. I was running out of energy for talking to men and getting feedback—real or imagined—that they didn't like me. For the first time in my life, the idea that I could be okay if someone didn't like me—if a *man* didn't like me to boot—was starting to form in the back of my mind.

It was not some fully formed feminist praxis that was leading me to not put all my self-esteem eggs in the what-men-think basket. It was more that I had used up all my energy caring about male opinions when I lived in a house with seven guys the year prior and I had kind of hit rock bottom in terms of mental health, so at that point I was in "Fuck it" mode. I actually could not muster the energy to keep caring what men thought of me.

Another part of my newfound lack of care was that I'd gotten so much shit from men online that I had reached another plane of existence and that plane was "If you fucking speak to me, I'll murder you." I was so done. So, so, so done with every cruel, condescending, or creepy thing a man had ever said to me, and so in a way, I was free. I knew that a lot of men didn't like me. I knew a lot of men thought—and *told me*—that I was a fat, ugly piece of shit. And I knew it wouldn't kill me to be rejected by them. You know how when you go into a job interview that you don't care about getting and you nail it? I had that energy.

That didn't make me less horny or desperate to hook up with guys. It's not like I'd fixed all the broken parts of myself and magically stopped equating any of my self-worth with how hot men found me. I'm not there even now, so let's not get crazy. Plus, I was newly able to actually go out to bars, and I finally lived with female roommates who wanted to do pretty much the same things I wanted to do every Friday and Saturday night, namely get drunk, try to find a bar to dance in to music that we'd actually heard before, and try to get laaaaiiid. My point is that being horny was still central to my being, and there was an app for that (Bumble). And I now had what could be perceived as confidence, but which was really exhaustion. Thus began what came to be known as Cocktober.

Cocktober commenced when I matched with a guy named Brandon or Braden or something like that who was in town from Ohio on a business trip. There is almost nothing better a man can be than "in town from Ohio on a business trip." Braden/on/yn and I both knew what we were dealing with, which is about as good as casual sex can get. He told me that he was being put up in a nice hotel downtown. The Marriott by LA Live, if you're familiar with Los Angeles. Apparently, I'm a sucker for a nice hotel, not that I'd ever really been to one before. Somehow, although I was absolutely wrong about this, I felt—and still feel—like nothing bad could happen to me in a hotel. Like if you murder me in your hotel room, you're going to get caught. Not that it matters if they find my killer; I'm already dead. Also, the search for my killer reminds me, if you're a member of my family,* please stop reading and skip to the next chapter, or better yet, the acknowledgments.

Anyway, I got a Bumble message from Brandon/en/yn that was like I'm here for three nights only, do you want to do this or not? Reader, of course I wanted to do this. He was a fit semi-fratty guy, which is not my type but it wasn't like we were going to be *talking* to each other. He was like, "I'm tired because of the time difference, so if you want to come over in the next hour or so . . ." and

---

* Mom, you count as a member of my family!

I, being the desperate slut I am, was on board.* There was nothing special about Brayden other than he was direct and clear that I could come over and have just sex, and that he offered a nice hotel to do it in.

The only problem: I hadn't shaved my legs in ages because I'm not fucking Bella Hadid. I'm a normal lady. So I broke out the razor and tried to speed-shave in my bathroom sink (didn't want to risk getting my hair wet in a shower). Then I put on leggings and an oversize zip-up hoodie that I'd stolen from the lost and found at work, which I thought made me look effortless.† Here's the thing, Past Sophia: he had sex delivered to his hotel-room door. He did not care about any of this shit!

I drove twenty minutes and then got lost because it turns out there are *two* Marriott hotels over by LA Live, and it turns out he was *not* staying in the nice fancy one. So I had to pull over into an abandoned parking lot where I ran over some glass and thought I popped my tire, which would just serve me so right for being a little harlot, wouldn't it?! And then I had to message him and get the actual address for the hotel, which was very embarrassing because it seemed desperate to be like, "HI I'M TRYING TO FIND OUT WHERE YOU'RE STAYING; I WENT TO THE WRONG HOTEL FIRST!!! BUT I'M STILL SO READY TO FUCK THAT I'M GOING TO KEEP REACHING OUT TO YOU." I'm sure that is *not* how it read to him, but I have anxiety, so it felt like that to me.

I finally found the Lesser Marriott, parked in the LA Live parking

---

* There is no such thing as a slut, actually. There's literally no way that you can have too much sex. Too much sex for what? It doesn't exist. There is no difference between sex a thousand times with your spouse and sex a thousand times with different people. It doesn't exist. *Slut* here just means "fun, horny girl."
† A sizable amount of my wardrobe is from the lost and found at various jobs I've had, and frankly, it shows.

lot,* walked a block alone at night to his hotel (safety second; dick first), and then went and met him in the hotel lobby, from where we shared a very awkward elevator ride up to the 1,004th floor.

Much like starting a run from your house,† there's no good way to transition into a hookup, especially when you're both sober. Sober hookups are excruciating. Like running, you just kind of have to submit to the awkwardness and get going. So we had a nice little chat about safe sex and went on our way.

He unzipped my hoodie and I wasn't wearing a shirt underneath. I had a good bra on (forethought!) and he was like, "I was waiting to see those." Which is just so gross and corny that I had to stop myself from laughing in his face. He'd apparently liked the Bumble photo of mine with cleavage, which, to be fair, I did look good in. But please, sir, cool your fucking jets. Then we got to the pants-being-taken-off portion of the evening, and that's when I discovered that I had blood running down my legs from shaving, which I tried to wipe off with my leggings while his back was turned *before* hopping into his bed with *extremely* pristine white hotel bed linens where all the blood would be very visible. I think I made it work; he didn't say anything about my bleeding legs.†

---

* I don't want to derail this perfect story but I do feel like I need to explain LA Live because it's so central to this story and to my Los Angeles experience. LA Live is this massive indoor/outdoor shopping/sports/entertainment complex. It's anchored by the Staples Center where the Kings, Lakers, and Clippers played. (The Clippers are eventually moving; in the future when you read this book they will be gone. Please don't write me mail to correct me.) Once Justin Bieber rented out the entire Staples Center to play the movie *Titanic* for Selena Gomez. There's also a movie theater which he didn't rent out, the Grammy Museum, and some restaurants. But they have extensive, if slightly expensive, parking, which is key for this story.

† Are you supposed to come out of your front door just running?

† Once, my friend was on a trip across Europe and she slept with a guy in his hostel (steamy, right?) and she forgot she was on her period and ended up getting blood on

Anyway, by the time the sex was getting close to done he was like, "Where should I come?" and I was like, "I don't care," and he said, "Is on your face okay?" and I said, "Sure." And he said, "My ex never used to let me come on her face." To which I said, out of politeness and a touch of duress, "Really?" To which *he* replied, "Yeah, that's why she's an ex."

There's a lot to unpack there (and I sincerely hope my parents followed my directions and didn't read this far into the essay) but one thing that needs to be asked is: Why the fuck did we have so much time to talk between when he said he was going to come and when he came? A mystery for Scooby and the gang!

Anyway, I got cleaned up and I'd unfortunately gotten a little come in my eye because that happens when someone comes on your face, folks. And then I just grabbed my shit and said goodbye and left, because, look, there are things Brennens from Ohio can do, and having a nice postcoital chat is not one of them. On the long ride down to the lobby I was in an elevator alone looking up at the mirrored ceiling when I noticed my eye getting kind of red and I thought to myself, *Fucking hell, if this is how I go blind, I'm going to die of shame.* How does one even explain to their parent that they lost sight in one eye because of the jizz of a stranger from Ohio?

I then had to basically bribe a man to let me back into the LA Live parking lot because that part of the parking structure was meant to be closed and he asked where I had just come from, and I'm a *fabulous* liar, and an even better one when adrenaline is coursing through my veins, so I immediately said, "The movies, but I forgot to validate." And he just shook his head and asked me if someone

---

his sheets and he was like, "What happened??" so she just said, "Oh, you're so big." And he was perfectly satisfied with that answer. I love that story and thought you'd want to know.

else had told me I could park there; I said yes, which was *another* lie. But no one had told me I couldn't park there after 10 p.m.!

I got in my car, unduly proud of myself for a successful random hookup, especially for someone who may have been going blind that very moment from come in the eye. And on the way home I got a Bumble message from Brayden, who was like, "You're the best blow job I've ever had."* Which is just true. He was from Ohio and the bar there is probably low. Also, who is giving it their all with a guy named Brayden? The answer is me, because I was overweight in high school. I said, "Thank you; glad you enjoyed it," because I'm nothing if not supremely awkward. And this motherfucker was like, "Was my dick the biggest you've ever seen?" I almost threw my phone out the window.

To answer the burning question on everyone's mind, the man had a very average-size dick, like almost everyone else. But he did have the distinction of kicking off Cocktober, which he doesn't even know about, sadly. Poor Brandon.

The next hookup came about a week later, which was a frequency I had *not* experienced before in my life. I was used to *maaayyybe* hooking up with someone once every couple of months. Maybe. I don't remember the name of the second inductee into the Cocktober Hall of Fame. I do remember that his Bumble profile had a photo of him with a kitten in his shirt pocket and my opening message was, "Nice pocket pussy." And then we met up in a bar where he told me that he was getting really into Charles Manson's music and that some of it was actually good, which is a red flag for two reasons: (1) the murder/cult situation, and (2) Charles Manson's music isn't actually good. Anyway, after a few drinks, and I guess not that many other red flags, he offered to drive me home even though it was very much out of the way—which I did *not* think

---

* Yes, I was texting at red lights; I'm sorry and I deserve bad things.

was him making a move, because I'm an idiot. When we got to my house, I was like, "Thank you so much for driving me extremely out of your way. Okay . . . bye." I walked in the house and got into pajamas. He messaged me on Bumble *from outside the house* and was like, "You could have invited me in, I would have said yes." Which sounds kind of creepy, but it wasn't! I just was very new to hooking up *after* getting drinks with someone and I didn't know how things worked. So we hooked up and he kept biting me *hard*, but again, it's sex with a straight guy, you can't expect it to be actually good. Afterward, I walked him out and said goodbye, assuming, of course, that we would never speak again. He stopped me and was like, "Wait a minute, give me your number. We should do this again." And I was very down for that because he was chill enough and hooking up is fun. So I gave him my number and he was like, "I'm out of town next week, but let's hang out after that." Again, this is all *him*—I had been ready to never learn his area code, never see him again in my life; I hadn't even invited him in my house. But I just followed his lead and a few days later I texted him like, "Do you want to hang out sometime next week?" And he was like, "Oh, I don't know my schedule yet. I think I have to stay in Philadelphia longer." And then he never texted me again.

We can assume, of course, that he died in Philly.

In my mind, Cocktober has loomed very, very large, and then I went back and read my journals from that time, which of course include details about 100 percent of the hookups I've ever had because each one felt like such an anomaly to me. It turns out I only hooked up with two guys during Cocktober, Charles Manson boy and eye-come Brandon. This may seem like Cocktober is a misnomer, like you've been lied to by Big Hookup. But what I also found when I reread my own report of that time is that I *almost* hooked up with a couple of more people, and in fact, I turned *them* down, for various reasons. One guy asked me to drive to Marina del Rey,* where he promised to leave me like a "hard-fucked rag doll." Yes, I'm as confused as you are! (Does he fuck rag dolls? I don't know.) My guess is had I *not* hooked up with two guys already that month, I probably would have driven all the way to his house and had incredibly dissatisfying sex and then gotten in my car and driven home. But I had Cocktober confidence on my side; for the first time in my life I felt like there would probably be another chance to have sex with someone and I didn't need to jump at every opportunity. What freedom!

One thing that rather surprised me about Cocktober is that I genuinely *liked* hooking up with strangers. I had fun having one-night stands; I felt I got something out of them. I mean, I'd *thought* I would enjoy it—I initiated it, after all—but I also had so many friends who had for years talked to me about how much they felt gross or guilty the next day. That isn't to say that my friends always had bad encounters, or that they universally felt shitty about the hookups they had, just that it was a very common experience for them.

It wasn't just my friends, either; there's a bunch of media out there reminding you that sex is better with someone you love, that hookups are dirty, that the morning after should naturally bring shame (to the woman, of course; the man is scot-free). And I simply didn't feel that way. I know sex is supposed to be better with someone you love, but *most things* are better with someone you love. Riding the subway is better with someone you love. Going to dentistry school is better with someone you love. Playing tennis is better with someone you love. That doesn't mean you never play tennis with someone just for fun; that doesn't mean tennis isn't still a nice little workout. Instead of these hookups making me feel small or worthless, I actually felt incredibly validated by them.

---

* If you're not familiar with LA, Marina del Rey is a geographical wonder in that it is somehow far from *everything*.

Part of it was likely all my aforementioned desire for male approval (and what could be a better sign that someone approves of you than them fucking you in a Marriott?). I had a good time, and part of that good time is likely inextricably linked with the feeling of validation. To some extent, it certainly felt like I was wanted, and being wanted always feels nice, whether it be a friend inviting you over to have a game night or a Tinder match being balls deep in you. Even if it wasn't long-term coupledom—which is not the only thing worth striving for in life, by the way—these hookups gave me a measure of self-confidence that obviously, ideally, I would not have needed to get from random men. But we do not live in an ideal world (otherwise acid reflux and genocide wouldn't exist), so grow up and get on board with me buttressing my self-worth with dick.

Sleeping with strangers wasn't some magical salve that cured me of all my personal shortcomings or anything. I still had a lot of anxiety; hell, I still *have* a lot of anxiety. But I felt calmer, more anchored, like I had experienced this thing that everyone else had experienced, like I had something to offer people, even if it was being good at sucking dick or telling funny, terrible hookup stories to my friends. I was doing things in my early twenties that other people were also doing in their early twenties. I was *finally* hitting milestones at the same time as my peers, something that I had not done before due to a heady combination of being overweight and overly responsible.

The feeling of having the *option* to hook up with someone, to get validation in that specific way, was such a windfall. Is that shallow of me? To base a large part of my self-worth on whether someone would hook up with me? Probably! But self-confidence, I've found, is somewhat like a snowball gathering in size as it rolls down a hill. The more little boosts you get, the more confident you get, which leads to more situations where you're boosted, which leads to more confidence. Hooking up with guys simply helped to push the snowball down the hill. By having the potential to have casual sex, by being valued in that way by some people, I started to like myself more. Ironically, it helped me to care about other people's opinions a bit less. Again, I'm not saying I'm not still an anxious disaster a lot of the time, that I don't worry about what people think of me, but I just have a deeper well of self-assurance to dip into.

Cocktober could have turned to Novmember to Dickcember—I was *ready* to keep using the "skills" I'd learned in a few short weeks, to capitalize on my newfound confidence—but then I stupidly went home for the holidays (a major dick interruptor) and came back and had a crush on my friend and started sleeping with him and then dating him. What can you do? Sometimes you love yourself so much that you accidentally get a too-good-to-pass-up boyfriend when you were just getting in the swing of sleeping around. I'm still dating that guy, and now I use the stone-cold self-assurance running through my veins to go approach people on behalf of my friends.

Oh, and I do still have vision in both eyes.

SECTION THREE,

in which I get very tired of trying so hard,
realize I was wrong about almost everything,
and save my boyfriend's life.

Kirkwood, Missouri

In case it hasn't been made *abundantly* clear by this point, I'm incredibly privileged—like the most you can get unless you have naturally perkier tits and a smaller rib cage and fewer chronic health issues. I'm a cis white middle-class lady with American citizenship. I'm disgustingly lucky. And for most of my childhood-through-teens I grew up warmly ensconced in that bubble. I thought that if you voted Democrat every four years that meant you were a good person; *clearly*, then, you couldn't possibly be racist or sexist or horrible. Obviously that is an incredibly ignorant opinion, which you might generously dismiss as part of being an eighteen-year-old. But my ignorance can't be pinned entirely on "just being a kid." I was (and am) white and middle-class (or upper-middle-class, depending on what the boundaries are) and the accompanying privilege—not my age—is what allowed me to be ignorant. Being white and middle-class is the reason I thought you didn't have any obligation to do anything other than vote every four years. I'm sure that it wasn't about being a teenager, because when I go home there are plenty of people who are forty-seven and sixty-eight who think the same things I thought at eighteen.

I grew up going to schools that taught only good things about capitalism and that conveniently stopped covering racism once Martin Luther King Jr. got shot. And often, even more conveniently, right *before* that event.

What's especially weird about this looking back, and when I say *weird* I mean "part of upholding white supremacy," is that I went to a school that was made up of about 30 percent Black students, most of whom were bused in from the city of St. Louis in a program people casually called "deseg"—short for *desegregation*. In 2010 administrators at our school were all saying "deseg"!!! And yet, no white person ever talked about race.

There is a small, small part of the town I grew up in that is predominantly Black. It's called Meacham Park, and every year it gets smaller and smaller due to things like gentrification and the need for a TJ Maxx *right there*, apparently. This tiny enclave is the only part of the school district that is predominantly anything other than white. It's not just white, either, it's a specific *type* of white. Almost everyone is Christian, a few Catholic. Being Italian is spicy for these people. There were very few Muslim students at my high school, and even fewer Jewish students. The entire thesis of the place was white Christianity.

Kirkwood—the city/neighborhood I grew up in—is about 90 percent white. Meacham Park is about 98 percent Black. Meacham Park is directly south of Kirkwood, and is its unincorporated neighbor, willfully neglected by those in power; if you live in Meacham Park, you go to Kirkwood schools and Kirkwood's city hall is supposedly yours. Kirkwood's money is not, however, put into your community. When I was in high school a man who lived in Meacham Park shot up a city hall meeting, due in part, supposedly, to the eminent domain project that saw much of Meacham Park being razed for the aforementioned TJ Maxx. Six people died, including our mayor. Still, no white person talked about race. At least, not explicitly.

Most of the white people I grew up around would describe themselves as someone who doesn't "see" color. They were people who would hesitate or whisper when describing someone as Black for fear that that word might be offensive, but they somehow always managed to include the detail in their story. If you make sure that the party line is "I don't see race," if you keep pretending that race doesn't exist, then no one can ever bring up racism. Heaven forbid a white person feel uncomfortable when confronted with their own racism.

For most of my childhood and teens I'd been taught that being racist was always overt and easy to spot, like "I won't swim in the same pool as people of a different race" racist. I thought that you had to *mean* to be racist to be racist. I certainly didn't understand all the ways in which I was racist, or all the ways in which racism benefited me. It was hard for white people in my hometown—myself at the time most certainly included—to imagine racism as much beyond slurs or people who flew the Confederate flag. It was *not* hard for white people in my hometown to have no Black friends, to make snide comments about being professional or the importance of "correct" grammar, to brag gleefully about St. Louis being the "most dangerous city" in the world, despite the fact that crime would likely never *ever* touch them or their neighborhood. I was in AP classes throughout high school, and for the most part the same group of kids was in most of the honors and advanced classes. I never once had an AP class with more than one Black student; no one seemed to ask *why* that was.

No one ever wanted to bring anything up that might topple the illusion that we were living in a post-racial, post-sexist utopian suburb. I grew up in a place that was big on the idea of tacit tolerance of people who were different. Anyone who spoke up violated the social contract of "niceness" that the (white) community had agreed upon; even people who were actually perpetrators of violence didn't meet the same censure as those who complained about it. The deal was that we all pretended everything was good for everyone, even when it so clearly was not, even when wealth and success were hoarded by a very specific set of people: white, straight, cis, able-bodied US-born citizens.

And I didn't *fully* understand any of this, the sheer whiteness of how I'd been raised, until I got to college. I mean, I'm still the equivalent of a fish living in an aquarium: the world around me has been painstakingly designed for me. I'm not suggesting that any of that changed when I got to college, or that I was forced to surrender a single ounce of privilege. But no one in my hometown had ever even used the word *privilege*; they preferred the term *blessed*. You know, the idea that God gave you these things. Of course God wants you in a four-bedroom 3.5-bathroom house with a fenced-in backyard and finished basement. God wants you, but not the people living a mile away, to be able to afford to send your kids to seven-hundred-dollar-a-week summer camps. This is God's doing, *not* the work of white supremacy. And when I did get to college and people were finally talking about privilege, I felt like I was *at least* four or five years behind. It felt like another thing that had maybe come in one of the forty-seven welcome packets that USC sent, maybe I lost that packet or it got lost in the mail. It really seemed like everyone else knew language about racism and sexism that I had never even heard. Even though I had heard plenty of microaggressions before, I didn't know the term until I went to college. I was still operating under the very basic "racism = bad" model. An equation that white people often reverse, and because they don't consider themselves bad, they therefore can't be racist.

I, as white people so often do, had the luxury—the privilege—of taking my time finding out just how much of America was built on racism, how many of our institutions were *still* deeply racist. I knew of course that the country was bad in the past. What I wasn't fully aware of was just how much of that past informed and *intentionally created* the present. And I *super* wasn't aware of how that present had shaped me. I'm ashamed looking back—not that my shame matters or does anything for anyone—at the ways in which I avoided learning more and learning better until I got to college.

I of course did not magically become un-racist all at once,* but my sophomore year of college, my life changed in some ways that helped me learn better. First, I broke up with my piece-of-shit high-school boyfriend who was far more ignorant than I on almost every issue. His political stances were the things we fought about most often,† and ultimately part of the reason we broke up, although it's pretty disgusting how long I stayed with a person who thought the things he thought; I thought my job was to teach him to be better. I thought that was the way to fix bigotry. But you can't change one ignorant person's perspective and act like it makes life better for marginalized people.

At the same time as our breakup, I started taking general education classes that were required, which put me in classes I probably *never* would have taken. It's not like I wouldn't have *wanted* to take Intro to Islam, for example, which became perhaps my favorite class I ever took at USC, but that I don't think I would have thought to look into the religion department at all as a theater major. Left to my own devices, I probably would have filled up my schedule with comedy writing and screenwriting classes, or more Shakespeare. That's the thing about being a white person: at every turn you're fed more self-interested shit to the point that it perhaps doesn't occur to

---

* Literally no one can do that. I'm not perfect—*CLEARLY*—or even all that good, and I'm nowhere near doing enough to dismantle systems of oppression.

† None of this stuff is actually political. It's not political to want Black people to stop being killed by police. It's not political to want ICE to stop deporting people, to stop policing and terrorizing undocumented folks. It's not political to want better lives for people, to want them to have money and health care and educational opportunities and to not be priced out of being alive. That's not politics.

you to look outside of yourself because you've been told that there *is* nothing outside of yourself. Luckily for me, I was required to take classes outside of my major and required to take classes that were not Western-centric or only about white people and white history and white art. I ended up taking a class on African American theater, dance, and performance, for example, where I was the only white person in the room. I took a class on women's involvement in revolutions in the Middle East. I took a class on money and capitalism. I took a class on the history of Judaism. I took multiple classes in the communication school about gender and race. I took all kinds of classes that I most likely never would have picked for myself, knowing what I know about the teenager I was. I would have likely picked the easy path, which was to focus on subjects I was already good at, to stay in classes that were mostly centered on white people's views and the views of men—stuff I had already been taught. And thank God I didn't.

Those classes, which I took at eighteen and nineteen years old, were the first to chip away at the outer layer I had around my brain that said, "I don't need to do anything for anyone else; this society is clearly a meritocracy and all you can do is try hard and be nice." Those classes challenged my preference for sitting on the sidelines, my aversion to activism or advocacy. They didn't do all the work, though.

What really un-taught me all the things I hadn't even noticed I'd learned—white supremacy, misogyny, transphobia, fatphobia, and on and on—was the internet.

The Internet Made Me a Better Person

I got a Twitter account in 2011 at the behest of my friend Devan Coggan, a brilliant entertainment writer now, who was then just a friend in my AP calc class who was sitting at the back table with me, ignoring Mr. Jonack's explanation of vertical asymptotes, most likely. She, like all people on the Kirkwood High School newspaper staff, had been required to get a Twitter and she urged me to join as well. Twitter was relatively new then and still somewhat fun. Do you remember 2011? LMFAO had one of the biggest albums of the year and the *Smurfs* live-action movie came out;* things were bleak, but in a simpler way. No one could name the secretary of education off the top of their head.

I knew my dad would be furious with me if he found out I got a Twitter, not for safety reasons like a normal parent or future-employment reasons like my ever-practical mother, but because it was another way to "talk too much" without saying anything.† Devan pressed me anyway. I told her my father would disown me

---

* The US also killed Osama bin Laden that year. Unrelated to LMFAO or the Smurfs.
† To be fair, he totally called it.

and, worse, that no one would follow me. "I'll follow you!" she insisted. To which I replied, "Great, I'll have one follower and no dad." Hence my Twitter handle.*

I figured that my Twitter would be like my Facebook, inane and irrelevant to anyone outside of my own high school and also most people *inside* my high school. To me, the big advantage Twitter had was that none of my family members or teachers were on there; I could start with a clean, anonymous slate. In the beginning, I had no conception of what I wanted to get out of Twitter. I used it to follow an *ass-load* of accounts that were suggested to me. I mean hundreds, if not thousands. Accounts like Ellen DeGeneres and Ferrari. I had no idea what the hell Twitter was for, and so I did what the app recommended and I followed Rob Delaney and the *Modern Family* corporate account.

At first, I didn't use my real name; I was worried about future employers or college admissions counselors finding me on there, which was a thing every child in 2011 was told to fear above all else. We heard horror stories of people being fired after getting a lucrative job and students having their acceptance letters rescinded after a school uncovered their social media accounts. Perhaps ironically, every single job I've gotten post-college, I've gotten from people I know on Twitter. But, at the time, teenagers were told the site was a threat to our future livelihoods. So I mostly just used it to read what other people were posting.

It wasn't until I got into doing stand-up my first week at USC that I actually had any use for Twitter myself.† In order to get better

---

* My father has yet to disown me, mostly because I'm the only one of his children who has sworn to keep his hair dyed if he's ever in a vegetative state. (I know the color combination, too. It's a mix of Just for Men A-45 and M-45.)

† USC did not rescind my admission despite my occasionally participating in hashtag games like #rejectedcandyhearts and #WorstVacationEver. I think they should have.

at stand-up, I planned on using my account to write as many jokes as possible, and the challenge was that they all had to be clean. This was a self-prescribed restriction, but I was still afraid of people I knew finding me. I wasn't, at the time, the type of person to put inappropriate language or thoughts online. Again, my parents and teachers had put the fear of God in me that someone would uncover a single instance of me saying "fuck" online and then ... I don't know ... bar me from ever working???*

The more time I spent on Twitter, the more I began to actually cultivate the experience into something I actually wanted. I went through and unfollowed every single account Twitter had suggested to me. I followed every comedian I could find. I went to a campus event once where Mike Birbiglia was performing and he called out Shelby Fero, who was my year at USC and who was sitting in the crowd; she had a big following at the time and he had her come up onstage and read her tweets out to the entire auditorium, which is, looking back, kind of an insane thing for him to do. But it made me seethe with envy and double down on my efforts to use Twitter to get to where I wanted to be in stand-up. I went home and followed her. I wanted Shelby Fero's life, not that I knew almost *anything* about it.†

At the same time that I was putting every single passing

---

* I still remember the first tweet I did that I didn't want teachers or parents to read, the first time I actively thought, *I'm making the choice to attach my name to this semi-sexual joke and I'm moving slightly away from being clean on here.* It was June 11, 2014, and I tweeted out, "I can't be responsible for where my nips end up in a sports bra." WHICH IS SUCH A TAME TWEET!!! But after that, the summer between my junior and senior year of college, I finally let myself get dirty.

† I know her better now and have actually spoken to her before and she's brilliant and hilarious and cares so much about people and is a very cool, fully formed, nuanced individual and not just a Twitter account. I fully admit that I was a weirdo at eighteen.

thought that came into my brain onto my Twitter,* in the real world I was getting very into doing stand-up. My parents aren't really fans of stand-up comedy; my mother loves Paula Poundstone, my father loves Robin Williams, and that's about *it*. I didn't even know stand-up was a thing until I was about fifteen years old. I had, however, been basically *doing* stand-up routines for my peers from a very young age. The summer before I was about to become a kindergartner, I used to sit on the tire swing at my preschool with the other almost-kindergartners and do a whole routine about how *we* couldn't be kindergartners and how we weren't tall enough. After doing it one day just off-the-cuff, the next day at lunch I had kids asking me to "yell again" at the tire swing. I was a mostly quiet kid, and I wasn't really yelling. I was . . . doing stand-up, although no other four- or five-year-old knew what to call it. Whatever the name, that became my whole personality in school going forward: I was the person making fun of everything.

So stand-up was a good fit for me. At USC, I joined a group of five to ten students (depending on the semester) who performed for groups of four to eight audience members in terrible venues around campus. One time, we got asked to perform during the honors dorm special monthly dinner where all the suck-up kids are trying to hook one of the professors who just came to get a free meal into being their mentor. We stood next to the serving line as people spooned dining-hall tortellini onto their plates and tried their best to ignore us.

I was usually one of only two women in the club, occasionally the only one—a demographic imbalance common in comedy. Junior year, my third year being in the group, we all went to the Laugh Factory to try out for the Laugh Bowl, which was a col-

---

* I haven't changed at all.

lege comedy competition between USC and UCLA. After your audition set, the host would give you notes. There were probably twenty-five or thirty guys and about five women. After my set, in front of *everyone*, the host told me that I shouldn't make too-inappropriate jokes because when I go onstage as a woman, everyone is already going to be thinking about having sex with me, and therefore I shouldn't mention sex because it would be distracting. Every other guy in the group I was with got notes on how to make punch lines more precise, how to make premises more creative, or where there was opportunity for a callback. Meanwhile, I was told not to talk about sex. On the walk back to the car, I was livid, and every single guy in the group—all friends of mine—was like, "Get over it."

I had been, for the first few years of college, going along with almost everything these guys said. I mean, I disagreed on occasion, but about things like whether Jon Hamm was actually as hot as Don Draper and which house beer pong rules we should instate. Never about my being treated differently as a woman. This felt like the first time I was asking them to have my back and agree with a simple "Yeah, that was bullshit," and instead they claimed they didn't see it. Maybe they really didn't! Honestly, I probably would have missed the sexism myself only a few months before. I had been the person who didn't see that women were often given short shrift in subtle, nonexplicit ways. I had been the person who thought people's sensitivity was perhaps turned up a little too high.

But something had shifted and that something was . . . Twitter.*

---

* I know I'm in the middle of writing an entire essay about this, but I think talking about Twitter off-line is excruciating for all parties involved. There's no way to bring up Twitter without sounding like a douche. Really, it's the most gross thing. That said, I don't think you can get a full picture of my life without me writing about Twitter and how much it shaped me. So here I go again on my own, walking down the only road I've ever known.

I was—and still am—on Twitter near constantly, partially because I have anxiety and use Twitter as an outlet despite clear evidence that it only makes my anxiety worse and partly because I've always had jobs that let me be on my phone and jobs are boring. Mostly, at the beginning, I was following funny people. Again, my goal early on was to use my account for comedy, which is why I sought out who I did. Also, at the time—before the 2016 election—Twitter was mostly comedy with a little breaking news mixed in. (Now it's the opposite.) At that time, around 2012, most big "funny" accounts were a mixture of stand-up comedians and TV writers in LA *or* regular people from small towns in Canada who had full-time jobs as something like an accountant or a teenager. Most of the very popular accounts were men, and almost all the men were white. Perhaps in an attempt to balance things out, outlets like *HuffPo*, *Esquire*, and Someecards started rounding up lists of the funniest women on Twitter. The lists were *full* of white women—and occasionally a white man who had an avatar that looked like a woman. Despite that most of the actually creative comedy being created on the site was made by Black people, almost everyone who got any attention from a media outlet for being funny was white. Lists of "funniest accounts to follow" leaned *heavily* in favor of guys in zip-up hoodies who were depressed and smoked a lot of weed. My point in all of this is to say that the Twitter I was reading from ages nineteen to twenty-two or so was bleak, and certainly not the place that you might *think* to introduce second-wave feminism* to someone.

When I first came to Twitter I was scared. I'm still scared a lot—shout-out to generalized anxiety—but when I was eighteen I was terrified of being wrong. I was virtually immobilized by it. Respect in my families, both at my mom and my dad's houses,

---

* I know that we're on like fourth-wave feminism currently; however, the feminism that I saw online from female comedians in 2012 was *not* that.

was usually predicated on being right. My mom always referred to herself and my older sister Lena as "right fighters," people who want to be correct and will needle you until you get on their side. My dad doesn't even have words for his deep conviction that he is always right. Look, not to dunk on my dad, who is a gem, but the dude has been wrong many, many times. He's the kind of person who decides to put IKEA furniture together without looking at the instructions because he *should* be able to figure it out, which is just not the case. (The Swedes running IKEA are *trying* to fuck us over and make us look stupid. You can't fight that.) Everyone around me thought being right was good, important, and achievable.

Unlike the rest of my family, I was not all that interested in being right—at least until I left for college. Most of the time growing up, I just sat on the sidelines and watched debates unfold. I felt genuinely confused as to where everyone was getting their deep convictions, their statistics, their anecdotes. My parents are both well-read and well-informed. And Lena liked fighting about things. I was none of the above. Conflict, even minor debates, made me want to crawl into a hole. I wanted everyone to get along. Everyone else in my family believed that you could argue with people and nothing would change, but I was less sure. The family had already split up once (divorce) and I had seen my parents argue with their respective spouses and partners quite a lot over the years, and how different are debates from arguments, really? It was much easier to feel calm when everyone was just agreeing. I liked keeping the peace. I certainly wasn't going to try to win a debate. It seemed like a small, simple favor to just let anyone else in my family "win" when they disagreed with me. I also genuinely had very few convictions. I was mostly interested in getting to college and getting out of Missouri. I wasn't political. I wasn't reading news. Through my privilege, I had the option to be completely uninformed as a teenager, to simply not know and therefore not care what was happening to other people.

I no doubt would have remained that way had I not gotten on Twitter.

Embarrassing as this is to admit, the white female comedians I followed gave me my first look at standing up for yourself, or any kind of advocacy. I'm not suggesting that they were all being feminists or anything, but following them and reading their tweets helped unfurl the idea in my mind that you could *maybe, perhaps, possibly* say things that men didn't like and not die from it. Or— and this was a massive shift in my worldview—you could even *not care at all* what men thought. A lot of these women were loud and combative and they weren't afraid of losing men's approval, or at least not as afraid as I was. And it felt revolutionary to me. Of course, as I look at it now I can see that these women—almost all white and fairly well-off—were in the safest position possible to not give a fuck about the opinions of men, especially the men in their industry. I also know, with the benefit of hindsight, that there was still *a lot* they weren't tweeting, that they couldn't tweet for fear of losing jobs and connections and friends and money. But seeing them tweet angrily, to see them speak up about how they'd been treated, to see them talk about what they desired or were owed, opened my eyes.

On top of seeing them talk about their *own* various instances of mistreatment—both off- and online—*I* started to get hateful, weird, and creepy messages. Of course, of course, of course ideally a person would not need something to happen to them to care about it. I wish I had cared more earlier. I wish I had cared more and listened more to people who had encountered this before me. I'm not saying that I didn't understand that the world was tilted in favor of men; I got the general idea that women globally weren't doing as well as men. But I certainly didn't *get* intersectional feminism, or even the burden of dealing with sexism day in and day out. Part of this, again, is because as a white, well-off, able-bodied teenager, I was about as protected as possible. I wasn't losing jobs because of my gender, I wasn't being assaulted or harassed,* I wasn't being relied upon to care for my ailing parents due to my gender; I simply hadn't faced much writ-large sexism, and when I did, it was infrequent enough for me to write off or not question. But Twitter helped change that—at least, the men on there did.

You cannot be a woman online and not get hated. There is not an opt-out option. In fact, there are also very few places *off-line* where you can be a woman and not get hated. It crept in fairly slowly for me. It started with fairly run-of-the-mill creepiness from strange men, which I was not used to at all, for a host of reasons, including being overweight and being sheltered; I found these replies off-putting and mildly scary, but not necessarily worrisome. I had seen this kind of stuff happen to other women; it just hadn't happened to me. At the same time, more and more non-creepy men became incredibly condescending to me. The more followers I got, the more often I got corrected. On *everything*. One time, as a game with myself, I tried to see if I could get someone to explain crosswalks to me—a man stepped in and helped me and my dumb lady brain out! It's easy to say that this stuff is innocuous, or small potatoes, but I don't buy that anymore. I used to, for sure. Back when I was still defensive of men as a group, I bought that these annoying and mildly creepy interactions were anomalies, that they were not representative of men as a whole. But if *every* time a woman gets a big enough following she starts getting mild harassment and constant belittling *from men*, it becomes difficult to ignore the overall pattern. And that isn't even touching on the genuinely scary, hateful shit that I got, that women get when

---

* Or at least I didn't understand when I was.

they're in public spaces. Once that stuff started—once I got rape threats and people contacting my employer because I said something "anti-men" online* and called a fat cunt about 284,058 times in various graphic ways—it was impossible to not see what was going on and why. My boyfriend, who used to be active on Twitter, could post essentially the same joke I did, and no one would say *anything* to him. No one corrected his jokes, no one "actually'd" him, no one threatened him in his DMs, no one sent pictures of dicks all day long. Certainly no one ever wrote an entire erotic play starring Mario and Waluigi and emailed him the script asking him to play the fairy nymph.†

After a few short years on Twitter, I realized that, wow, actually, you *are* treated differently if you're a woman; no, this isn't a conspiracy. I started listening better to more and more people about what they thought was unjust. I started following people who weren't comedians—they were writers and activists and scientists and academics. Some were just people who were really good at explaining tough concepts via Twitter. Most of all, I started following more and more people who were not white. I started wondering why all the people who I *had* been listening to were white, why that felt so comfortable, what was left out of what white people said. I started to realize more and more of the gaps—chasms, really—in my fundamental beliefs about the world. If I could understand the disparity of treatment of women when held up against that of

* I said something about male comedians not calling out other people because they benefited from sexism, and some random person tried to tweet to David Spade and GQ to fire me, as if David Spade knew who I was or as if Mr. GQ was going to call me and never let me write again.
† One of my favorite details about this insanely creepy thing that did in fact happen to me is that the guy who sent me that script—and a few more!—always pretended that he was Shigeru Miyamoto, the game director of Nintendo, emailing me. But he used his own email address, which had his name in it.

men, it seemed to me incredibly easy to understand how a similar dynamic of oppression would extend to trans people, Black people, people with disabilities, undocumented people, indigenous people, and all marginalized communities. I'm not saying that I read one tweet about intersectionality and *snap* got it. I'm just saying that after realizing that women definitely had it harder and worse than men in a general sense, even if not on every individual level, I understood better how that might apply to lots of issues, and how identities could intersect and overlap. And of course, I didn't really learn this from Twitter—Twitter itself taught me nothing—but from the activists *on* Twitter, especially Black women, whose voices I probably would not have heard had I not been on the site. I would not have heard them because until Twitter, I wasn't trying all that hard to stay informed about things; I was luxuriating in the white teenage space of "If something is not happening to me, I don't know much about it." However, I also suspect that even if I *had* tried to be more informed on more topics, the places I would have gotten my news from would likely *not* be publishing stories from, for, and by marginalized people at the rate I was reading their words on Twitter.

Perhaps the thing that cracked open my worldview the most, and I readily admit that this came *way too late*, was Mike Brown's killing in 2014 in Ferguson, Missouri. Ferguson is a suburb of St. Louis to the north of the city. I grew up only about twenty minutes away; my mother and father both still lived there. My siblings still lived there. I was actually the only one in my family *not* in St. Louis in 2014 when Mike Brown was killed. The trial took place in the suburb my dad lives in; they closed off access to his neighborhood because it was close to the courthouse and some of the wealthy white residents were afraid of looting during the trial.* You had to show ID to get

---

* Disgusting of them.

in. I say that because it's not like this didn't touch my parents' lives. And yet I somehow knew *so* much more of what was happening than they did, while living two thousand miles away. And it was *all* because of Twitter. Every time I found someone who was tweeting *from* Ferguson, someone who was actually there, actually protesting, actually showing up, I followed them. Then I followed anyone they retweeted, too. I read everything I could. I donated to bail funds. I retweeted every piece of information I could find. Not that doing any of that is anything, obviously. I couldn't imagine why it had taken me so fucking long to pay attention. But of course the answer is, because I didn't *have* to. I got to wait until I was twenty-one years old because I was white.

Could I have found out about this earlier, about just how much of our nation is predicated on white supremacy? Absolutely yes. It's not like Twitter was the first place to report on police brutality. I'm not suggesting that I had no choices for places to go to do work and read and listen and learn better. But Twitter was a wonderful tool for sharing information rapidly,* and for getting that information to people who might not otherwise seek it out. I know that's not good or ideal. I know that I should have been outraged sooner. It should not have taken years of other people's pain for me to catch on; no one should have had to be harmed ever to begin with.

At first, I joined in in being loud about injustices. Whenever anything unfair happened—anything racist, sexist, ableist, homophobic, transphobic—I yelled about it. I figured that joining in and repeating what I was reading was a good way of showing support. I was angry *a lot*. For the first time in my life, I was gaining actual convictions. I believed that things were right and wrong, or, more accurately, harmful or not, and I was upset when people didn't see it that

---

* Most of the time. Obviously, sometimes false information spreads quickly and widely, too.

way, or didn't care. I am still upset and angry *a lot*. I'm furious that so many people in our world are not just okay with but happy about the suffering of others. That so many people don't want poor people to live, that so many don't care that trans people get murdered at such high rates, that so many don't care about the lives of refugees, that so many believe that climate change won't affect *them* and therefore isn't worth addressing. It's horrific. But back in 2014–15, I was a little tornado of ire about every issue under the sun. If I had been a chill girl in the first few years of college, people on Twitter helped me make the hardest of one-eightys. I didn't allow *anything*; I had a hair trigger and I couldn't figure out why everyone else wasn't on board.

Of course, *I* hadn't been on board a few short years before. I don't want to make it seem like I didn't know that racism, sexism, homophobia, ableism, and other forms of bigotry were bad before 2014. I knew. I just didn't think I had any personal responsibility to do anything about them other than to not be a bigot. I didn't realize the full extent to which the world was tilted in my favor, and I didn't understand how living in a patriarchal white supremacist colonizer capitalist state might color my entire worldview. I had to unlearn a lot of information, like the myths that America is a meritocracy or that voting once every four years is enough to help people. And as soon as I did learn otherwise, I was upset that other people weren't on the same timeline. Of course tons of people were light-years *ahead* of me in their understanding of social inequality—many were the very people posting about it on Twitter whom I found and read and listened to and then often regurgitated.*

It felt very *good* to be right—which is what I thought I was. I felt like I finally had ground to stand on. I felt smart and wise and

* This is very wrong! You can't just rephrase what marginalized people are talking about and then post it. Just share what they said! Share their writing!

empathetic. I knew I didn't know everything, but I thought I knew a lot. I thought I was being a good person. I thought I was helping people and being supportive. I was not. I was 100 percent wrong about that. I was a classic white feminist taking up space and being loud for the sake of being loud. I didn't have ill intent, not that that matters at all. It was more that I thought I was unimpeachably right—for perhaps the first time in my life—and I wanted to fight people who were wrong because they were, in my eyes, harmful. But my impact was ... terrible. I was a loud, obnoxious white lady who no doubt talked over Black and brown women, even if I was agreeing with them. I don't remember every single thing I tweeted or said, but I'm 100 percent sure there is a lot there that I would cringe to read today. It's not that my beliefs today have simmered down or been tempered at all—if anything, I'm much more radical now than I was then—but eventually I finally, *finally* learned better how to stop centering myself. While everything felt brand-new to me, it was *of course* not new to the communities experiencing harm. But it felt good to feel like I was fighting for something worthwhile, like perhaps I was doing for other people what activists online had done for me. But I'm not an expert; I'm not an authority. It was simply not my place to talk.

What I know *now*—what took me longer to learn than it should have—is that adding *my* voice isn't what the situation calls for, most of the time.* I've now learned how to listen better and amplify other voices, how to let other people talk of their experiences and speak for their communities, rather than trying to take up space. To put it simply, I learned how to shut the fuck up, that I did absolutely not need to weigh in on everything. That in fact I *shouldn't*. It's not like I'm perfect at this. I'm not even close to perfect at almost any-

---

* Seriously, like 99.9 percent of the time, no one is asking me to weigh in.

thing!* I'm still angry and upset all the time. I'm still worried constantly; news stories frequently completely unmoor me. But I'm not talking or, God forbid, shouting all the time anymore. I've learned how to support better without taking up space. How to show up but not make it about me. And I learned it by being really, really wrong for a long time and then listening to other people and adjusting my behavior.

It's not particularly pleasant to be confronted with the reality that your previous behavior sucked for someone else, that it was harmful or uncomfortable. It's shitty to hear, but it's *necessary* to listen to. And the more practice you get with humbly accepting that you've messed up, the less harm you do, because if you're *really* apologizing, that means you've absorbed what you did wrong and you will change your behavior. I've found that a lot of people want to support marginalized communities in ways that make them feel good or look good; most unlearning is a lot more painful than that, frankly. It's usually pretty excruciating or at least embarrassing to look inward at what you've done and how you've harmed people intentionally and unintentionally. It isn't meant to make you feel good.

I learned all of that from people online who often *had* to be aware of bigotry and hatred because they were experiencing it, unlike me. I learned from all their work and writing, and for that I'm very grateful, not that my gratitude is necessary or helpful or asked for, or that my individual learning is the goal.

But, when people say, "You won't change people's minds on Twitter," I have to disagree. I wouldn't hate billionaires and corporations and fossil-fuel executives were I not on the site. I wouldn't understand all the ways in which I unintentionally uphold and ben-

---

* I do make a really good arugula salad that is a hit pretty much everywhere I bring it. But other than that . . . no.

efit from white supremacy. It probably would have taken me much longer to figure out how often I encounter sexism on the smaller scale. I never would have learned how to be wrong, how to apologize sincerely, how to separate my *intent* from my *impact*. Every day I read more and learn more and listen more to people who aren't white, who aren't cis, who aren't in power. Access to those voices has immense value, and Twitter gave me that. Twitter made me a better person. Even if it also gave me Shrek porn* and hundreds of men calling me a fat cunt.

---

* If you are unaware of Shrek porn, it is exactly what it sounds like. No need to look it up unless you're actually interested in seeing Shrek in a sexual light, and then by all means.

Imaginary Dinner Party

I assumed, perhaps like many children of similar upbringings (who watched a lot of movies), that adulthood would include dinner parties. I assumed my attractive partner and I would host them together; he'd be the kind of hot guy who can pull off a turtleneck—like a male model or a professor. Ideally, an ex–male model professor.

This is the type of party where guests would show up with bottles of wine, despite that we—the model-professor and I—already had dozens. In this fantasy, I am a red-wine drinker, which is just about the chicest thing I think a person can be. I am not a red-wine drinker. I drink champagne. All the time, without regard to occasion. But at my fantasy dinner party we are not drinking champagne. We're red-wine drinkers here, in this house.

Speaking of the house, I think the setting of this dinner party is paramount. You simply must envision the dinner party I'm hosting in a vaguely '70s-style home with beautiful original hardwood floors. Throughout.* Plants and expensive chairs fill the house. Everything

---

* People *love* saying "throughout" after "hardwood floors." Fuck "cellar door"—"hardwood floors throughout" is actually the most beautiful phrase in the English language, if Zillow is to be believed.

looks both cultivated and effortless; you would believe me if I said that the person who lived here before me robbed a flea market at gunpoint and took the best stuff and I simply inherited the furniture. Of course, there are modern touches here and there. A glass-door refrigerator in the kitchen displaying emerald San Pellegrino bottles and fresh produce. Nary a processed food in sight. But those are offset by the custom built-ins, shelves laden with obscure books and one-of-a-kind souvenirs.

A record player is setting the mood, though in my fantasy there's none of the work of actually changing albums and resetting the needle. I don't know the logistics, but somehow I've made a vinyl mixtape album that plays for hours. This is a fantasy! Go along with me! Here's the playlist: "Didn't I" by Darondo, "Do What You Gotta Do" by Nina Simone, "Give Me Just a Little More Time" by Chairmen of the Board.

I've cooked for us this evening, because of course I have; those cooking lessons I took in Piedmont two summers ago really paid off. I worked on this meal all day, but it's casual. There's handmade pasta and homemade pesto with basil fresh from my garden. My "famous" arugula salad on the side. *Cipolle ripiene*, probably. We'll begin with a happy hour of charcuterie so no one gets too hungry. There will be specialty cocktails and a fully stocked bar, and of course, red wine. Anything you want, it's yours. Help yourself!

My model-professor partner will be regaling everyone with stories as I finish getting ready—I've spent all day cooking, remember. Though of course he's been helping out; I'm not going to have a fantasy partner who isn't helpful. Maybe he's a desserts guy; that would work nicely. Yeah, he's made tiramisu to keep with the Italian theme. Good for him; we'll get that out of the refrigerator later when we need a . . . wait for it . . . pick-me-up.

I'll go into the master bedroom and change into a dress that somehow is both stunning *and* effortless. It's intricately made and uniquely designed without being fussy. Also, you've never seen me in it before, but I've had it for years. I'm wearing delicate gold jewelry, the kind that good dinner party hosts can always pull off. And I'm tan—glowing, even. I must be getting a lot of outdoor activity; I insist it's just from tending my herb garden. After slipping into the unmatched dress, I throw my hair up into a chic almost-French twist. It's messier, looser—pieces are falling out. You know that look. Of course, in my fantasy, putting my hair up doesn't make me look like the Trunchbull. It makes me look ethereal, goddess-like. Oh, don't forget, I'm wearing the best-smelling perfume you can even fathom. Or maybe that's just what I smell like. You've always wondered, because I always smell so good. Is that bergamot? Citrus? Who knows!

I come back out from the master bedroom to a good-size group of people already here, people who have arrived magically at the same time, so no one is feeling weird about being the first guest at the dinner party. Every guest is interesting and talkative without needing to be the center of attention. Conversation is flowing freely; we're talking about politics, love, philosophy, art.* We're laughing so hard we keep knocking over wineglasses, but I'm cool about it. "You can't ruin anything in this house! It's no big deal!" I say with a laugh, grabbing nice tea towels to wipe up the spill.

We eventually move out to the back patio to continue drinking and laughing around the firepit. I have two or three very beautiful, impeccably trained dogs, who are roaming around the well-curated lawn.† There are hanging lights and citronella candles and a copse of lush fruit and olive trees, making it feel like we aren't in a city but rather a Mediterranean orchard.

No one even says, "We'll have to do this again sometime," because we all *know* we will. Soon.

---

* TV shows.
† Please note that while I'm calling it a lawn, there will not be grass, because grass is bad for biodiversity. I will have a lot of native plants that attract pollinators and lots of drought-friendly landscaping.

Not to Be Cliché, but I'm Going to Talk About My Vagina (and Tits)

There comes a time in every memoir written by a cis woman where she has to talk about her vagina. I know because I read a lot—*a lot*—of memoirs. They're my favorite genre of writing. I want to know how everyone is faring. I want to know how their dad's death affected them, how their first restaurant job went, how their first kiss came about. I love that shit. Someone spent the time to write down the hot goss in their life! Thank you! I just want to hear about the lives of strangers without the risk of meeting someone who might be boring or tell me about being a hedge fund manager, or that they think 5G networks are killing us, and *that* is where memoirs step in. It's like meeting a new person but you don't have to have your pants on and you can walk away at any time without being rude.

Anyway, in a lot of cis women's memoirs (basically all of them), things come back to the vagina. I read two books in a *row* this January where an entire chapter was devoted to periods. Frankly, menstrual prose is not my favorite genre of writing. Unless you've got some really good/weird/bad shit going on down there, I'm pretty neutral about the topic. I'm not *against* anyone having their own vagina monologue; I'm not grossed out or scandalized by it, as I would've been at fourteen, but I still don't usually feel like I connect with these stories. They often feel too common, too pedestrian.

Aside from some negative, shameful feelings about getting my first period, I never really had strong feelings about vaginas one way or another. I didn't want to talk about my period, and I didn't want to celebrate "becoming a woman" or anything (a phrase which I now realize is incredibly trans-exclusionary, but which I was just personally mortified by at the time). Beyond that singular experience, I was not thinking about my vagina almost ever or at all. I certainly had reason to think about my vagina; I've had really long, bad periods most of my life. Like some that have lasted fifteen days. Every doctor has just been like, "Maybe if you lose weight, it will go away." They've given me birth control pills and IUDs— sometimes both at the same time, which is just cruel, because the point of the IUD is to *not* have to set an alarm on your phone for 4 p.m. every single afternoon of your life. For most people, these methods make periods go away almost entirely; mine is still here, eager bitch that she is.

Still, I'm not that passionate about my vagina one way or another. She has never really held any allure or deeper meaning for me. I mostly feel the same way about my vagina as I do about my knees: sometimes they bother me or don't work correctly, but not in a way that's tied into my identity. The same goes for my boobs. Other than extenuating circumstances, like when I'm forced to buy a bra for an exorbitant amount of money due to my unusually large rib cage, or the time the guy I was deeply in love with in college asked me, "What happened?" upon seeing my titty stretch marks, I'm dispassionate about my boobs.

I understand, of course, why many people *do* have stronger feelings about vaginas and any other reproductive organs, especially those involved in being pregnant. I understand that as someone with access to birth control and abortion, and health care in general, I'm privileged enough for those parts of my body to be an afterthought. I understand that as someone cis, I'm allowed space to go whole days or weeks without being reminded about my genitals or any other body part that a stranger might feel is their business. And that, perhaps, is why it was such a shock to find myself for three years on end deeply entrenched in caring for my boobs and vagina.

It started, as many auspicious moments do, in the shower. For some reason unknown to me—and I have thought about this *a lot*—I decided to feel around under my boob in the shower. A lackadaisical check for lumps. This isn't a crazy thing to do; monthly tit checks are advised once you reach a certain age or if you're bored. But at twenty-five, I wasn't in the demographic for lumps *and* I had just two days prior—two days!—gone to a gynecologist who had done her own titty check (professionally known as a breast exam).

If your doctor does a titty check, usually you can go ahead and assume that they would have told you about any lumps. You can assume that you're in the clear for a bit. Which is why I have *no clue* what my hand was doing under my boob during that shower. Was I just washing off my boobs and I felt something? Was I actively looking? I don't remember and I can't figure it out, but either way I felt a lump.

If you've never felt a boobie, they're lumpy as shit. I distinctly remember reading one magazine that said, "Boobs can feel like a bunch of grapes," which is just such a weird thing to compare them to, but they made a point which is: boobs are *odd*. They feel odd, they do odd shit. They can have cysts and abscesses and infected ducts. There aren't rules. Titty tissue is like the wild, wild West. When I was fourteen, I found a lump under my armpit that I thought was breast cancer and my doctor was like, "No, you're fine; it will probably go away. Chill out." So when I found the underboob lump, I was about 55 percent chill. The other 45 percent of me was like, "I'm gonna die of breast cancer this year and I should probably quit my job and move home to spend time with my family before I pass."

Logically, I knew this was probably what's medically known as NBD (No Big Deal). I called up my doctor, who had just examined me two days prior, which I felt a little weird about doing. It feels kind of rude to be like, "Can you please go back and check your work on #7 and show me how you arrived at this answer?" I tried to get an appointment with my Other Gynecologist, and yes, I have two, because Los Angeles is a nightmare for gynecologists and most of them can't fit you in for an appointment until August, even if it's February.* Anyway, the Other Gyno couldn't fit me in and the gyno I had just gone to had left for a *monthlong* trip. She took one look at my vagina and left town.

Luckily, another doctor in her office agreed to see me on short notice because titty lumps are sometimes important. She felt me up and was like, "Yeah, this is a real lump, but it's not a big deal. I think you should go get an ultrasound of it, but it's not cancerous or anything, so don't freak out. But go get an ultrasound today. Right away."

Mixed messaging, if you ask me. Also, who knew (outside of the medical world and probably a lot of people) that ultrasounds were the technology we were using for titty tumors? I was like, "Don't we want like an MRI? A full-body scan to make sure I'm not *dying*???"

The closest place to get an ultrasound the same day was the ritziest† breast center in Beverly Hills. The waiting room of this boob clinic had nicer furniture than I will ever own. They had chandeliers hanging from the ceiling. They were a few streets over from Rodeo Drive and next door to a chocolatier that I could not afford to walk

---

* There is a nationwide shortage of gynecologists, by the way. As if life weren't bad enough already.
† The word *ritzy* is so funny to me. Ritzy!!!

into. An entire boutique for rich people that just sells chocolates. Just chocolates!

Anyway, I did not belong. I don't remember exactly what I was wearing but the odds are it was overalls. I walked in on Birkenstocked feet with a slip of paper that said I needed an ultrasound and sat next to women who said words like *coiffed*, women who wore kitten heels and blouses. Blouses! Imagine owning a blouse!

I finally got to go into a room after making it a third of the way through an issue of *Vogue*, which, as with any reading of a rich-people periodical, left me riled up. A nurse asked me to take my top off (the second time that day! Nice!) and she squirted preheated ultrasound gel onto my tits—imagine food-stand condiment bottles coming on your chest. Now, if you've never had an ultrasound before—I've now had dozens and dozens—you can tell when you're in a fancy place when they heat up the gel.

One weird thing about getting an ultrasound anywhere on your body is it looks, feels, and sounds exactly the same as the ultrasounds you get for a baby, or at least the ones I've seen on TV. I kept wanting to ask, "Is it a girl or a boy?" just to get a joke in, but I didn't because every four seconds I was gripped with the fear that I was going to find out that I was dying. Also, because I bet someone's done that bit before and I didn't want them to think I was unoriginal.

I'm *very* afraid of dying, so afraid that I had played this scene out many times in my head, although never in a Beverly Hills office with paintings of orchids hanging on the wall. In some sense, I was like, "Okay, I knew this was coming. I have been right all along to be afraid of my body killing me. They're going to tell me I have two years to live and I will be vindicated." My family makes fun of me for all the medical problems I think I have. One time, I got really concerned that I had pancreatic cancer because there are usually no symptoms for pancreatic cancer and I was experiencing no symptoms. My family does have a little bit of a point, but also my body is a shitshow and I have lots of random *real* medical problems. Recently, I got diagnosed—by a doctor—with LPR (a.k.a. silent acid reflux, which despite the name is *not* silent at all; it just doesn't include heartburn) and my mom was like, "You're such a hypochondriac." It's not hypochondria if you *have it*, Mom.

Anyway, I got called back to an exam room by a beautiful but serious nurse. The room was in the far back of the office and she apologized for the construction noise from next door. Buzz saws were frankly the least of my concerns; I was waiting to find out if I had cancer. The nurse peeked around in my boobies and told me that she saw a lump at three o'clock. My right tit was now a clock. She was very confident that it wasn't cancer (phew!) but she wanted the doctor to come take a look at it. She handed me two washcloths for my boobs to cover up the ultrasound gel but told me not to wipe it off. Just hold them there like a makeshift bikini.

She left and I waited awhile. There is no good way to wait on an exam table. The very act of lying down on a *table*—cushioned or otherwise—with your top off in the middle of the day, waiting for another adult to come in and inspect you, is weird.

Finally, the nurse came back in and announced, "We actually have to move to room 1 because it has a better ultrasound machine. Pick up your terry cloth–covered titties and let's go." Not those exact words, but you get it. She carried my belongings as I shuffled across the entire doctor's office to go to a room with better equipment. It's a Beverly Hills doctor's office whose *only* focus is on breast cancer; why would you even *have* a room with a bad ultrasound machine?

Room 1 was admittedly much nicer. There was a massive gilt-framed mirror on one wall (so you can watch your reaction to getting a cancer diagnosis?), another painting of an orchid, and classic rock hits being lightly pumped into the room. The very volume of the music said, "We understand you have breast cancer; we're here for you." Room 1 was for people they would *never* ask to hold wash-cloths over their tits.

My doctor arrived eventually, the most glamorous woman you can even imagine. She was wearing a lab coat and heels. Her smile was genuine but her teeth were either professionally whitened or veneers. I would bet veneers. She didn't seem to have pores. She radiated competence, the kind of competence the people of 90210 are paying for. She was also kind and warm and funny. She came over to stand above me like a Reiki healer with her hands hovering over my boobs and said, "Don't tell me! Let me see if I can find it!"* It could have been alarming for my titty lump to be a game for her, but instead it spoke of her casual relationship with tumors, which seemed reassuring.

She *did* find the lump in record time (it took me a whole shower, and my previous gynecologist never found it at all), and she quickly set to work scanning that little bitch. A Tom Petty song came on, "American Girl," I think, and she started lamenting how sad it was that he had died so young; I wondered if it was good bedside manner to mention people dying young in a situation like this, but she was the professional. This was my first time maybe being diagnosed with cancer, and the nurse said it wasn't cancer, so I had no right to get too miffed. She then asked me if the music was okay and if I had any requests, and I was like, "Is the tumor so bad that you're letting me pick the music as my last make-a-wish moment?"

It turns out the lump was actually at four o'clock, not three o'clock, on the titty-clock face. So the nurse had been wrong about that. The lump was the size of a peanut M&M according to my doctor. When she told me that, I replied, "I wish it *were* a peanut M&M," and we both laughed, me nervously, her politely.

And then she told me that the edges of that peanut M&M lump were actually rough instead of smooth, which usually means cancer.

---

* I've never actually been to a Reiki healer, so maybe it's nothing like that.

What.

The.

Shit.

We transitioned seamlessly from peanut M&M jokes right into "You might have breast cancer and we need to do a biopsy." I really wanted to be like, "Oh no, no, the nurse—that nurse that was just in here, who gave me these towels—she said it wasn't cancer and the gynecologist said it wasn't cancer too. You're actually my third opinion of the day and I reject this one." She also broke it to me that even if the lump *wasn't* cancer, we were going to have to do surgery.

The good news, according to her, was that it had not spread to my lymph nodes, and she was very confident that we could get the whole tumor out. Which is like, definitely good news, but also I know a tiny bit about cancer and one thing I know is that a peanut M&M clump of cells is a lot of cancer!!! Anyway, it was Wednesday and I'd find out on Monday if I had cancer. If I have any advice for you, it's to get all your medical testing that might be serious done on a Monday to give you the most business days possible in a row after your test.

I got the biopsy, which hurt a lot (which is bullshit; I didn't realize biopsies hurt), and then I tried to call my mom, who didn't pick up because she was at a fancy dinner event with her husband or something, and then I called my boss and was like, "I can't come in tonight for work because I think I may have breast cancer, is that okay?" So the first person I talked to and cried to was my boss, and I kept apologizing for crying. And then I got in my car for an hour-and-a-half commute home because LA is like that.

Then I entered a purgatory that anyone who has ever had to wait on medical results knows. It's Schrödinger's biopsy. Until you get the results back, it might be nothing and it might be death and you can't actually start mourning or grieving anything, but you have to sit around *knowing* that on Monday morning literally every aspect of your life could shift. Waiting is hell. Waiting over a weekend for results is double hell.

Luckily for me, it turned out that the lab was very fast and I got the results early and I did *not* have cancer. I had a very, very rare type of tumor. Did you know that most tumors in boobs *are* cancerous? That cysts and abscesses and fat deposits and scar tissue are incredibly common but noncancerous tumors just aren't? But I got lucky.

A week or so later, I went in for surgery to remove my titty tumor and it was heavenly. They put you under a very warm, heated blanket because the surgery room is so cold and then you pass out and somehow wake up with no memory of any time passing, which is trippy as hell.* And when I got out of the surgery my glamorous doctor came over to me with the tumor in a clear film canister—well, it probably was not an actual film canister, because that seems unsanitary and not official—and was like, "Actually, your tumor was the size of a Reese's cup and had started to grow on the muscle, so we had to take more than we thought, but the good news is, the titty looks normal and we think we got it all." Obviously, your question is, what type of Reese's cup is she talking about? The big flat ones that come in two-packs or the individually foil-wrapped ones? I don't know!

I got a call a week after the surgery from my doctor, who said, "Good news and bad news." Which is a phrase that almost never means *mostly* good news and just a sprinkle of bad. Dr. R was like, "Okay, good news, it's not cancer." And I was like . . . I thought we had already established that? And she said, "Well, we like to double-check." So the good news is something that I thought I already knew, that I didn't think was up for discussion. Can't wait to hear the bad news.

Reader: they did not get it all.

---

* Fun fact: we don't know how anesthesia works!

The second surgery was going to be *way* more aggressive, because apparently this fucker was starting to grow on bone and wrap itself around things, and this tumor was a fast-growing tumor and I needed to get it out before it turned into the size of a chocolate Easter bunny or whatever the next-size chocolate item was. Are all doctors measuring things in chocolate? I don't know.

A couple of weeks later I went under again, and when they opened up my titty area (chest), they had to do a lot of . . . rearranging. When I woke up, my doctor told me that the surgery had been more extensive than they'd expected and that what was left looked like a "shark bite" (her words) on my rib cage. She told me she'd had to take out more of my boob than planned and that my boob would be a bit uneven.

What.

The.

Shit.

I mean, good news: not cancer. Good news: they thought they got it all for real this time. Good news: I had survived two surgeries. Good news: I could still breastfeed (presuming I have time to have children before climate change renders the world uninhabitable).

Bad news: I had a surgical drain coming out of my boob, collecting blood and fluid in a clear grenade-shaped plastic canister,* and also: now I had a wonky titty??!? At age twenty-four?

I didn't even like my boobs beforehand! Like at all! They were mediocre; kind of deflated and covered in stretch marks from gaining and losing and gaining and losing weight. They were not twenty-

---

* I have a lot of bad things to say about the experience of having a surgical drain, and I only had to have one—many people need more, and many people need drains for life—but one thing is that they are potentially a great way to sneak alcohol into a stadium if you get a brand-new one. Also, one time someone saw me with my surgical drain and gave me a free latte. So win some, lose most.

four-year-old tits, which feels like the most embarrassing possible thing I could admit to you, somehow. I don't know why six chapters back or so I was fine with talking about come on my face but admitting that I have mediocre boobs is just a bridge too far, apparently.

And now they were uneven?!? COME ON.

The perhaps exciting upshot of this story is that I worked with my doctors and insurance company for two years trying to get a reconstructive boob job. I paid thousands of extra dollars in health insurance each year in the hopes that the cost of the surgery would be lower, and I finally got approved. So now I have new tits and whenever people, usually men, are rude about plastic surgery—which happens all the time!—I get to be like, "I had a boob job." And then they backpedal. And then I get to say, "Because I had a tumor." And then they try to backpedal faster. And that's what they get for trying to make someone else's body their business.

But for two years I had a slightly wonky tit mocking me for all the times I *didn't* appreciate having nice-enough (albeit stretchmarked) perfectly even titties. Throughout this titty imbroglio, I kept expecting to feel *something* about womanhood. I was waiting, trying to figure out the right time to really *feel* connected to my womanhood via my lost boob chunk.

Retrospectively, this was a weird fucking feeling for me to be expecting, since it's not like I *normally* believed that boobs had anything to do with womanhood. Many, many, many women don't have boobs, of course. I was waiting for a Chicken Soup for the Noncancerous Breast Tumor Survivor's Soul moment, though. I was waiting to be like, "Who am I with a wonky tit? Why do I feel less female?" I didn't feel less female at all—OF COURSE.

I felt ashamed of Ol' Wonky Girl, especially the first time I looked at her two days post-surgery when there was still severe bruising; my boob looked like if you took an abandoned baked potato that you found in a CVS parking lot and stapled it to my chest. I cried so hard after looking in the mirror that night that I woke my boyfriend up. I was 100 percent sure that he was not going to want to have sex with me and my tater tits ever again. I *never* let him see my boob until it was fully healed because sometimes you can't unsee stuff and what if we're having sex and he keeps thinking of my innocent boob at her very worst?

Eventually, this medical drama abated. Potato tit healed and I moved on to fighting with my insurance about the reconstruction. I had a cool ten months where the worst problem I had was severe neck and shoulder pain from TMJ that made two separate doctors ask if I had been in a serious car accident.

And then my vagina was ready to take center stage.

It started with a regular-degular run-of-the-mill UTI, so I naively thought. I went to an urgent care center because, as mentioned above, gynecologists are in short supply and UTIs hurt like a motherfucker. I have a pretty high tolerance for pain; I have *no* tolerance for chronic discomfort. I would much rather a very painful four-second spasm happen every two hours than an all-day background pain. UTIs give you *both*.

If you have never had a UTI, don't talk to me ever. Even if you're a close friend or family member. We have nothing in common and I have nothing to say to you. Just joking! For real, though: if you're a close friend or family member and you've read this far into my essay on vaginas, sorry we can't talk anymore.

Look, I'm a responsible sex-haver. I know about peeing post-coitus to try to avoid UTIs. I know The Rules. Sometimes things happen, though. Bodies are shitty and I was fine with that truth. I got my antibiotics and went on my merry little way. The problem: my UTI did not. Oh no! She stuck around. I went to another urgent care (you have to play doctors off one another!) and spent fifty dollars to have them tell me that I was fine and that maybe the antibiotics just needed longer to work. I'm not a doctor, but I do not think that's a thing.

Still, she was sticking around. Again, painful, annoying, nightmare shit. For weeks. Imagine feeling like you have to pee the worst you've ever had to pee in your life 24/7 and no matter how much you try to go it doesn't help. It's like the food-turning-to-ash curse in the *Pirates of the Caribbean: Curse of the Black Pearl*.

Finally I went to a urologist who specialized in erectile dysfunction and he was like, "Maybe you have an overactive bladder," which is, if you don't know, a very real and scary health problem because guess what? There's no cure and sometimes medicine doesn't fix it. And the medicine that *does* fix it has been linked to causing Alzheimer's later in life. I was trying to be twenty-six, flirty, and thriving!! Not to have a bladder issue!!

I'm going to skip the boring parts of this tale, but basically, I did not have an overactive bladder despite taking strong medications that may later cause a rift in my family when I eventually get Alzheimer's and some of my children want to put me in a care facility and the other children don't think they can afford it. But I kept coming back to this doctor who kept prescribing me higher and higher doses of this fairly risky drug that gave me such severe dry mouth that I lost my voice a bunch and had to buy gels and lozenges to be able to talk. On top of this, because I didn't have the issue that he was prescribing medicine for, I wasn't feeling any better. It turns out that I had chronic UTIs that magically no one was testing me for. At a fucking urologist's office.

Finally—FINALLY—by the grace of some god somewhere, I found a uro-gynecologist who specializes in vagina-pee problems rather than dick-pee problems and *he* was straight up with me and told me this little fact: many, many, many people with vaginas will have a year or so in their twenties where they just get chronic UTIs and yeast infections and then eventually it goes away and the best thing you can do is treat them as they come and stop eating sugar.*

Every time I took the medication for UTIs, it made my body go fucking nuts and I got a yeast infection from it. Is this too much info? I don't know! Probably! It took this Fairly Good Doctor and me a year to get my body to calm the fuck down and not have a nonstop UTI. And neither of us know what actually changed! No idea! The problem could be comin' back 'round the mountain at any moment.

After all the shit I went through with my body—two tumor removals, not having sex for a while because I was so afraid that I would get another UTI, a suggested bladder surgery, having to put pills *up* my vagina for months on end (which is just funny)—when my doctor finally admitted, "We have no idea what's happening with your body, sorry," that was the moment that made me finally feel a blip of connection to womanhood, or non-cis-male-hood. This was it! After a year that included nineteen doctor's appointments for my vagina alone. NINETEEN. The only thing I want to do nineteen times a year is go to Target. What it took was being told, "Yeah, your body is a mess. We give up. Good luck. We don't know. But it happens to lots of people!" for me to finally feel a real kinship to womanhood via my body.

A perfect example of the dismissal of women's health as important is the wildly racist and misogynistic history of the speculum—a tool I've now had inside of me more times than I can count. Speculums haven't been updated much since 1847, when a piece-of-shit slave-owning doctor started using gravy spoons to look up the vaginas of the women he enslaved, despite being vocally disgusted with the body part. The speculum that he eventually "invented" is basically the same thing we use today. What other medical devices

---

* Obviously, I did not stop eating sugar; I'm not a freak.

haven't been updated since then? Why are people stuck getting chronic UTIs in their twenties for months on end with no solution other than waiting it out? If cis men were getting UTIs and yeast infections this often, I have no doubt medical care would have advanced to address those issues—as it should! Why are women's symptoms of heart attack mostly unknown to the general public? Why do Black women have astronomically higher maternal death rates than white women? Why does Plan B not work reliably for women over 175 pounds? Why is women and femmes' pain and especially the pain of Black women, indigenous women, disabled women, obese women, LGBTQ+ women not taken seriously?

Having your pain be ignored or misdiagnosed or minimized, it turns out, is way more intrinsic to the female experience than a body part could ever be. The reason that so many women are writing about boobs and vaginas in books—about bodies in general, actually—is because while our bodies are objectified and sexualized to the point where they become a synecdoche for us, they aren't actually cared for. When we try to get care for our bodies, when they don't work, when they cause us pain, society loses interest. We all have been dismissed and belittled at doctor's offices, often with incredibly serious consequences. The story of having horrible pain that goes undiagnosed, or having a body issue that we're asked to be quiet about because it's not "polite" (miscarriage, pelvic pain, endometriosis, gender-affirming surgery, mastectomies, breast reductions, etc.) is an experience so common it has become a trope. I mean, the French Open banned the type of outfit Serena Williams played in—a catsuit she wore to help prevent blood clots. This right here is the common bond: your body is your entire worth, but also it's not worth keeping healthy, cared for, pain-free. This is why there's always a chapter.

There Were Two *Different* Songs Called "Miss Independent" in the 2000s. Why Is No One Talking About This?

The first time I ever made out with my boyfriend Dave, we were both ... pretty drunk. It's very difficult, although certainly not impossible, to make out with a close friend while sober. I'd had a crush on him for a month or so at this point, and we'd been friends almost a year; we were walking in a group from a bar to a friend's house at the end of a long night of drinking. A very common romantic setting, obviously! And by the time we got back to her house we were making out. Everyone was blitzed and we were not sneaky whatsoever and we found a back bedroom and kept making out and finally he was like, "Do you want to come back to my place?" No one had *ever* asked me that in person before, and of course I was like, "FUCK YES ARE YOU JOKING WITH ME?" So we went back to his place and hooked up and then the next day all our friends hung out *again* and I was like *doot doot doot*, I'm just going to play it off like I didn't wake up at Dave's house and be super chill about this whole situation and say NOTHING. We all watched *Straight*

Outta Compton and I don't remember a single minute of that film because I was freaking out about sitting next to Dave after having slept with him the night before.

For the next month or so, we started hanging out multiple times a week and hooking up fairly frequently, but I always felt like *I* was the one taking the initiative, and therefore I felt like I clearly liked him more and that he might not be into me. Also, I had been told pretty much all my life that men didn't want serious relationships, so I was like, "Okay, cool. I'll be chill about this and not mention dating." Except the problem became that I really, really, really liked him and I was like, "I don't want to date other people and I don't think I want you to date other people." But I didn't say that to his face. Because I had never had an "Are we exclusive?" talk before and I was dreading it. Plus, again, it didn't seem chill and I really wanted to impress him. Even though this was well past my college chill-girl phase (by about one year), I still found myself frequently reverting to the (wrong) opinion: that I needed to be low-maintenance in order to not scare him off. Eventually, I gave up on *him* bringing the topic of exclusivity up and I had my best friend Emilee sit on my bed and practice, *using the voice memos app*, the conversation I wanted to have with him.

She made me repeat what I wanted to say again and again until I got it right and until I wasn't being apologetic or meek or a doormat, which is a very good-friend thing to do. So the next time I saw him, I was like, "Listen, bitch! We should date exclusively!" (I did not say it like that.) And he was like, "Oh, that would be wonderful. I've been wanting that." And I demanded to know—because I was amped up from Emilee hyping me up and from him agreeing to date me—"Okay, why didn't *you* ask *me*, then?" And he looked at me very confused and said, "Because it seemed like you didn't want that."

I assumed he was taking his cues about my desires from my Twitter, where we knew each other from originally. I certainly talked a lot on there about hating men and not wanting commitment or to date anyone, which was mostly true except for this guy, whom I *did* want to date. I was miffed that he'd taken my Twitter persona so seriously, even if it was fair of him to do. So I said that. And then I was like, "You could have just asked me what I wanted." And he looked even *more* confused and he explained, "Well, the very first night that we ever made out, you stopped kissing me, pulled back, and said, 'Just so you know, I'm not looking for anything serious.' So I took that as your stance."

Yeah, he hadn't been reading my Twitter for clues *at all* because he's a normal-ass person. No, I had apparently *told* him that I didn't want anything other than a friends-with-benefits situation. Only I didn't remember saying that specifically. As soon as he said that I had said as much, I was like... *Okay, well... that does sound exactly like a thing I would say and do.* Every single time I told a friend that story, they were like, "Yeah, that sounds like you, Sophia."

The thing is, I grew up believing that the worst thing that a woman could do is be needy, and by that I mean have needs. I had seen the women around me get left by men because they were too "difficult." (At least, that's what I had thought I had seen.) I wasn't particularly afraid of being left; to be honest, I figured I would survive that. I was beyond that fear. I was afraid of needing anyone at all, ever. See, if you don't need anyone, it doesn't even matter if they leave you. Even better, if you never commit to anyone, they can't leave you and you don't have to leave them and there's none of this sad, drawn-out-endings business.* But beyond that, if you're a woman and you don't commit to anyone, if you don't need anyone... you're cool.

Obviously that's not actually true at all, but that is what I believed

---

* Please feel free to play "I Am a Rock" by Simon & Garfunkel, which beautifully distills the themes of this paragraph into lyrical poetry: "And a rock feels no pain / And an island never cries." Chef's kiss on the emotional vacancy, Paul!

because I was about twenty-three years old and twenty-three-year-olds believe stupid things.* I believed being "independent" was cool not because I was a massive dolt, but because I had been told that thousands of times across pretty much every media platform imaginable. There are infinite TV shows and songs and movies and books about the lives of young single women and how being single is about freedom and power, and that needing a partner or having a "happy ending" is sappy and feminine (in a bad way, of course).

We've got this idea that the way to address inequality between men and women is to ask women to be more like men, and therefore no longer need men. Of course, not everyone even *dates* or is attracted to men, so the messaging to women really becomes: Provide everything for yourself. If you're *really* a strong woman—which is the apparent goal of this oversimplified imitation of feminism—you won't debase yourself by wanting romance. Sex, perhaps, but not emotional intimacy. To want a partner, to actively make moves to commit to a partner, is painted so frequently as weak and bad. The "strong" thing to do, according to this hyper-capitalistic fantasy of girl power, is to give your everything to your career. Settle for anything less than that, we tell young women, and you're compromising your goals and dreams for the sake of someone else. God forbid your goal is a loving partnership. Good women are strong women, per this encyclical. And strong women are above love.

Strong women, too, conveniently behave much in the same way men behave. Coincidence? Probably not! Modern women are encouraged to want sex, but not commitment, to never stay over the night after a hookup, to not want to get tied down right now, to never have even contemplated getting married, to focus on their careers, to not call or text too much, to eschew romantic gestures.

---

* I still believed at that age that one day I would get health insurance from an employer, ahahahahah.

Don't get me wrong, there are a lot of pieces of that that apply to me.* But I think a lot of the reasons I have the proclivities I do is because I was taught that operating more like a guy in almost every arena, especially romantically, was better, preferred. The reality is, though, that men get lauded no matter what they do. If men don't want to date, they're bachelors (which is cool), and if they do date a lot, they're players (which is cool), and if they date someone long-term and they're committed, they're a good partner (which is hot *and* still cool). They don't lose anything by partnering up *or* staying single; meanwhile, it's pretty much lose-lose for women.

While you can't say that you *want* to date someone or get married or start a family—which would be sad and pathetic and needy—you also can't totally eschew that stuff forever, which would be sad and pathetic and lonely. As a woman, you're asked to be open to having casual sex without commitment for a bit, but not *too* long, and then you must magically find someone to date seriously and eventually marry (while being chill about it!!!!) before you're *too* old. Ideally *you* did not express any desire to get married (embarrassing); your partner brought it up! You weren't even sure you ever wanted to get married! You're a chill girl!

The other day I was watching *Selling Sunset* because everyone I know watches it and I don't want to feel left out ever. On the show, a woman who was in her early thirties and who had been dating her boyfriend for *years* expressed publicly that she wanted to get married soon, and that she was hoping for her boyfriend to propose. I felt embarrassed for her. My initial knee-jerk thought was, "Why would you admit that on TV?" I had an initial gut reaction of "WE DON'T TALK ABOUT THAT!" As if it might make some other off-screen guy feel uncomfortable or pressured.

Marriage and weddings expose some of the most glaring dou-

---

* The very idea of roses or daily "good morning" texts makes me want to diiiiiie.

ble standards for how we treat women and romance. If you are a man who expresses that he would like to get married one day, perhaps to the person you're dating, perhaps just in general, first of all, you're brilliant, because marriage is a very good arrangement for straight men. But second of all, you will get treated in one of two ways: "Awww he's so sweet." Or, "Wow, your female partner must have pressured you into this." If you are a woman who says that she's interested in marriage, the narrative is that you are either dragging your unwilling partner down the aisle kicking and screaming—a dynamic you can even get as a cake topper!—*or* that you're some pathetic bundle of need who wants a man more than a career,* a woman who is desperate to have children, which is somehow sad for reasons that are mostly unclear.†

There used to be a café near my boyfriend's apartment, where I was basically living at the time because that is what new couples are like, sorry. Anyway, we'd walk to this café and every time we'd pass a high-end wedding-dress shop. I did everything in my power to not look at the wedding-dress shop, in order to not make things weird, which of course probably made things much weirder. I was terrified that my then new boyfriend might find out that I knew about matrimony. Like if I glanced at a wedding dress in a shopwindow he might bolt, or worse, have a long, sincere conversation about how he isn't ready for that yet, but that he *understood* I was obsessed with getting hitched. And I would have to be like, "No, no, no, I don't want that either. I'm not into freak shit like holy matrimony! I'm normal and want things on a normal timeline. I hadn't even remembered that it was possible for us to get married ever. That

---

* That's right, ladies, you have to choose!
† Please note that if a man wants children, it's never desperate or pathetic of him, it's only ever about passing on a legacy or being a great father someday. It's cool if a guy does it and sad if a woman does it. Remember!

truly had never occurred to me. I didn't even know those were wedding dresses, honestly. I thought this shop just had a thing for the color white and intricate beading."

And even that avoidance of shopwindows made me feel shitty, because so what if I wanted to get married? So what if he thought I wanted a wedding someday? The semi-reasonable part of my brain knew that what I was doing was a ridiculous charade. I *wanted* to look at the wedding dresses, not because I had *any* interest in getting married immediately to this specific guy (and who cares if I did?) but because they were ass-ugly and I wanted to judge them. It's nice to judge consumable goods being presented to you. The best part of going to the movies is the trailers and sitting there getting to be like, "Never in one million years would I see that!" Or, "Yes, bitch!! If I don't see a heist movie starring Marisa Tomei opening day I will die." Let me look at wedding dresses that cost more than my car and decide if I hate them in peace!

But I was terrified of my boyfriend finding out that I knew about marriage and him concluding that I was a psycho. I'm not alone in this. My sister was with her boyfriend for seven years—they'd bought a house together and adopted a dog—and she said she still felt slightly embarrassed bringing up the idea of them getting married. My best friend had to get drunk before even admitting to her boyfriend that she wanted to get married *someday* (to which he was like, "Yeah . . . I assumed"). Another friend of mine called her boyfriend—they were both committed and exclusive—her "dude" for months and refused to say "I love you" in order to not look too attached. I mean, sorry, but if you're spending the night at his place and posting Instagram pictures together and trying anal sex, you guys are attached!

So if you aren't allowed to want marriage, what are you supposed to build your life around? Your job. Careers have been sold to us as the solution, the substitute for the all-consuming satisfaction women were meant to get from their marriage and children in the '50s. Careers are the dog bone everyone keeps throwing at women to keep them quiet. It's not that women aren't allowed to have life goals, it's that those goals must be about work. This shift from homemaker to office worker ends up helping a whole lot of people.

Firstly, it helps men. The one thing they were bringing to the table in past relationships was, frankly, financial stability. Of course, men still outearn women, and women are systematically kept out of the workplace and high-paying jobs. But now men don't have to be the sole breadwinner anymore. The pressure is off. Any woman who is asking for or expecting that is generally thought of rather unkindly as either a suppressed-conservative housewife or a gold digger.

The other people who benefit? Companies that women work for, and since the US government counts corporations as people, I'm doing the same for the sake of this paragraph. If you just keep telling women that the reason they aren't getting ahead as quickly, the reason they aren't making as much, the reason their title isn't as prestigious, etc., is that they simply aren't working hard enough, you can keep moving the goalposts. All you have to do is convince women that they could be a #GirlBoss if they just would #LeanIn. Corporate feminism in *so* many ways feeds into the idea that women ought to base their lives around their jobs and their career goals, and to do otherwise is anti-feminist. In this warped perversion of feminism, you become weak and unenlightened if you aren't "hustling," if you aren't keeping up with the guys and trying to get the corner office. Meanwhile, that same company will gladly fire you for getting pregnant, give you insufficient maternity leave, or penalize you for not being available to stay late because you have to pick your kids up from school. Please keep in mind that you cannot be a #GirlBoss if you, say, run a daycare out of your home or care for your ailing parents. Being a successful career woman is all about making it in a specific, male-dominated corporate world. Men's work is valid, women's work is not. The goal always is to be more like men, because clearly they're killing it.*

Meanwhile, most workplaces I've ever been in and the men in them have been extremely hostile toward women, but *especially* toward women who are in committed, serious relationships. Not only is it more likely that that's the time when you're going to have children, which might cost your company money (God forbid they lose your labor for a millisecond), but also women who aren't single aren't usually available to fuck. And men want to fuck their coworkers. They at least want to want to fuck their coworkers. They want the possibility to be available. I have worked at many male-dominated jobs—a hockey warehouse, on TV shows, doing stand-up. Technically, stand-up is not a job, you're correct. Let's move on. All of those jobs, in general, I've done better at when I was flirtatious and when I put in the effort to look good and be appealing to the men around me. Recently, I worked at a TV show where there was only one woman over thirty-five and only one who was overweight in the entire office. The number of men who were overweight and over thirty-five was . . . very high. There were also almost no women in senior positions; every woman was someone's assistant. I mean, I like being around people I want to fuck, too. But I wouldn't—or at least I hope I wouldn't—create an entire workplace around that. And once you become a woman in *any* male-dominated space who for *any* reason isn't going to fuck the guys there, you lose value. People don't listen to you as much, even if it is subconsciously. Your choices in male-dominated workplaces are basically to be ignored or to be harassed, neither of which is a good option and both of which make having a successful career incredibly difficult.

---

* Frankly, it's a little hard to say that men are "killing it" with a straight face when men make up like 95 percent of magicians.

Of course, instead of addressing the behavior that is aimed *at* women—the ignoring and the harassing, the belittling, the overlooking, the creepiness—we decided to try to address women's behavior in the workplace by telling them that they just needed to try *harder*. That if they focus even *more* on their careers, if they write thank-you cards after interviews, and bring brownies, and have more sales than anyone else, *and* ignore Creepy Ted in Accounting, they will eventually get ahead. At some point in mainstream feminism, there was an immense amount of pressure to refocus any energy, even—perhaps especially—caretaking energy, on the job. You don't need to be a homemaker anymore; your life is now work. You answer emails on weekends, you get in before everyone else and leave after them, and you never say no. Of course, *a lot* of people feel that pressure, but men are so much more likely to have a spouse they lean on for support, for childcare, for family emergencies, for a healthy meal to come home to. Women aren't supposed to expect that *ever*.

Part of why I think this myth of the "badass career woman" who doesn't need a man was glommed onto by so many people—men and women alike—is because it was a great way for men to abdicate any financial and emotional support (your job should fulfill you, or therapy should, or your friends should, but God, not a man!!!) while seemingly being about giving women more power. It also left women single and potentially free to fuck. If commitment is down, and being single is cool, men ostensibly have more casual sex partners. Being told to focus on our careers and to not ask for romantic entanglements—as if the two are in any way mutually exclusive—results in more single women out there to hook up with. Meanwhile, of course, someone shrewdly branded the entire idea of being career-oriented as being a tenet of feminism. Because of course we did! Having lower romantic expectations is empowering! Somehow! This isn't to say that every woman wants commitment and that no man does. There are plenty of women who don't care for long-term love and plenty of men who are looking to settle down. I'm just saying that the model we have right now gives preference to how men were taught to think and act; it says that you should be one of the guys, but that you shouldn't get any actual support from a guy.

Women receive so much messaging about how they have to be able to do it all, even with less money and less time than men, and do it mostly, if not entirely, alone. Women have to have our shit together if we want to get anywhere (unless you're white and ultra-wealthy, in which case there are no rules). If we want a cleaner house, we have to do it; if we want to bring a gift to a kid's birthday party that they actually like, we have to find it; if we want birth control, we have to pay for it. It's up to us! The best you can hope for as a woman when it comes to help is other women helping you. I have never had a male friend offer to run an errand for me when I was sick, and I've never seen them do it for each other, either. When they need care, they turn to women too. This pressure to figure it out on your own doesn't exist in the same way for men.

They get help all the time! They get help every step of the way in ways they don't even realize. Despite their belief to the contrary, almost no man I know is handling shit on his own. A fact that is beyond cliché, but true and therefore somewhat illustrative is that I have three sisters and one brother and guess which one is the only one who doesn't know how to do his own laundry? Guess who needed help applying for colleges and remembering deadlines even though his three older sisters did it mostly on their own? Guess which of us kids had jobs during high school and which didn't?

It's not like our parents *wouldn't* have helped us, had we asked. Or that my brother isn't smart enough to figure out laundry: he's on his school's robotics team; he's brilliant. But, Lord, women have been so used to figuring shit out on our own *and* taking care of other people that I'm not sure it occurred to any of my sisters to ask our parents to step in and keep track of when applications were due or by what date we needed to sign up for AP tests. I'm not saying we were perfect, that we never procrastinated, that we never got help. I'm just saying the drive for my brother to be independent isn't there. Not from him, and not from my parents. This isn't just to roast my brother either. He's a great person, hilarious, analytical, and kind. He can do all kinds of shit I can't, like basic math, but he can also get away with a lot of shit I can't, and most of my family doesn't want to admit that. And my family is not alone in this. Starting from childhood, girls on average spend more time doing housework and helping with tasks like childcare and cooking, while boys in general average an extra *hour* a day of leisure time. It's bigger than a tiny smudge of inequity in my childhood, though. I mean, God, if that were my main gripe, I'd be an ass. It's that the pattern continues.

Men in general are used to relying on others—specifically women—and that isn't shameful for them. It's not shameful for men to be reminded about a doctor's appointment by their mother. It's not shameful for their girlfriend to call in and ask about what a store's return policy is when they bought the wrong size joggers at the mall and don't know how to exchange them. It's normal for them to emerge into adulthood unaware of how to clean a bathroom or hold a baby while supporting its neck. It's expected that men's emotional growth in their early twenties will be built on the backs of the women in their lives. And this frees up time in their schedules to be the fun uncle or the fun dad or fun friend, the person who doesn't have to follow the rules or adhere to responsibility because guess what? Someone else is taking care of it. (And that someone is almost always female.) Men still get to abdicate work at home despite no longer being the sole financial providers, because someone else will always pick up the slack.*

Women don't get the luxury of relying on someone else to step in and do unpaid labor. If we get a break it's from someone we paid to give us one. We have to be competent in every sphere. We know about soothing teething infants and which day trash day is and how to stop mail service when we go out of town *and* also how to be an actuary *and* the rules of basketball *and* what a Roth IRA is. And we're expected to actually *take care of* all that shit. And we're not supposed to want, let alone need, a partner in any of this! We're doing more than ever before and getting less help and being told to want less. Less romance, less intimacy, less connection.

I still think of myself as pretty romantically independent. If, for some really depressing reason, Dave and I were no longer together, I think I would do well single (after a period of deep sadness that involved *a lot* of donuts and weird fashion choices on my part). Before Dave, I loved being single; I'm not saying I loved every single moment, but I *like* doing things on my own. However, I'm not entirely sure how much of that is really who I am, and how much of that I cultivated because I thought that was the cool, good, strong thing to do. I find myself shocked that I'm going on five years of dating the same person; I did not think that I would ever do this, and frankly, I never specifically *wanted* to date long-term or pick out shower curtains together. I didn't see the benefit of commitment. No one showed me the good parts. Rom-coms cut off right after the wedding or the big declaration of love; movies about marriage are usually gritty or unhappy; songs about being happy in a relationship are usually cartoonish and over-the-top. There isn't much art out there right now that is a celebration of good long-term partnership,

---

* In fact, in straight partnerships where women earn *more* than their partners, men do even *less* housework than their breadwinning counterparts.

the day in, day out boring sweet bits.* I didn't really know what to expect when Dave and I started dating and then *kept* dating.

I thought that the world would forget me when I wasn't single. I thought I would become reliant on and consumed by my partnership. I thought I'd stop being creative, stop having strife, stop experiencing excitement. I thought it might be boring to only be wanted by one person.† I expected to lose out on a lot of male attention and friendship, which did happen to some degree, but I expected to be gutted by that, and mostly it's been relaxing.

I worried I would become dependent. That all the parts of me that I liked and valued—being smart, being hardworking, and yes, being independent—would be or even could be erased by wanting to date someone seriously. I still find myself occasionally seeking out ways to prove that I'm not just a girlfriend and that my life doesn't revolve around Dave. I try to travel alone when I can. I try to hang out with friends without him. I try to separate our lives enough that we still have things to say to one another. I still don't bring up marriage much; I'm not convinced it will change anything for us other than maybe I'd get a ring, which would be tight, because rings are delightful. I try to not do too much PDA. I don't care much for romantic gestures, which I find *deeply* embarrassing. I try to let other people see that we're—that *I'm*—independent, that I don't need him, that he doesn't need me. I still try to assert that I am not weak or needy, as if those are the worst things a person could be.

Here is the root of the root and the bud of the bud and all that: it's completely normal to want someone to go through shit with. Or

---

* The one song I can think of that feels anything like the happiness of a steady relationship is "Our House" by Crosby, Stills, Nash and Young. And the couple from the song (Graham Nash and Joni Mitchell) only were together for two years, which is still the fun, easy part of a relationship. Let's be clear.
† As if when I was single I was wanted by loads of people. Ha!

even if you're like me, and you *didn't* want that, to find out that you quite enjoy love, even if it *is* most often boring, as you suspected. Love is not flashy or thrilling most of the time. In the words of Samantha Irby: "Real love feels less like a throbbing, pulsing animal begging for its freedom and . . . more like, 'Hey, that place you like had fish tacos today and I got you some while I was out.'" It's totally natural and human and lovely to want to have someone bring you home fish tacos. It's not weak. It's not pathetic. It's not unworthy of your time or desire or effort. I'm not saying that doing twelve vodka shots in a night and grinding on a stranger isn't dazzling. It is! I'm not saying that dissecting every single social media post your crush has ever engaged with to figure out if they're really a good fit for you despite being a Sagittarius isn't a fun time. It is! I'm just saying it's okay to want someone to send stupid tweets to, to laugh with when the dog falls off the couch, to ignore when they suggest that *Love Actually* isn't a good movie. Love (actually)* is a worthwhile endeavor, and it doesn't make you any less independent.

Plus, who can afford to live in LA on their own?

---

* Sorry.

How Exactly to Be Likable

1. Be mega-hot, but in an approachable way. A way that makes people think that you might one day be hot around them or even toward them. Think young Jennifer Garner, but obviously not exactly young Jennifer Garner, because some people don't like her.

2. Admit to no vanity, for the love of God. Remember, the reason you look this good is that you drink water and always wash off your makeup before bed. NOT Botox, La Mer, good genetics, and generational wealth that led you to always have enough money to see dentists and dermatologists.

3. Spend your free time caring for the emotional needs of others, but don't smother, okay? Check in the right amount. Keep it light, but be available to be emotionally dumped on at a moment's notice.

4. Make it clear that you do stuff for other people, but don't showboat too much. Have a trusted friend leak good things about you. When doing stuff for others, be careful to take up causes

that everyone agrees on; animal rescues and delivering food for old people are relatively low-risk. Obviously, there's room to be disliked because you haven't gone far *enough* in your activism, so do watch for that.

5. Have a perfect ass. Your friends keep trying to explain what cellulite is, but you don't really *get* what they're talking about. You have compassion for them, of course! That must be rough!

6. Stay fit, but don't go wild. Never mention how you stay in shape unless fitness is a part of your personal brand. You can offhandedly mention specific trendy workout gear you use; however, you don't want to seem *too* worried about material items. There are people dying. You *can* admit to enjoying a sunset on a hike, but do not mention that you're hiking more lately because your body dysmorphia has gotten bad recently. Remember to always mention that you're working out for your health or to feel better; never allude to the pressure to be thin.

7. Decorate your house in a way that doesn't cost you money, because spending money on interior design is gauche, but also have a home filled with priceless statement pieces. You can do flea markets; most people like flea-market finds. But also your entire place should have a cohesive feel that is modern but *not* trendy. We're going for contemporary timeless here; what the fuck are you doing with shiplap? That's *sooo* 2016 Joanna Gaines derivative.

8. Be down for *whatever!!!!!!!!!!!!* But be chill about it.

9. Read, but don't talk about it unless someone else brings up a specific book, because people who talk about loving to read are fake

and annoying. Especially people who read in bars. Don't *ever* read a book sitting alone in a bar unless you can guarantee that only men who find that hot and won't think it's an affectation will see you. In that case, reading in a bar alone is good and likable and an easy conversation starter. (For them. Not you.)

10. When you eat with other people, eat whatever you want that isn't *so* unhealthy as to be gross to others (who are somehow involved in what you're putting in your body), but also not so healthy that you're bullying others with your choices. Turkey burger can straddle the line, though of course there are questions as to the ethics of eating meat.

11. Do not sleep with people too quickly, but don't be a prude about it. Don't talk about having sex unless you're being flirtatious and no one else but your intended sex partner can hear, but again, don't be frigid about sex when it comes up. Joke, but don't be crass. Certainly don't ever say "making love."

12. Respond to texts in a timely—but not clingy!—manner.

13. Be a leader at work without being a bitch. Don't be hands-on or hands-off. Your hands should be lingering over the project like those of a Reiki healer.*

14. Be warm without being overly chipper. We want enthusiasm, but tone it down. Again, you need to be approachable *should* anyone—especially a straight white cis man—want to talk to you. But don't approach him, unless being bold is his whole thing and he loves it when people approach him. Then you

---

* Still unsure if this is how Reiki works.

should do it. But even if you do approach him and that *is* his thing, don't give him the wrong idea. If you're there to talk business, don't wear clothes that would make him think about something horny like shoulders, okay?

15. Not sure what to tell you about nipple appearance. I'm personally confused on this one. If you know what's "in" for nipples, let me know. Basically: whatever nipples you have and wherever they are is probably wrong.

16. Be outdoorsy, but don't go overboard with it. No one likes people who talk about their little weekend camping trips or how many national parks they've visited. Boring! Post a couple of photos every month where you look hot (while outside) in your Instagram stories and be done with it.

17. Know and appreciate art and have clearly formed opinions based on that wealth of knowledge about what is good and bad art. Have conversations but not debates, and frequently concede that the other person is making good points. Make sure your tastes are refined and unique. You don't want basic-ass Art History 101 opinions, okay? But also don't show off about how much you know about art. That's tacky.

18. Keep your carbon footprint at zero. By accident.

19. Be interested in sports, but not more interested than your closest male friend or lover. They should know more than you, but you should be an attentive listener if they want to talk about it. Do not correct them or teach them anything. Occasionally demonstrate arcane sports knowledge, but only if you're agreeing with and building on their point. You may tease lightly if

you meet someone who is a fan of a rival team, but don't let things get actually heated.

20. Do *not* watch reality TV of any kind; double no to anything from the *Bachelor* franchise. *The Twilight Zone* is fairly universal, but be ready to critique it if need be. Have well-informed, positive opinions on *The Sopranos*, *The Wire*, *Breaking Bad*, and *Mad Men*. Do not watch shows with female leads unless the show is universally acclaimed and beloved.

21. As for film, documentaries are mostly acceptable as long as you aren't *too* into them, as are some—not all!—films with Leo DiCaprio in them and some—not all!—Steven Spielberg productions. Don't get smart about it. You can enjoy classical rom-coms but only the really good ones (ones with male main characters). *The Godfather: Part II* was the best movie sequel of all time, but you also loved *Magic Mike XXL* (unless you're talking to someone who would be threatened by a male stripper movie) and *Paddington 2*. You've never seen *Mamma Mia!* or *Mamma Mia! Here We Go Again*, but depending on the crowd, you've either been meaning to watch it or you don't get the hype.

22. Be allergic to something that doesn't ruin everyone else's good time because it's a fun little quirk but we don't want to all have to stop eating shellfish around you.

23. Own a KitchenAid mixer, but one you didn't pay for (again, gauche to spend that much on a mixer!). Maybe you got it when your old roommate died? Her mom wanted you to have it? But if you do say where it's from, be a little poignant about it. Don't just say, "It's my old dead roommate's."

24. Do NOT win too many Oscars!

25. Do NOT receive too many birthday wishes on Instagram!

26. Do not complain, ever, about any of the things you are experiencing on any level, other than the occasional nod to your grandmother's brave fight against breast cancer. Nota bene: you remain upbeat about her prognosis.

27. Don't talk about it or anything, but have a cool job title. No one needs to hear about the day in, day out of your perfectly nonthreatening job. Obviously, you don't want to be too ambitious, so it's not like you're at the *top* of your field, but you are respected. It's a good job in a competitive market, but you didn't take it away from anyone who might deserve it more, like someone's nephew.

28. Never smell bad, ever. Even after a seven-mile hike in 90 percent humidity.

29. Have a hairless asshole. Your butthole doesn't even need waxing. It's hairless?? Somehow?? (Unless hairy buttholes are hot to the person you're showing your butthole to. Then, well, it's butthole wig time.)

30. Like music. When confronted with new music, you reply, "Oooh, I really like this. Who is it?" and let someone introduce you to a new artist. Everything that you've already heard before? Love it. Unless it's bad, of course.

31. Love yourself, but don't go nuts, okay? And don't hate yourself out loud. No one wants to hear that.

Sorry, Dove, but I Am Never
Going to Love My Body

When I was sixteen, I lost a bunch of weight. That is the easy, painless baby-shoes-never-worn way to tell the story. The truth is that when I was sixteen, like pulling the emergency brake on the highway, I switched from one eating disorder (food addiction) to another (anorexia). I would love to show and not tell you what happened then, scenes of how I counted calories and starved myself into submission, but I don't think what I did belongs on a page. People describing their weight-loss efforts—both healthy and unhealthy—still often triggers my brain; it makes me think, *Hey, you should probably not eat for a while*. And I don't want to put anything like that into the world. I don't want to make it seem cool or okay or even effective. It was painful and awful. I couldn't concentrate at school a lot. I fought with my mother constantly. I missed my period. I was tired all the time and hungry even more often. But being thin felt like being good.

Everyone around me, with the exception of my mother, loved my weight loss. Doctors congratulated me on a BMI that was finally "healthy," relatives were proud of how little I ate, friends told me how good I looked, I got better roles in the school play. I was still larger than most people my age, so it was likely difficult to see from the outside what was really going on, and what it was was self-harm. There's no other way to put it.

Right in the throes of my own anorexia, my cousin died from the disease. She was ten years older than I was and had been anorexic for many years. No one knew it was coming and no one thought her situation was that dire. After my cousin's death, my mother became fanatical about my health, understandably, if not helpfully. What had been concern before turned into a full-court press against the disorder. Of course, while she did everything out of love and desperation, no one can decide for you when you're done with your eating disorder the same way no one can make you be less depressed.

I would love to tell you exactly what helped me recover from anorexia, but mostly I think it was just the passage of time. My inclination to starve myself tapered off slowly in fits and starts. I saw mental health experts who may have helped and ones who certainly didn't. I hope dearly that if you are experiencing any kind of disordered eating, you seek out the help of professionals, because disordered eating is deadly. But I cannot tell you specifically what worked for me. What I know is that I went from fat to average-size and I did it in an unhealthy way and everyone was happy for me. I still hated my body.

"Learn to love your body to boost your daughter's self-confidence." That is the title of a real page on Dove's website. (Dove calls their campaign the Dove Self-Esteem Project, which makes me want to crash a board meeting and projectile vomit on their CEO.) The company that also owns Axe body spray wants to remind you that stretch marks are tiger stripes or some corny shit. Click here to learn how to *love* your fleshy container.

Someone over at Corporations decided that the best way to help women to not feel like shit about their bodies after years of making them feel like shit about their bodies was to simply tell them to love their bodies. Sometimes this is also said as "Love yourself!" Because as we all know (and love), women *are* their bodies. Where men are allowed the nuance and grace to be any one of dozens of things—a pilot, an asshole, Christopher Walken, sensitive, the best third baseman of all time—if you're a woman, you *are* your body until proven otherwise. Corporate America said: we know you've been taught to hate your body, to obsess over it. We're not going to change that fixation. We agree. You *are* your body. But we can't tell you you're ugly anymore (it's not the '70s), so instead, we'll put the onus on you to *love* your body. With the help of our products. Remember, ladies: you are not a person *with* a body, you are a body with a person inside.

Even if you get into Harvard Law School—what, like it's hard?—people will go out of their way to make sure to let you know that they've consumed your body and what they've concluded. You could be the most famous model in the world and people you will never meet will still let you know that they wouldn't sleep with you. I get a lot of messages from people on Twitter that are very kind about my writing, which is lovely, and I can't say enough how much it means to me. However, about 90 percent of the messages from men include a note about my appearance. I'm not exaggerating at all; I'm probably underestimating. It's always some version of, "Sophie,* I loved your article this morning. You're very smart. Keep up the good work! And also, you're sexy in your profile picture. I thought I had to tell you. If you're ever in Boston, let me buy you a drink!" What the fuck, dude? First of all, I'm never getting a drink with anyone. Secondly, leave my body out of it. My big honkin' titties didn't write the piece; leave them alone. Somehow, because I'm a woman, the

---

* Creepy men always call me Sophie. Perhaps it seems more diminutive? Or they literally just don't care at all to notice that I don't go by Sophie? I don't know. I don't care at all about people calling me Sophie, but it's usually a red flag in Twitter DMs.

way I look is relevant to my work and how much these people support it. It's relevant all the time because I *am* my body!!!

Remember, ladies: you *are* your body and you better fucking love your body.

Well, guess what? I'm never going to get there!

This is not to say that I don't love *other* people's bodies or that I think you ought *not* to love yours. There is no good reason—not a single valid reason—that any of us have to not love our bodies *in theory*. The problem is practice. The problem is fighting against all the messages we receive that our bodies are less than, shitty, broken. The problem is European beauty standards, the problem is objectification, the problem is our obsession with thinness, and if not that, then thinness disguised as fitness or thinness disguised as health. The problem is doubled and tripled and thousandfolded if you're not white, if you're not able-bodied, if you're not cis, if you're nonbinary.

All the "Love your body" messaging leaves absolutely no room for people who have body issues or body-image issues. Just look at the way the movement treats people who have just given birth. It tells them their stretch marks are battle scars and that they have to be thankful for their belly skin because it gave them a baby. Let me be perfectly clear: it's *lovely* if you genuinely feel that way about your body post-baby! But what about people who don't? Imagine going through a process where you gain twenty-five to seventy-five pounds (or more! or less!). Your vagina rips to your asshole, you shit yourself in front of strangers, your bladder never works quite right again, your abs get shredded (and not in the six-pack way), your feet change size, your hair falls out, your boobs sag forevermore, and there is *no room* for you to talk about how hard that might be to cope with because you're supposed to love your body the whole time. Even as American society has made it clear that mothers we'd like to fuck are the exception rather than the rule. And God forbid you go through any of those body changes without a baby to show for it!

Well, I'm not going to love my body. I've been told too many times in too many ways what is wrong with me (my body) for me to realistically get there. I've been told by Target clothing sizes that my rib cage is too big. I've been told by Kelly Ripa getting plastic surgery on her earlobes that mine are too stretched out. I've been told by ad campaigns that I'm supposed to (I think?) bleach my asshole, even though I have no earthly idea what that means or does and very little interest in looking it up. Loving my body is not an achievable goal. I've done lots of cool things with my body. I've played ice hockey and eaten an entire pan of Rice Krispies Treats in one day and given a blow job in a bathtub. I've had eight surgeries and I'll probably need more. My body has done cool shit and I still don't love her and I don't think it's a realistic aim. The same body that has allergic reactions to everything? The body that has IBS and chronic UTIs? The body that has bad hips at age twenty-seven? The body with the titty tumor? The body that gets shoulder acne every single time I work out no matter how fast I take off my sweaty sports bra? Not happening! I don't have the fucking energy!

The reality is I'm allowed to hate my body and not hate myself. I'm allowed to look in the mirror and not like my thighs. Are my thighs beautiful? YES. Is someone else with exactly my thighs hot? YES. Is it okay if on occasion I absorb the harmful messaging of the world and agree that my cellulite is ugly? YES. It's not *my* fault. I am not my body—a lesson I learned from a somewhat ironic source: body dysmorphia.

When I came into college, I was still anorexic. I was better than in high school, but I was not in the clear. I worked out constantly and felt guilty every time I left the dining hall. By the end of my sophomore year, I had relaxed my insane calorie counting a bit—mostly because of the unpredictability of college and how hard it was to keep up with, and also because I was tired, honestly. It's very,

very, very exhausting to use up your brain space knowing the exact calorie count of every type of fruit. I have slowly gotten better and better at labeling unhealthy thoughts, at recognizing when I'm trying to harm and punish my body. I stopped weighing myself three and four times a day; I even went about six years without weighing myself or knowing my weight at all. At the doctor's office, I would make them *not* tell me what I weighed. Is it perfectly healthy to know that I might become emotionally unmoored just by hearing the number? No. Probably not. But it's healthier than checking in on that number every six hours. I stopped working out every single day eventually. Mostly because I got busy and worked about sixty hours a week, not out of any true sense of health or balance. Once I got busier, however, once I had things to actually do and take care of in my life outside of trying to be thinner, I got better at not starving myself. Slowly.

But despite my eating habits stabilizing, my body dysmorphia didn't abate. I don't know when exactly it started, because by definition, body dysmorphia is about not knowing what your body really looks like; I don't know precisely when the two images of my body—the real one and the one in my head—diverged in the woods. If you don't have body dysmorphia, well, frankly, I don't even know how you operate. What must it be like? One time someone tweeted—and I can't find the tweet, or otherwise I would tell you which brilliant angel wrote this—that body dysmorphia feels like they made your whole brain out of the deep shame response you feel after you've come and porn is still playing. Like your whole life is that weird, disgusted-with-yourself feeling.

And at its worst, that is how I've felt. Now, however, after years of eating disorder recovery and reminding myself that my brain cannot be trusted in matters of personal body shape detection, mostly my body dysmorphia manifests as me having no fucking clue as to what I look like. I think it's why I've always been so fascinated with mirrors. It's not out of a sense of vanity, which I assure you I would own up to. It's because before I arrive in the mirror, I have virtually no idea as to what I'll see. I simply don't remember what Sophia Benoit looks like. I cannot conjure up an image of myself in my head. In a way, I became separate from my body.

I probably first became unattached from my body when I got fat. When you're fat, people *love* to remind you that you are not *really* your body. Your *real* body is hiding somewhere under there, only a few decades of starvation away.* I suppose it was messaging like that that first led me away from my body. Because you're supposed to believe that you aren't a fat person, that you're a thin person waiting to get out of a fat person's body. And in the meantime, everyone is going to keep reminding you constantly that you *are* currently fat. It's like if you were stuck in a well and every single person in the town gathered around the well every morning to shout down, "Hey, you're stuck in a well!" Fucking thanks! I got it!

My body dysmorphia, and years of weight changes and hyper-focus on my appearance, has made it impossible for me to figure out what the hell I look like. I have a warped, distorted memory of myself where sometimes I completely forget that I don't look like an Instagram model who has been a size 2 or less her whole life, and sometimes I assume I look like a trash bag full of mashed potatoes that was left out in the sun for six days and then dressed up in clothes that you found in the lost and found of a small-town ice rink. Sometimes I forget that I have (or am?) a body that can be seen by other people at all! I used to beg my college roommate to point out people who were my size so that I could see what I look like; she (rightfully!) refused. I find myself *shocked* when people recognize me after

---

* Of course, you are also *only* your body, too. You are fat and nothing else!!!! Got it?? As soon as you lose all that weight, let us know so we can all finally comfortably resume life.

a few interactions, even if *I* recognize them, too. I live next door to a pizza place and I walk my dog past the front patio at least three times a day and I still was surprised they recognized me when I dyed my hair blond. I'm never sure what I'm presenting to other people and therefore I assume everyone else is unsure of what I'm presenting to them.

One of the best tools for fighting off my body dysmorphia came from the most unexpected source: selfies. You know in *Peter Pan* how Peter loses his shadow and has to chase it around so that he can sew it back to himself? Selfies became the sewing needle for me to figure out what the hell I look like, for me to reattach my body to myself. If not completely, then at least a little bit.

Selfies became big in my world around 2011. Obviously, people were taking photos of themselves long before then, and who can forget the horrendous Myspace profile photos of the early aughts? But selfies became A Whole Thing around 2011. I immediately *loathed* them. I railed against them. I joined in with anyone I could find—and it was almost always a man—to shake my fist at the sky and holler about how selfies were attention-seeking displays of self-absorption, tangible demonstrations of fatuity. I was embarrassed *for* the people taking selfies. I wanted them to feel shame at being so bold as to post a photo of themselves online for people to see.

I wanted them to feel shame, of course, because I felt shame. Because I couldn't imagine putting a photo of myself up online that I *liked*, that I wanted to claim. This was still in the era where Facebook was alive but losing its grip as the main social media site, commandeered by fiftysomething women named Marilyn who shared recipes, grandbaby pics, and wild conspiracies about the government. Instagram was new and gaining ground, at least among hot people. I hated it. I hated it all. I hated change; I didn't want to learn a new app. I certainly didn't want to download an app where the sine qua non of success was either hotness or wealth. I didn't want to find more ways people could be better than I, and photos were something I *knew* I wasn't going to win at. Every photo of me up until that point had been put up online mostly without my permission by well-meaning friends who thought *they* looked cute in the picture. Which is fair!! But I looked like dog shit, or at least I thought I did. I certainly didn't think that more photos, and photos with me as the centerpiece, would be the answer.

But as with most things that I've railed against because I've actually just felt left out, I eventually succumbed and tried taking a selfie. Sometime in 2013, I was in my apartment, which was really an off-campus dorm, and I was next to the bathroom mirror—I still remember what I was wearing—and my hair looked *stunning*, so I tried taking a photo of myself with my phone and it worked (because it was designed to!). And for the first time in my life I *knew* immediately that I had a photo that I felt good about. I was in control. This seemed as revelatory as if they had all of a sudden put me in control of the Federal Reserve system. You see, women aren't supposed to have control of their own image. We're supposed to be *in charge* of it, of its upkeep, its maintenance, of making sure it pleases visitors—much in the same way women used to keep houses but never own them.

Most of my life, being photographed felt like picture day at school where some strange adult you'd never met before corralled your hair with a disposable comb, posed you like a doll, and then barked weird orders at you while you tried to hold still and then after all that, you didn't see the photo for weeks and weeks until the day arrived to take the big paper packet of photos home. And they were always ugly. I mean, mine pretty much *always* looked like ass. I'm not going to sugarcoat it. I love myself, so I'm not trying to be cruel to nine-year-old Sophia, but the pictures were bad. It always felt like everyone else's photos were wonderful. The popular girls—

girls with names like Lauren and Amanda—always hid theirs and pretended like theirs were terrible so people would beg to see them and then they'd finally reveal them and the photos would be *gorgeous*. No one begged to see my photos and they were ugly anyway, and that was the process of having your photo taken, in my mind. I had no say over my self-presentation and it turned out bad anyway. Selfies offered a way out of this. All of a sudden I got to watch myself in the camera *before* the shot was taken. And then I got to take two million more shots until I got it right, which, yes, you could do with a digital camera to some extent, but digital cameras didn't have front-facing lenses and you always ran out of room on your memory card and it was a whole ordeal.

I was a year or two late to the selfie craze compared to everyone at USC*—which feels *very, very* late when you're in college—but as soon as I let go of the shame I felt for taking and later posting them, I was in. I felt a genuine *rush* every time I saw a photo of myself that didn't make me recoil in self-hatred. And then, when I would occasionally share them online, it was always done with a dollop of self-disgust for being so public about *not* hating myself, and usually paired with a self-deprecating caption. I knew where the self-censure around taking selfies was coming from, of course, because only a few short months before, *I* had been appalled by people doing the same thing. I didn't immediately overcome my own shame or judgment, but I *loved* the thrill of being adjacent to being attractive, and that outweighed my embarrassment. I was not the hottest girl, but my God, I could figure out angles and lighting and take forty-eight photos and have one turn out well and that was good enough.

---

* *Selfie* was the *Oxford English Dictionary* word of the year in 2013, which means that they started becoming popular *at least* eighteen months before then because we all know the *Oxford English Dictionary* is far behind the real world. Hence, if I took my first selfie that year, I was similarly delayed.

When I took selfies, I could, for a moment or two, see myself as I was. I could see the outtakes, the ones where I blinked or blurred, the ones where I had a double chin or something in my teeth. I could also see myself in good lighting with good hair and a smile that wasn't too gummy. I could see myself for a short time and know what I looked like and I didn't have to be surprised by it, like I am when I look in a mirror or when someone else takes a photo. The very act of selfie-ing with a front-facing camera means control. Control of self, control of image, control of body. I finally had some say over not only how others perceived me, but how *I* saw myself. And it helped a lot. Eventually, photos of myself became less evil. Eventually, I understood that you can look your absolute hottest and then take forty-seven photos of yourself and thirty-nine of them will turn out positively *god-awful*. The odds when a stranger takes your picture are not in your favor.

As photos lost their potential to harm my mental health, my body in general did, too, since that was my best window into what I looked like. After I started taking selfies, I had proof that there were good versions of my body, preserved in my phone and in the cloud. There was hard evidence that I had liked my body before and could in the future.

Despite the help of selfies and staying busy and learning how to actually do my hair, despite being fairly far along in the recovery process from my eating disorders, I'm still not going to *love* my body. On some days, I still don't always remember that my body and I have anything to do with each other, and on other days my fixation with her is back. A good photo of myself is just as shocking to me as a bad one—I find it difficult to identify with either most of the time. I still don't know what I look like! I don't. I'm somewhat more connected to my body, but I'm not perfect at linking the internal world where I think about the Spice Girls performing with Pavarotti with the stomach I see when I look down. I still have urges to punish myself with starvation. I still know how many calories almost every single food is off the top of my head.

But I'm doing better. Not perfectly, but better. I go hours sometimes without thinking about my body at all. Days without the urge to weigh myself. Weeks without wondering if I should skip a meal. I'm doing okay. My body is fine. She's here. I don't always know what she looks like, but she's along for the ride. My attitude is akin to what it would be if I got a shitty rental car for a long road trip: okay, we're stuck together; what can I do but make the best of it? I just know I'm *never* going to love my body even if I give birth to five kids or run a marathon or do any of the other things the Love Your Body community brags about their bodies having done. Probably I wouldn't love it even if I got a ton of plastic surgery, but I am willing to find out if that's the case if anyone wants to pay for that. At my very best, I love myself and I'm indifferent toward my body, and *that* feels pretty close to bliss.

How to Be the Life of the Party in 28 Easy Steps

Being the life of the party is, of course, the pinnacle of human achievement. Once, when I was about sixteen, I googled "How do you have charisma?"* because I'm clearly the most pathetic person alive. Being beloved has always been a goal of mine, and I've even achieved it at one or two gatherings. It's rare, mostly because my bedtime is midnight at the latest, and because I find social interaction excruciating after the two-hour mark. That said, with maximal effort, it is possible to be the star of the shindig, the queen of the clambake, the belle of the banquet, the nonesuch of the night out. I'll show you how:

1. First, you must understand that being the darling of a social gathering requires preparation far in advance. If you can start in early childhood to cultivate a personality that others like

---

* I always include the question mark in my Google queries, something that I *think* started ironically, but now has become integral to me.

and are drawn to, a general ease among others, that would be ideal. If you can't scrounge up an agreeable temperament at home, store-bought is fine.

2. About three weeks before the event, you should get started on any hair removal or deep exfoliation that you need to do. Smooth, supple skin does not magically arrive overnight. I'm not saying one *need* remove body hair to become the life of the party; I'm just saying if you're going to do so, start early, so that by the time your little get-together arrives, you're in a maintenance zone rather than a demolition project.

3. Four hours before you're going to leave your house for this soiree, you're going to need to start Getting Amped. Ideally, you take a small dose of recreational Adderall, which will give you just enough buzz to get through the evening but won't keep you up all night. If you don't want to take a rec-Addy, that's perfectly fine; your body, your choice. You're gonna need to guzzle an energy drink. If you're pregaming to go out, you can mix this energy drink directly into the alcohol to speed shit up. If you're going to make it past ninety minutes of socializing and still be Fun to Talk To, you need either a massive dose of adrenaline—the kind that only comes from hanging around the deepest crush of your life—or you need artificial stimulants. If drugs/alcohol is not your thing, that's totally fine, but I don't know what to tell you. Fake it?

4. While getting ready, which you should treat as the sacred ritual it is, you should have a bomb-ass playlist going. This is technically a part of the Getting Amped section, but I can't overstate the importance of a pregame playlist. You want songs that make you feel like dancing, fucking, or singing along.

Think "Man! I Feel Like a Woman,"* "Fast Car," "Every Day Is a Winding Road," "Just a Friend," and "It Wasn't Me." Nostalgic songs that your brain knows every single word to work best; if the song was played at your middle school dance, that's a green light. (Other than "Cotton Eye Joe," which is a no. The vibe is *not* country line dance.)

5. Carve out an hour to get dressed. While the act of putting on clothes takes forty-two seconds, standing in front of a mirror pinching and cinching various body parts, trying on three different bra styles to see which one makes your boobs look least weird, and loathing every outfit you've ever owned takes fifty-nine minutes and sixteen seconds, minimum, and let's give you a grace period. Frankly, I agree, the first outfit you put on was trying too hard. Anytime—every time—you purchase new clothing for a big event, it ends up looking like ass. What looked chic and sophisticated in the forgiving light of the Zara dressing room now makes you look like a person who is going to a business conference who plans to cheat on their partner.† You try on an old trusty outfit—an iridescent bodysuit—something that used to be a surefire shortcut to self-confidence, but which tonight makes you feel like an impostor. Back to the business-y outfit, on to Instagram to see how people your age actually dress because you've suddenly forgotten, off with the business clothes; now you're going to try to pull off bike shorts. Let me save you time: bike shorts suck and

---

* Shania Twain did say she'd liked Trump's no-bullshit attitude and would have voted for him, but then she walked that back, so only play this song if you already own it and you won't be giving her any streaming money.
† I actually can't afford Zara; I'm just trying to sound relatable. I shop at Target and occasionally H&M.

they're a scam invented by thin rich women to make the rest of us feel uglier. How about a chill vibe instead? You could be a Chill Person tonight. A funny graphic T-shirt and cute jeans says, "Oh, I just happened upon this party. I had other options tonight. *Billy Madison* is the peak of cinema to me. I have older brothers." Fuck. You look like your dad. You just do. You look like your dad in that outfit. Sorry. Back to the bodysuit. Oh, wait, maybe that really tight dress with two pairs of off-brand Target Spanx under it.

6. Finish your drink, pee one last time, make sure you have your ID and gum, deodorant. Call an Uber.

7. Panic, cancel the Uber, and go and change your clothes again. Go with the chill outfit, please; I implore you. You will need to be comfortable in order to be the life of the party tonight. Being hot is obviously important, too. If you need to jazz up the chill outfit, do so with fun shoes or earrings or a jaunty hat if you're one of those people who can pull off hats. But if you feel uncomfortable, you will not survive as the center of attention. People don't like watching other people experience discomfort; have you ever been to a stand-up show where someone is bombing? It's awful. You don't want to spend the entire night adjusting the straps on your sexy little tank top, or rebuttoning that dress that always comes undone. I have a friend, Tam, who is a delight to be around—everyone loves her, desperately—and she has never once in her life felt uncomfortable; earlier this month, her whole titty popped out on a Zoom call because she was wearing a blazer with no shirt under it. She didn't care at all. I don't even know if she remembers this happening. She is the kind of person who can pull off wearing "uncomfortable" clothing because she's so comfortable with herself, because

she's so naturally dazzling; unless you, too, could pull off a wardrobe malfunction on camera without a care in the world, you, my friend, should choose comfort. So my advice is: If you can muster it, please remember to never once in your life feel uncomfortable. This will help loads with our goal of making you the belle of the ball.*

8. Take a shot; try to force yourself to pee again even though your friend's house is like twenty-five minutes away and not a four-hour road trip; move your ID and gum from one purse to another because it goes better with your outfit; spritz on perfume or cologne (people love a good-smelling person);† call an Uber.

9. Get carsick in the Uber. Psych yourself out about the whole night. Question why you're even going to this event. *Who do I even know who is going? Is Carli actually going? When is she planning on showing up? What the fuck almighty am I wearing? Why am I sweating so much? Specifically, why am I sweating so much in the butt region?* Question who the fuck you think you are. *Have I ever spoken to a person where they have enjoyed it? Who am I to try to go to a party? Isn't that just so fucking cocky of me, to think that people like me enough to want to be around me? Jesus, people probably hate how self-assured I seem, showing up like this to an event. The gall!!!!*

10. The very moment that your Uber driver starts to slow down, tell the Uber driver, "Here's fine!" even if you have no idea

---

* And by "ball" I mean semi-intimate gathering that the coolest person from your work is hosting, which feels like your *one* shot to become friends with her.
† I personally have a *very* strong If You Can't Look Good, Smell Good policy that has served me impeccably well.

where "here" is or if it is actually "fine" or even "in the vicinity of your drop-off location."

11. Okay, well . . . you're here. You spent thirty-six dollars to get to this stupid-ass event that you're going to hate and despite what the sunk-cost fallacy suggests, you might as well go inside. Fuck off, game theory.

12. The buzzer seems to be broken? Text your friend to come let you into their apartment, the very act of which, despite your having been instructed to do so by their Facebook invite, feels desperate. Is everyone else such good friends that they come over here all the time and know the door code? How did they get inside? Okay, no one is answering your texts about letting you in. Should you call? Is it desperate to call to be let in? It feels very weird to call and practically beg to be let into this party. Oh. Okay, someone has answered. Thank God. They're coming out to get you. You, the weirdo alone in the dark on the sidewalk, text-begging to be let inside.

13. Let out a very high-pitched "Hey there!" when you arrive that you then spend the next three minutes playing back to yourself in your own head. Are you even a "Hey there!" person? Why the hell did you say that?

14. Here is where you need to Pull. It. Together. You've got to give 'em the ol' razzle-dazzle. Under absolutely no circumstances should you utter the phrase "give 'em the ol' razzle-dazzle."

15. Assess who the hottest person in the room is. This is vital. The hottest person in the room isn't always the literally best-looking person in the room. It's the most attractive person. The person

whose cues everyone else is following, whose jokes always get laughs, whose suggestions are always heeded. This is the person you're here for. You need to pretend this person is an ex and that you are attending this party to devastate them with your blithe nonchalance. The goal is for them to fall right back in love with you, not that you'd even notice if such a thing happened. (But you *must* make it happen). One of the best ways to get your ex to fall back in love with you is to make everyone else around them fall in love with you. Your job is to be irresistible. Stop hiding in the corner, hoovering up pizza bagels, and start dazzling.

16. Get a drink. I think I forgot to tell you this because I was too busy yelling at you about the pizza bagels or saying "razzle-dazzle" a lot, but get a damn drink. It does not need to be alcoholic, but you need something to do with your hands. If you have a purse/keys/phone/etc., put that down somewhere in a careless manner that suggests that you don't give a shiiiiit about what happens tonight! Wooo! You'll find it later! (But seriously, just leave it all by the door.) Your hands need a drink in them; holding a cup is the universal symbol for "I am not a threat." If you're camping and you see a bear and you have a drink in your hand, you're safe. The bear knows you have chill vibes.

17. Start small; dip your toe in the water of socializing. Turn to someone, anyone who is not talking to another person, and ask them a question. The question itself can be awkward; that's fine. Just keep asking questions. You want to hover somewhere between interrogation and an interview for a job where your best friend is the manager and this is just a formality. Why? Because everyone likes getting asked about themself. We're all

addicted to it. Ask where they grew up, how they know Tony and Annette, if they think Hello Kitty or SpongeBob would win in a fight. It doesn't matter. Get to talking, but don't get stuck with one person. This is a ground game situation. You need to shake a lot of hands and kiss a lot of babies at this bash.*

18. Make excuses with person number one (e.g., "I have to go to the bathroom," "Oh, did Kaitlyn just get here?," "All my parakeets died last night; I need a minute alone on the balcony") and move on to the next thing. Go refill your drink in the kitchen, then join in the discussion about the Lindbergh baby† in the living room. Mingle, mix, be. The verb of the moment is to *flit*. Yes, flit. Flit around finding new people. Ask these new people questions! If you're interested in other people, people will think you're interest*ing*. Of course, don't *only* speak in interrogatives. Drop a personal anecdote every once in a while.

19. Be hilarious. Sorry if I forgot to mention it earlier, but you're going to need to be at least a *little* funny during these interactions you've been having. The only way to get around this requirement is if you are 10/10 hot and very, very kind. Like not nice, *kind*.

20. Make friends with the pets. Everyone loves their pets and that means you need to love their pets. I mean, you should anyway—animals are angels and I'll never forgive humans for

---

* If there are actual babies at this party, you are probably not going to be the life of the party because new parents don't give a shit about who the life of the party is, they just want to drink half a Lime-A-Rita and talk about something other than *Paw Patrol*.

† He definitely killed his kid, didn't he?

stamping out biodiversity. Play with the dog. Pet the cat. If it's a hamster or a tree frog, I'm not suggesting that you go in and scoop it out of its cage and try to be Steve Irwin. Just appreciate the pet! Comment on how cute they are. Remember its name. Make the dog like you the most of any of the guests. This could unlock the whole thing.

21. Circle around the hottest person at the party, occasionally throwing in the absolute quippiest, funniest lines that make everyone roar with laughter. "Is she serious?" ARE YOU? You don't even know where the joke stops and the truth begins, hahahaha funny!!!! FUN! You're funny!!!!! Sardonic, even!!! Get a little close to being "too dark" and then pull back and be effervescent again!!!

22. The energy drink and the adrenal rush of being around a bunch of people who are performing loose approximations of Having Fun is making your mania reach new heights. You feel like you're in a low-budget commercial for vodka. Ask people more questions! Bring up a funny joke from forty-five minutes ago: "Hahaha, remember Mona at the fridge trying to open the beer?" More questions! Start flirting if you haven't been already! Tease people about their home state (classic flirt); steal a cute person's hat and put it on your own head (a flirt that happens in movies a lot); laugh so hard at a medium-funny joke that alcohol almost comes up your nose and then laugh at yourself for that (one of the best flirts of all time). Someone call you Bob Dylan because you are freewheelin'!!!!

23. Everyone loves you. You can tell. You know everyone loves you. People are saying it. They're like, "Oh my God, you're so funny!!!!" and "I love you!!" and "We should totally go to

Cinespia* this summer," which you heartily agree with, even though you are not the kind of person who can sit on a picnic blanket on the ground for three hours without major hip pain. The more they love you, the deeper in you go. Their adoration is fueling you. You're riding a high that rivals drugs. I don't know enough about drugs to tell you which drugs it rivals. Maybe you do? Great.

24. You've had a lot to drink and you make the mistake of going to the bathroom. The relative silence of the bathroom is suffocating, almost . . . poetic? You look in the mirror while washing your hands and start thinking about how your world really only exists in the bathroom; who knows what's going on outside the door anymore? Isn't it crazy that you're *you*?? Like, you're having your life experiences while other people are having their life experiences? This is the most alive you've ever felt; the most you! Here in this bathroom and, oh God, you're really drunk, huh? Shit. Okay. Pull it together. Collect yourself. Get back out there!

25. In the two minutes you've been in the bathroom—it has been two minutes, right?—somehow the entire party tone has shifted. What a betrayal! Everyone is sitting down now. People are on the couch; some are even under blankets. There is scientifically no way to be the life of this kind of get-together. People are sleepy, they're worn-out. This makes you think: perhaps you were the linchpin holding the party atmosphere together; no one could hold shit down for two minutes while you peed? What role are you supposed to play now? Are you supposed

---

* This is an LA thing where you sit in a famous graveyard and watch classic movies on picnic blankets.

to stick around for the maudlin, waterlogged end of the party? Are we all gonna watch *Step Brothers* on Blu-ray? Are we doing raucous commentary over it or are we falling asleep scattered across the apartment like a litter of puppies?

26. Panic.

27. Don't say goodbye to anyone; they don't care that you're leaving. Why the fuck would anyone care that you're leaving? Are you going to go around to each person and offer your condolences regarding how much they'll miss you after you're gone? Deranged. No. Wait until the focus is on something not-you (everyone trying to get the TV to work, a new person who just arrived with an edible arrangement, the hottest person in the room speaking) and then slip out the front door into the night, Uber arrival time be damned.

28. Stand and wait in the wet grass (grass is always so wet at night!!) while your eyes adjust to the dark. Ahh, it's so nice and quiet out here. And you were just the life of the party.

I Check to Make Sure My Boyfriend
Is Still Breathing When He's Sleeping

I have written about sex and relationships for quite a while. I got into it basically by loving only to write (and read and talk) about being horny and by never actually becoming an expert in anything else other than Fleetwood Mac intra-band drama. I've had a relationship advice column in some form or another for years. After reading this far into this book, you may question my ability to give advice, which I think is fair of you! Anyway, perhaps the number one question I get in some form or another from women and nonbinary folks is: Am I crazy?*

Am I crazy to leave this person who treats me poorly? Am I crazy to leave this person who treats me well? Am I crazy for being sad that my parents didn't want to come to my graduation? Am I crazy for asking my partner to be kinder to my pet? Am I crazy to be offended when my partner asks me to dress differently? Am I crazy for moving in together, for wanting children, for demanding he get a divorce before we date, for

---

* While it has happened once or twice, it is *incredibly* rare for a cis man to ask me this question.

275

asking her to stop commenting on how much I eat, for being mad that they locked me out of the house?

That's the big question on everybody's lips:* Am I being unreasonable?†

Women are near-constantly being told they're being unreasonable; this is the sternum of the question, "Am I crazy?" You do not ask, "Am I nuts?" unless you've been told over and over again that you are. Women obsessively check in with one another, relying on consensus as a barometer of their behavior. We have been made to distrust our instincts, to question our requirements, to lower our standards. To believe that if something is upsetting us, we must be responding to it wrong, somehow, because the other person must be right. We must be crazy.

This tiny flame of self-doubt burns across all kinds of interactions. The late-night requests from your boss, the weird, shitty phone calls from your dad, the way your friend's boyfriend talks over you all the time. *Am I being crazy for asking for better treatment? For expecting more?* The answer is (almost) *always* no.† No, you are not crazy for finding your partner's friends' pranks mean. No, you're not unreasonable for asking your girlfriend to meet your parents. No, you're not a bitch for insisting that your roommate take out the trash as often as you do.

The thing is, women are—generally speaking—not supposed to have boundaries or expectations of others. It kills other people's vibe, and if you have one job as a woman, it's to not in any way harm the

---

* On their chapped lips.

† *Crazy*, of course is the more stigmatized, more insulting, more common term.

† On occasion, all of us are unreasonable and, even worse, delusional about it. All of us have outsize expectations of others, expectations that go unexpressed, making them even *more* unreasonable. We're all poor communicators, impatient and imperfect in our relationships. But when I say "us" I don't mean me, of course. Or you. Obviously, you and I are perfect.

vibe. This is especially true in romantic partnerships. In fact, there are few places where the stakes feel higher, where there's more pressure to go along with someone else's expectations, than a romantic relationship.

In the beginning, it's little things that you're asked to put more effort into, like staying over at their place instead of yours every time, hanging out with their friends more, engaging in their hobbies but never asking them to engage in yours. Anything to fit into their life easier, while they make little to no effort to fit into yours. All of this is especially true if you're dating a man. If you've dated straight cis men, you've probably sat and watched at least one of them play video games as part of a "date." No man has ever sat quietly and watched me read romance novels. You might be asking, "What the fuck would he get out of sitting there and watching you read romance novels?" Well, the same exact experience *I* get out of sitting there watching him play *Call of Duty.* But early in a relationship women are often asked to explicitly signal that we will not disrupt a man's life in any way. Women are, as a general rule, extremely good at reading the room and then catering to the desires of others. And nowhere does the need to track and manage someone else's preferences manifest more strongly than in the early stages of a relationship, when becoming something other than yourself always seems so appealing.

Obviously, everyone shifts a little during the opening salvo of dating. None of us brings our full whole self to the table on the first date. I don't come in a bar, plop down, and say, "Let's be honest, I shut down a lot in the face of minor criticism and need a lot of attention." We *all* perform a shinier version of ourselves for potential partners, but one of the ways that a woman excels at being appealing is by molding herself into whatever her counterpart wants, or whatever she thinks they might want. And we're pretty good at it. We pick up the other person's expectations and shift ourselves so subtly as to make it seem *brilliant* of them that they like to hike. *What a sexy hobby you have. I'm so down to go on that hike; I've never been. Can you believe it? I've lived here four years! What an adventure. I've been meaning to be more outdoorsy and then you came along and created an opportunity for me to be a better person by taking up your hobby.*

There is a subtle, albeit meaningful shift, after the relationship becomes "official" (as if you've registered the fact that you're dating a guy named Connor with a bureaucratic body somewhere). As soon as a hetero relationship gets serious, gendered expectations morph a bit. Namely, they become more care-centric. Here is how I've seen it play out among my straight friends and acquaintances: the woman slowly starts taking over small tasks like remembering if a friend's birthday is on Friday or Saturday, bringing a bottle of wine for dinner, scrubbing the grout in the bathroom. Then the tasks get a little bigger—doing friendship maintenance for her boyfriend, planning the unfun part of vacations, calling Spectrum and yelling at them about how the bill goes up every month. Somewhere in there, these tasks become something that the guy they're dating doesn't value; sometimes, he claims he doesn't think those tasks need to get done at all.

It's a stroke of genius, really. To have someone take over the unfun parts of your life. Then when they say, "This is too much work for me," you can reply with, "Well, *I'm* not the one who cares if this stuff gets done." As if they made up the concept of living in a clean house and maintaining personal relationships. What a fucking cop-out. How antagonistic to the very thesis of romantic relationships, which is—or should be: I would do anything (within reason) to make my partner's life just a little bit better.

The truth is, men likely *would* care if that stuff didn't get done if there were actual consequences they suffered. Obviously, this all varies by task. Some people are never going to bring a bottle of wine over to a friend's house, regardless of gender, regardless of their partnership status. Additionally, some of the people who claim they wouldn't miss these tasks are simply people who don't care about other people, about generosity, about the social contract we have with others. And *that* is what women are to men in these instances: a way out of caring about other people, about norms, expectations, and chores. If someone else simply does the caring for you, you get to be carefree.

Women do not get to be carefree almost ever (unless they're wealthy). Certainly poor women, Black women, women with disabilities, and trans women rarely do. Cis able-bodied white men get to be carefree all the time. You know why? Because they have delegated caring to someone else. They've made the women they have relationships with—whether familial, romantic, or friendly— do the caring for them. The women around them will do the care work that keeps up the appearance that this is a guy who participates meaningfully in society.*

And it's not just care of others that women track and manage and execute for their male partners, friends, sons, and brothers. It's care of self, too. It's women urging men to go to the doctor, asking them not to take certain risks, making them get that mole checked out, pressuring them to apply SPF, talking to them about their drinking habits in ways that aren't alienating, cooking for them, buying water filters, dusting fucking baseboards, calling the landlord to make them look at the mold in the bathroom. The list of ways that women keep men safe is endless.

I love my boyfriend a rather disgusting amount. (As a former Chill Girl Who Hated All Forms of Vulnerability, yes, I'm appalled by this admission.) I have approximately 2,498 kind things to say about my boyfriend, and I know good writing is all about specificity,

---

* Lest you think I'm overlooking the contributions of stay-at-home fathers, a study found that stay-at-home dads do less childcare on average than working moms.

but I don't want any praise of him in published writing, okay? I'm not a fool. I don't need him bookmarking this page and bringing it up later. Instead, I will frame his good traits as a recommendation of myself and my good taste. I would not, for example, ever be with a guy who wouldn't help me with something around the house simply because *I* was the one who cared about it getting done. I have incredibly high expectations of what a partner is and he exceeds them (because I am good at picking boyfriends now. Again, Dave, don't get cocky).

That said, we both fall into the occasional hetero-relationship cliché. Take the time we went on our first couples' trip to Mexico City. Neither of us had been before, and we, stupidly, were not entirely prepared for how much the altitude would effect us. Mexico City is at 7,382 feet above sea level. Somehow, in all the research that we'd done about what to see and do and eat and experience, we hadn't taken *just* how high that is into account. Especially coming from 285 feet above sea level.

Soon after we landed and checked into our Airbnb (in an apartment on the fourteenth floor of a building, which is even higher up), we both started to feel the effects of being over a mile up in the air. I felt light-headed, which is super common for me, but also my hands started to swell and my fingers felt like they couldn't bend. I was tired and had a headache, but again, my body is pretty shitty, so it's always hard to tell what's going on. We were both determined to push through our minor suffering and enjoy the trip, though. After all, it's just altitude sickness.

I looked up the symptoms of altitude sickness and how to treat it, because I'm a hypochondriac and because I wanted to get rid of the feeling as fast as possible. We took ibuprofen and drank water and went out into the city. We started with a seven-mile walk into town, which perhaps was not our most inspired idea. Dave felt mostly fine but a little more tired than usual, and I was . . . struggling. We found a place to get food (for me) and beer (for Dave) while debating what to do next, and it was at that restaurant that I noticed that Dave's hands were kind of . . . blue.

Now, as someone who had only hours earlier read the entire WebMD page on altitude sickness, I could say with clear authority that when your extremities or lips turn blue, you are experiencing *severe* altitude sickness. It's likely to be worse if you came from a low altitude (check) or if you're drinking alcohol (check). I begged Dave to not finish the beer; I was like, "WebMD says you're dying right now. We should find an urgent care!" And Dave was like, "I feel totally fine. Honestly, you're struggling more with the altitude than I am."

Which is a logical-adjacent argument but *his hands were fucking blue!!!!* That's like the last stage of altitude sickness before you *die.* It's never a good thing when your hands turn blue. It's not like, "Oh, that happens when I eat tomatoes; it's no big deal!" It's your body not having enough oxygen! To be fair to him, severe altitude sickness does not usually start at the elevation we were at; it's more common when mountain climbing. But when your fingers turn blue, it's *only* ever bad.

Dave kept insisting he was fine, that he felt fine, that he really wasn't that tired or light-headed. He wanted to keep going. I was walking gingerly next to him the entire day, waiting for the moment he would collapse on the sidewalk, imagining trying to scream for medical help in bad Spanish. We finally made it back to our Airbnb that night, where the air felt impossibly thin to me, the worrier, and we both lay down to try to sleep. I kept surreptitiously looking up how far it was to a hospital and trying to *hint politely* that we should maybe think about considering maybe visiting an emergency room possibly. Just a little bit! A little hospital visit as a treat! Dave was at his breaking point and I was at mine. He finally got upset with me because he'd already told me about fifteen times that, no, he did not want to go to a hospital and that he was fine.

Dave turned over to go to sleep and was successful almost immediately, aided by travel, beer, and a day of being heavily monitored by me. I, however, felt deep in my bones that Dave was going to die in his sleep and I would wake up next to his dead body in a foreign country where I speak almost none of the language other than travel basics, in a rented Airbnb. *Who do you even call when you wake up next to a dead body in a foreign country? Is that just a police thing? Is the number for the ambulance separate? Do I need to testify that I had nothing to do with this? How do I bring his body back to the States? He wouldn't care about his body, but I'm assuming that's a step, right? You can't leave your boyfriend's body in another country, surely. Do I plan the funeral? We've only been dating a year. I don't know what kind of funeral he wants, other than "open bar."*

I'm in bed running through how him dying is most certainly going to ruin my vacation, and I start to get a little miffed. I've never been to Mexico City before. I finally got days off work from my *three different jobs!!!* And he might die on me? He won't even go to urgent care *and* he's mad that I keep bringing it up? At this point, I'm running on spite. I've now looped around from concern over him to anger at him and I don't even *care* if he dies! In fact, when he dies, I'm going to be a single twentysomething woman in a foreign country; I'm going to kick up my heels and flirt my way around the city without him! Mexico City has a fabulous bar scene! GOOD NIGHT AND GOOD LUCK, PAL!

I checked on his breathing many, many times that night like the mother of a newborn.

Obviously, he woke up the next morning. (Imagine if he had died and this was how I wrote the story?) He *had* survived the night, so I agreed to go back out again. We spent another morning walking around the city, strolling through gardens, eating delicious food, mapping out monuments we wanted to see, stopping in cafés. His hands were blue, but holding steady; he swore he didn't feel bad at all. I had entered the point of grief over Dave's certain death where I just wanted to appreciate what time we had left.

At some point in the afternoon, we made it back to the Airbnb because I needed a nap; I kind of always need a nap, to be honest, but especially after this shit. I shucked off my clothes and crawled into bed while Dave headed to the tiny, confusing* bathroom to shower. As I was about to drift off into my first peaceful sleep of the vacation, from the bathroom I heard, "Babe?"

"Yeah?"

"Guess what?"

"What?"

"I figured out why my fingers are turning blue."

"What is it?" (At this point, I'm annoyed because he kept me up all night and now we're playing goddamn Blue's Clues.)

"You know how I bought new jeans for this trip . . ."

That is correct. Dave's hands were turning blue because he'd put them in the stupid pockets of his stupid brand-new jeans and they dyed his stupid hands blue and I lost a night of sleep over it.

I almost lost my mind. I mean, thank God he was okay, but also, come on! Are you kidding me?!

I was talking to Dave about this recently and he was like, "You know, if you hadn't been there, I wouldn't have even noticed my hands turning blue." Which, with the knowledge we all have now about indigo dyes and how this story ends, is fine. But what if he *had* been dying and was simply oblivious to one of the most glaring and obvious signs that his body was completely shutting down?

Was I crazy? I don't know.

I don't think it's crazy to worry about a partner having blue hands, actually. I think I was in the right. I also think that a respon-

---

* I've never been to an Airbnb anywhere in the world that didn't have the most disorienting bathroom experience. It's part of the fun! What *does* this knob do?

sible adult *would* worry about that. Again, hands turning blue is not medically a good sign *ever*. But, by virtue of how things turned out, the story has become an anecdote about how much of a worrier I am, how high-strung and overwrought I can be. That would not be the narrative if he had ended up being seriously ill. Why is it so easy to dismiss women's concerns? As a couple, we rarely dismiss his concerns. I can't think of many times when *I* told *him*, "Don't worry about that. We'll just ignore it." Part of that, of course, is our personalities; he's not a worrier by nature. But also part of that is about who is *asked* to be vigilant about health and safety. It's not usually men. So when things go right, the women who worried—and sometimes who prevented things from going wrong—are painted as hysterical.

Here is another story from when we started dating. A story I hate because I don't think I come across well. Also, a story that is painful to retell. I would like to start this story with a spoiler, because the point of the recounting this is not to find out the outcome, but rather to tell you what happened. So here's the spoiler: everyone involved is lovely. We all meant well and acted poorly. Everyone hurt and everyone got hurt. Also, spoiler: none of us die in this story or even get altitude sickness.

When I first started dating Dave, he lived alone in a one-bedroom apartment with no roommates. The glamour that has! A one-bedroom apartment! Are you the Queen? I was living with two roommates who frequently left dirty plates on the couch or in their beds. *In* their beds. Meanwhile Dave did his dishes after every meal. Dave is a "party boy," which is what I call being an extrovert because I can; he likes having people around all the time. When I met him, the people who were around all the time were two friends of his, a guy and a girl. They all knew each other from Twitter, and I, in turn, knew Dave from Twitter, which is as embarrassing for me to write as it is for you to read. I understand.

Anyway, they were over at his house almost every single night, and they all three hung out pretty much every single day. They watched anime and *Game of Thrones* and the Olympics together. They went to the same bars, and when someone couldn't afford to go out, they stayed in together. They smoked a lot and drank a lot and generally did friend shit. And then I came along.

I had known Dave for a few months from a different Twitter friend group, and I had, because of a misunderstanding in a loud bar, thought that he was dating someone else and that that someone else was male. So I had been friends with him for a while under the assumption that Dave was both gay and taken. Which made me feel very comfortable talking to him. And then, after a few months, I found out that he was both single and into women and within a month I had a crush on him. Dave was not someone I expected to ever have a crush on; he was not exactly my type at the time: namely, he did not treat me like shit and ignore me. So when I got invited to hang out at his place with people I didn't know, I was *of course* going to go, despite that they all hung out in *Pasadena*.* I was trying to get laid.

Well, I was triumphant. I started sleeping with Dave almost immediately, but I tried my hardest to keep it out of the friend group. Years of being overweight had taught me that there was something shameful about someone wanting to sleep with me, plus I was trying to be low-key. Casual. Blasé. "Oh, you like me and want to hook up? Ehh, I'm fine with that. I'm amenable. We don't have to advertise this."†

---

* Non-LA-ers: this is very far away from wherever you are. It literally doesn't matter where in LA you are; Pasadena is far away.

† I was practically shitting my pants with anxiety every single day over how to talk to a guy I liked who seemed to maybe like me back?? One week I got so nervous that I lost my appetite, which has never one other time in my entire life happened. I have never not wanted to eat. I was a train wreck.

Eventually, we got more "serious." We told other people we were hooking up/dating/whatever. We eventually agreed to be exclusive. Things were rolling right along despite my pathological fear of ever being in a relationship again—a thing which I had hated the last time it happened years before with Hockey Warehouse Guy. The one bugaboo other than my abject horror at the mere suggestion of commitment was: his female friend.

I have all kinds of character flaws. You could unfurl a scroll longer than a CVS receipt listing them in six-point font if you wanted to. One thing I did not think I was was the type of person who gets romantically jealous, especially not of female friends. To be a little fair, it's not like I had any issues with any of his other female friends. He had many, many other female friends whom he hung out with both in groups and one-on-one that I had no problem with. (Of course! Because friendships are great!) Why would I *not* want my boyfriend to have friends?

But this one female friend of his seemed different. There were big things, like the fact that she had a key to his place, that she came over more often than I did, that she cooked for him often and left bathing suits in his bathroom. There were small things like foreign hair ties on his bedside table, photos of them that looked couple-y, the way he greeted her first (and with more animation) when he walked into a room. There was the fact that she was extremely hot, something friends of ours brought up often. There was the fact that she had older brothers and knew how to attract male attention and what to do with the male attention she inevitably garnered. There was the fact that he laughed more at her jokes (in fact, I think that might have been the worst). There were a million tiny moments where he chose her preferences over mine. At least, that's how things looked from my end.

It's not that I thought they were sleeping together, although of course I wondered on occasion; I reminded myself frequently that they'd had the option to sleep together at any point in their friendship before we got together. Like, why would Dave even *start* dating me if they'd been hooking up? I really didn't think they were. I don't think they were at all romantically inclined toward one another. They were just intertwined and I was left out. And it drove me nuts.

I wanted Dave to understand where I was coming from: Didn't *he* think it was weird that he saw more of her than me? Didn't he think it was odd for her to nap in his bed sometimes? Was I *insane* for telling him that I had a problem? That I wanted different boundaries than what he found normal? Did it make me a bitch? Jealous? Needy? I kept checking in with my friends, maniacally, frantically, *repeatedly*, to see if I was in the wrong.* If I was being unreasonable. If I was crazy.

To chill out, I reminded myself that either they *were* sleeping together, which I didn't think was the case—and what am I gonna do about it if they are?—or they *weren't* and then no big deal! But that wasn't even my problem; that wasn't my concern. I thought their boundaries were weird. The issue wasn't about a dick going in a vagina. It's not like I thought they wanted to be dating. It was about small looks and sweet favors and the way he looked to her for care and the way she looked to him for emotional support.

All my female friends understood this. Every single one. Most of them had been in a similar situation, trying to describe to other people (usually men) *why* they had a problem with someone based on small, tiny moments—feelings, even—rather than concrete Certified Bad Events. Most of us, too, had, upon telling men, been told we were simply jealous or competitive or petty or bitchy.

Let me reiterate that I don't think I was completely correct, especially not in *how* I went about expressing myself to Dave and to his

---

* Sorry if you were one of my friends during this time. I was ... obnoxious.

friend. I was trying to override my feelings, to be chill about them, to let go, but then every few weeks I would drink one sip of alcohol and then every thought I ever had came bubbling up and spilling over and I was at a ten and crying, which is not the best way to express yourself or have calm, rational, productive relationship conversations. I think I wasn't listened to, wasn't understood (or maybe I wasn't understandable), and it made things worse. It made me *feel* worse. I felt like I had no grasp on reality. I wanted, just *once*, for one of them to say, "Yeah, we're very reliant on one another. Perhaps too close. Sorry if that is uncomfortable sometimes." The message I was getting was that I came second, because she had been there longer and she needed him more than I did right then and I could not and should not expect otherwise. I kept getting told, "This is friendship. Don't threaten our friendship. This is how it is." Which is fair, too. I'm sure Dave also felt like I wasn't listening to him, like I didn't get it, like I wanted him to not be friends with her. Which was *not* the case, but I'm *sure* it felt like that.

I can't tell you what changed; as with most of life, there wasn't one moment, one turning point, where we all got on the same page and stopped hurting each other. I think we all just got used to living differently; we all had to mourn and grow and change and those things are uncomfortable. Eventually, she started dating someone, and then she moved out of Los Angeles with him, and the distance and her relationship status shifted how we all interacted. But Dave and I still disagree about what happened and why. About who asked for what and if they were reasonable.

Was I crazy? I don't know.

We all got through it by being well-intentioned toward one another, by being kind and patient. It all worked out, big picture. And now? Now I'm very close with her. I love her; she's a magnificent friend to me. I think the world of her, and in many ways the issues from years ago feel like they happened to three different people. Close friends of mine, perhaps. Part of me didn't want to write this because why kick up dust?

Well, simply because I'm not alone in this. One of my best, best friends is going through the same thing right now and is wondering how to approach the situation. She keeps saying that she doesn't want to seem crazy or needy, she doesn't want to seem like she's asking him to end his friendship with this person. But she's also like . . . well, *Why does your friend keep calling you "baby" in front of me? Why is she commenting "I love you" on your Instagram posts?* And the worst part of it for her, as it was for me, is *How do I express discomfort with this without you thinking I'm being competitive or possessive or obsessive?* Here's how I felt at the time and here's how she feels now: I don't want to be talking about this. I want this to go away. I want this to not be an issue.

I cannot tell you the percentage of letters people write to my advice column, almost always from women, that I get describing the same *exact* thing. The letters always start with a plea to me, a plea that amounts to, on some level, "Please believe I'm not insane. Please, I'm begging you to believe that I'm not a jealous bitch. I'm reasonable normally and I think I'm being reasonable now, but everyone else is acting like I'm not." It should be noted that many people in similar situations experience a more insidious ending. The friend they have a weird feeling about actually *is* something more. But even when the story does not end in emotional or physical cheating, it is *not* crazy to have boundaries, to ask your partner to understand nuance; it's not crazy to feel left out, to ask for more or better or different. You're not nuts, and people *will* at some point try to get away with treating you poorly by insinuating that you are, that your needs are irrational, your concerns absurd, your boundaries nonsensical.

The truth is, you are not crazy. You're being reasonable, most likely—and even if you aren't, we are all allowed moments of unreasonableness. Obviously, you're not allowed to be harmful, and you must still cultivate self-awareness, but it *is* reasonable to ask for the things you need in your relationships. Your requests and boundaries have merit. It's normal to ask for things. It's normal to feel hurt, annoyed, and even envious from time to time. And it's normal to check in on your partner when they sleep to make sure they're still breathing.

A Short Letter to Responsible People

Dear Responsible People,

First of all, thank you for reading this letter. I knew you would; you do what is asked of you. But I'm thanking you because most people *don't* say thank you to you for doing what is asked. Most people assume that you will do what needs be done, and that you don't need recognition for it. It's assumed that you will double-check the credit card statement for recurring charges and schedule the dog's yearly rabies shot. No one else is even thinking about buying a radon test kit for your house. (Radon is the leading cause of lung cancer in the US among nonsmokers. Did you know that? Of course you knew.) You know where the Band-Aids are and whether you're out of ibuprofen and if the dinner plates are microwave safe. You know where the copy of the lease is and which of your friends can't eat walnuts. You're holding shit down.

Here is what I have to say to you: you will never, ever, ever, ever get a break. You will never, ever, ever, ever get a break, because you will not give one to yourself. Even if you have brief moments of respite courtesy of friends and loved ones who take up the mantle of responsibility, you will never get a week off without worry. You will never be able to fully cede vigilance. Accountability is at the very core of you like a heartbeat and, like a heartbeat, it's designed to never end. (Until The End.)

No one will ever plan Thanksgiving airport pickups the way you do, or turn immigration forms in correctly and on time as well, or apply to as many fellowships. No one will ever hold shit down like you do. And no one will thank you for doing any of this stuff. No one will rejoice at having you in their lives to take care of things, at least not in any way that is proportional to your work. You deserve a parade every quarter, or at the very least a $250 Target gift card. But who would step up to organize that?

Being responsible will cost you. You will sacrifice. You will *pay*. You'll pay in fun, in excitement, in thrill, in leisure, in free time, in relaxation, in blood pressure readings. Even though you know you're sacrificing—are you *ever* going to get to go to Mallorca, get blackout drunk and dance on a table? No. Probably not—you beat on, boats against the current and all that jazz. You take care of yourself and you take care of others and you show up and you do your best, and not in the "I'm doing my best" divorced dad forgetting to pick kids up from school kind of way. The *real* doing your best. You never say no; you rarely say you can't.

Your responsibility will cost you so many funny stories. Yeah, the lead singer of Third Eye Blind invited you to his Malibu home to write songs together, but that's sketchy at best and Malibu is far and you have work in the morning at your day job and songwriting for Third Eye Blind is a great story but no one at the Los Angeles Department of Water and Power gives two shits about that story, they want you to pay your bill on time. Plus, you're not a songwriter, so why the fuck is he asking you anyway? Seems suspicious. Better to play it safe.

Many, many times you will ask yourself, "What the fuck am I trying so hard for?" And, "Why does everyone else get to be a fuckup and still turn out okay?" And, "Why can't I just take a break for once in my goddamn life?" And, "Why can't I fail simply because I didn't feel like trying?" And the answer to most of those questions is simply: Because you're responsible. Maybe at one point you *had* to be, but now, even if you wanted to abdicate, you won't, because this is what you know.

You will have to mourn. There is a whole lot of mourning to be done in life that has nothing to do with the death of a loved one. There are all kinds of little deaths to mourn along the way. One thing you will have to mourn is all the shit you missed out on because you were busy being well-behaved. Being a good kid. Making enough money to set yourself up well for the future. Not taking risks that were too big. Not trying that drug. Not heading home with that person. Not breaking into the chemistry building. Not getting your nose pierced. Not dyeing your hair a fun color. Not studying abroad. Not jeopardizing a job. Not quitting a job. Not picking a riskier career. Not having hot sex with a stranger. All of this is a loss.

It sucks, and I frankly think you should get to scream at the sun for one straight hour a day. You should have gotten a life that let you be irresponsible, that didn't punish you for your dalliances. You deserved four thousand safety nets. I'm sorry you were forced to be good instead.

Eventually, you'll reach a level of acceptance with your responsible self. It's much easier to do once you're past your mid-twenties, when everyone is slooooowly getting more and more accountable and less and less likely to climb onto roofs at 4 a.m. I'm not saying you're going to wake up one day and love that you pack the right (ugly) shoes for vacation or that you'll start to feel like eating healthily is its own reward. It's just that you'll give in eventually and stop fighting responsibility so much, someday. Sometimes that's its own kind of relaxation—the letting go of the fun, fancy-free person you thought you'd be.

You'll make friends with other responsibles, too. You'll plan together. You'll ask clarifying questions before renting kayaks on your friend-vacation. You'll remind each other about sunscreen and heartburn tricks and mutual friends' birthdays. You'll send links to pillows that help with bad backs. You'll help each other figure out the unemployment benefits website.

It's my strong recommendation—not that you asked—that should you date or fuck or marry (or kill) someone, you pick a fellow responsible person. Someone else who had to help around the house too young, who raised their siblings or got a job at sixteen. Because it's very hard to love someone who has never known vigilance, who has only known invincibility, who isn't going to ever recognize the extra work you do. Surround yourself with people who understand that the world is onerous on a good day, people who understand that it is in and of itself worthwhile to try hard and put in effort and give back to others and to *care*.

Just don't hold your breath for anyone to thank you; they're having too much fun.

Love,
Sophia

Riding Shotgun with My Hair Undone in the Front Seat of Margaux's Truck

When I was a freshman in high school, I met one of the most delightfully singular people I've ever met in my life: Margaux Meyer. Her name alone in a sea of Kathryns and Caitlyns and Kaitlynns let you know what to expect—the glamour of that *X*. She was a grade above me and we met making costumes for a musical; I'm not sure why *she* was making costumes—it was probably a capricious whim of hers. For me, it was because I loved the theater department but couldn't sing, so for the spring musical each year all I had to offer was costuming help. We sewed dress after dress for *The Pirates of Penzance* and over pattern cutting and sash attaching and bust measuring, Margaux and I became friends.

Margaux was the kind of person who was not necessarily popular, but rather beloved. She awed people everywhere she went. She wore rain boots with dresses and drove an old pickup truck and ran cross country and had short hair and guys liked her *a lot* and she would tell you *precisely* what she thought at any given moment, which was often terrifying to witness. She was unflinchingly honest, just *wildly* herself all the time. Oh, and she *loved* Taylor Swift. And this was like early country + god Taylor. It was *Taylor Swift*, *Fearless*, and *Speak Now*. It was what the popular girls who actually loved Jesus listened to. It was *not* what someone like her was "supposed" to like. I'm not sure Margaux even noticed; she just *adored* Taylor Swift, and that was that for her.

It made me itch, to be frank. When she gave me rides home my freshman and sophomore year before I could drive, she would *blast* Taylor in her beat-up pickup and I would sit there mortified. It wasn't that I didn't like Taylor Swift's music or Taylor Swift herself or anything—I did. But I felt sure that this was not the stuff I was supposed to like. Mostly, I felt it was waaaayyy too girly, which I presumed was a turn-off for guys, not that any guys were (a) around to see us or (b) interested in me. I also felt the music was not just girly, but dumb. I figured this kind of music was embarrassing to listen to and I couldn't figure out why Margaux refused to be ashamed of it.

In fact, I often felt embarrassed *for* her, as if I was following her around, cleaning up after a messy toddler, but instead I would follow her around and try to stay small and try to express contrition with my body language just in case she pissed someone off. It didn't occur to me that she didn't need me to do that, that in fact her very purpose was the opposite.

Instead of ever discussing it, I just observed Margaux's confidence, her insistence that she get to be allowed to be herself, without a hint of self-editing. I wish—God, how I wish—that I had simply picked up what she was putting down, that I could say I left high school having learned that being anything other than yourself doesn't just lead to an anemic existence, but to bone-deep exhaustion. But I didn't learn that. When Margaux left for college my senior year, I was nowhere near ready to actually be myself. The thought utterly terrified me, even as I felt slivers of envy toward Margaux for barreling through life no-holds-barred.

I eventually talked to her about it a year or two after I graduated high school, during a college break when we were both back in St. Louis. She said that she had been so loud and confident and weird in high school on purpose, with intention. She figured that if she could be odd and loud and utterly herself, it might invite other people who felt less sure of themselves to take small steps to do the same. I still wasn't there myself, but I loved the sentiment. After a year or two in college, I finally at least *wanted* to shed my insecurities, my shame about simply being alive and being a woman. Margaux was never worried about her femininity being held against her. She cried in front of guys; she was dramatic, impulsive, loud, and critical. She was exactly what straight cis guys would describe as "too much." And it didn't kill her. I admired her so much, but I didn't feel like I would or could ever get there. For a few more years after our talk, I didn't. I would privately cringe when she would tell me the latest thing she did to get a guy to ask her out, or how she drew firm (and sometimes unusual) boundaries with people because she figured that if they cared, they'd adhere to them. I would shudder at her boldness, the way she called people out. I was still indoctrinated in the school of "Impress Straight Cis Men at All Costs and Never Mention That They Messed Up." When Margaux was moving in with a guy after a third date or living in a bus with a man, perceptions be damned, I was still a clenched fist of nerves around pretty much everyone, especially men and authority figures and hot people and my family and anyone more successful than me in my industry. I just wanted to make sure they all liked me; God forbid I ever say out loud—or *do!*—something I wanted.

But then, slowly, something happened: I got tired. Not just tired, but exhausted. I wish I could say that I finally gave up on impressing my family and my bosses and people online and, perhaps most of all, men simply because I realized it was the right thing to do. I wish that I had woken up one day and been like, "Okay, wait a minute . . . this is bullshit." But that wasn't the case. The truth is, I just got tired. I got tired of feeling like every minuscule decision I made had the potential to make or break someone's opinion of me. I got tired of feeling like other people's opinions of me were my business, and not just relevant to me, but that they *mattered*.

At first, I didn't know what the alternative was to caring what everyone thought. (Yes, the answer might seem obvious but I was also about twenty-two years old! Please!) I was just tired; I was tired of feeling like I couldn't win no matter what I did, that someone, somewhere, was always going to be a little upset. It was, I realize now, a dynamic I was familiar with as a child of divorced parents who each wanted me to live at their house 24/7. No matter what you do, it's not enough. That was the messaging of my childhood in many ways, and it became the messaging of my teenage years and college years and eventually my adulthood. No matter what you do, it's not enough. And I couldn't think of an alternative to caring about that truth. I felt bad—genuinely bad!—that I couldn't do enough, be thin enough, write enough, read enough, tweet enough, work out enough, call home enough, stay up late enough, be friendly enough, be quiet enough. I felt sorry that I didn't succeed in pleasing other people. But I ran out of fuel.

Eventually, after enough time of being tired and being a bit angry that I was so exhausted for the sake of other people—which in itself is tiring—I discovered that I had given up. I didn't realize it at first. I didn't recognize immediately that I no longer cared because it didn't happen at one particular moment. It happened in fits and starts. Some days, I would leave my house wearing ugly clothes and go to work with no makeup on and all the men in their thirties and forties would talk to all the young twenty-year-old interns instead of twenty-four-year-old me and instead of feeling shame for not being appealing enough, I was like, "What a relief to be left alone!"* Some days, I *wouldn't* stand in the mirror for twenty-three minutes and catalog everything I hated about how I looked; I just didn't care to spend my time that way anymore. I knew I didn't loooove my body. Okay. Boom. Next question. I'm busy. Some days, I told people to not use certain words around me. (Preferably not around anyone ever, but what can I do?) Some days, I told white male actors to shut the fuck up when complaining about not getting parts because they were white and male.† Some days, I still cared a lot!!!

A lot of the time, especially when I worked at the improv theater—which had a revolving door of new people in all the time, creating opportunity for hundreds of first impressions a year—I got told I was intimidating. I wasn't. There is nothing I was doing that was intimidating at all, because *intimidating* is simply the descriptor being used by the person being intimidat*ed*. The only thing that I was doing actively was not caring if I was likable. Nota bene: I was extremely professional and good at my job. But I didn't care if people didn't like me for not bending rules for them. I didn't care if guys were flirty with me in order to get what they wanted. I didn't care

---

* I also made it very clear to all the young interns that if they wanted to escape a conversation ever or report someone or have me yell at a guy, I would. And I often did!!! Flirty straight men in workplaces often hate me!

† Because I was at work, I didn't use the phrase "Shut the fuck up." I said it in a way that was *just* professional enough to not get me fired. Like giving them a hard Paddington stare and saying, "Are you being serious?" Which is usually enough for a person to realize that they are wrong.

how I looked, I wasn't trying to get ahead, I wasn't trying to dazzle anyone. I just did my job and minded my own business. Anything else genuinely felt too tiring.

Gradually, this exhaustion-cum-detachment seeped into more and more parts of my life. I'm not saying I don't care about people—I do, very deeply. I'm also not saying that I don't care at all what people think of me—I still do, very deeply. But I care less and less about people with power, people with influence, people who demand that you impress and suck up to them. I care very little about people who insist that you can never do enough for them. I care less now about being likable and more about being a good person.

While I certainly learned from my own depletion, my own weariness at trying to behave for other people, I can't claim to have done this alone. I did it with the help of Margaux, and my mom, and my sisters, and my best friends, and my aunts. I did it with the help of thousands of women online. I did it because people before me showed me what it could be like to let go of being well-behaved. No one woman did it alone or did it constantly—all of us are still hemmed in by and upholding and celebrating and rejecting societal expectations on and off and on and off again and again. No one is constant. But the moments when I saw other women be unafraid mattered a lot to me.

I hope you got some of that feeling out of this book. This book was not intended to be instructional—can you even imagine if it were? Yikes! All I wanted to do was lay bare what it took for *me* to get away from trying to live my life for other people. I wanted to tell you the truth, which in my experience is: you're fucked. You're fucked no matter what you choose. This axiom is shitty, yes, but I encourage you to find it freeing as well. The truth is that when anything you do will be met with criticism, when anything you do will get you objectified, ignored, belittled, dismissed, etc., then you can do anything.*

The really good news is that, like in *High School Musical*, we're all in this together. Not in the corny, two-dimensional Zac Efron/Vanessa Hudgens way. I'm not claiming that something as flimsy as surface-level unity will fix oppression. I'm not saying anything like, "We all just need to get along and support one another!" When I say, "We're all in this together," what I mean is this: you're not alone. You aren't the only one trying to figure out how to be a good person. You aren't the only person who feels like they're getting conflicting messages about what a good person looks like. You are not alone, and it's not hopeless. Some days you're probably going to conform, some days you're going to buck the system. Sometimes you're going to try to get straight cis white male approval and some days you're going to be like, "Okay, why the fuuuuck was I trying to get straight cis white male approval last Thursday??? Idiot!!" But you aren't an idiot; the system is set up for you to fail. You fail when you try, you fail when you don't.

Sometimes you'll do a really excellent job of living fully for yourself and then two months later your crush comes around and you act like a completely different person, a person with opinions on *The Lord of the Rings* or something. It happens! It's fine! As far as any of us can tell, it's your first time on this planet; you are bound to get things wrong. Especially in a world where no matter what you do, you're fucked, you've disappointed someone, you're not good enough.

My hope for you is just that you choose to behave in ways that suit you, that benefit you, that affirm you as often as possible. I hope that you get away from trying to please others at the expense of your

---

* Within reason! You can't harm people, obviously.

own desires whenever you can. I hope this book made you feel like there's someone else—lots of people, even—experiencing some of the same pressures and strains that you are. (Not all of them, of course. I'm still a cis able-bodied white lady with US citizenship.) My story isn't everyone's story; it isn't even most people's story. This book isn't saying, "Here's what it's like to be a person." It's saying, "Here's how it was for me. Maybe you recognize some of the pieces. Isn't this shit absurd?"

That is the way in which we are all in this together. We all have a story about figuring out who we want to be and how we want to behave and treat other people, and often in other people's stories we recognize ourselves. We read something and go, "Ahhh, yep yep yep. That's it; that's what it's like to be alive sometimes." And I hope you had moments of that in this book. (Hopefully the time that guy Brandon got come in my eye was not a moment you also experienced.)

Maybe—and perhaps it's unfair for me to hope for this—maybe this book released a little tiny amount of the pressure. Maybe it made you think, "Yeah, it *is* fucked-up that there are no older women in my industry," or "Yeah, it *is* fucked-up that I'm expected to care for my parents but my other siblings aren't," or "Yeah, it *is* fucked-up how much I've normalized my own experiences with sexual assault."

The world is mostly hard and often lovely and here's the thing: you can't be so good that you don't get hurt. You can't behave so well that you reap a ton of rewards and everyone loves you and you learn how to do that whistle with your fingers in your mouth and you get a walk-in closet and you have a dog that doesn't bark and thirty-seven very close friends and no one is ever mad at you. You just can't. All you can do is try your best and take a lot of naps and be good to people and go really easy on yourself. Find people who seem brave and kind and surround yourself with them and emulate them* slowly until you become braver and kinder, but in your own ways, according to your own values. (I don't know; that's what I did and now I barely even notice what straight cis men think anymore! It's great!) Seriously, though, when you have the ability to—which is admittedly not always—I hope you take the chance to just do shit your own way, to set your own boundaries, to live up to your own expectations. It's a lot less exhausting.

---

* Not in a creepy way!

Talking Too Much

I learned from a fairly young age that the biggest knock against someone's character was that they talked too much. This, I'm sorry to say, I learned from my father. I picked up early on that my father enjoyed quiet. (No offense to him, but maybe don't have five kids if that's the case.) My dad and I would often have completely silent forty-five-minute car rides; I clearly remember him commenting on how great it was that my brother stayed so quiet in the car, as opposed to his daughters, who were prone to jawing, as he calls it. When I got tattoos, he expressed his disappointment because he thinks tattoos are too often "another way for people to talk more." He wasn't worried about their permanence or appearance but rather that they were, in his opinion, "loud." (Please bear in mind that my father has a lime-green car.) He is fundamentally against the idea of talking for talking's sake, something he seems to believe he is the arbiter of, which I believe to be wholly subjective.

My dad does not use filler words. He doesn't use "umm" or "like" or "uhh" or "well." It can take him half an hour to tell a five-minute story because of how precise he is with his language. He used to charge us a quarter every time we said "like." He never let a "less" go when it should have been a "fewer."* Words were precious to him, and not to be bandied about willy-nilly. Grammar was the way of appreciating those words, the equivalent of going to church to worship the thing you believe in most. I want to be clear that my dad does talk to his kids and he does *like* talking to us, but he also lets it be known that people who talk too much or about the wrong things—based on his judgment—are annoying.†

"Annoying" is one of those words that so infrequently gets lobbed at straight men. If it isn't gendered, it is at the very least lop-sided. One of my greatest fears, along with spiders, the vastness of the ocean, accidentally killing someone with my car, and enjoying a Smash Mouth song, is being seen as annoying. It's a rather absurd fear, in the scheme of things. I mean, the ice caps are melting and I'm worried that maybe my presence bothers people. There are 82.4 million refugees right now who have been forcibly displaced from their homes and I'm over here stressed that maybe I'm doing too much. Too much *what*? Too much. The specific complaint I'm *sure* people have about me is that I talk too much. No one has actually *told me* that I talk too much; in fact, when my boyfriend and I started dating‡ I mentioned that I talked too much and he said that he thought I actually didn't talk *enough* and I think I fell in love with him a little bit right then. (Not sure what he thinks now, not gonna ask.)

---

* Obviously, this made me *quite* the cunt when I grew up, because I thought that correcting people's grammar was good and helpful, or at the very least a cool thing to do that made me seem superior. It is not. Don't correct people's grammar. Ever. It's not an emergency. If you understood what someone said, then they spoke correctly.

† He finds a lot of people annoying for the most bizarre reasons (although I will say that the label often falls on women he's not attracted to, I think), and most of the time we just roll our eyes. But one time he told me he didn't like Dolly Parton and I fought with him. I really don't allow that kind of talk around me. There are things you can say and things you can't and not liking Dolly is a cardinal sin. Papa, if you're reading this, I do not forgive you.

‡ Hooking up.

I simply enjoy talking to people—talking *with* people. I was shy as a young child: many of my earliest memories involve hiding behind my parents' legs avoiding strangers. Some of my first words were *too loud*. I am, by nature, an anxious person. I'm consumed with making sure everyone around me is having a nice time, which often means social situations take a whole lot out of me. I can't really be around most people longer than two hours without needing a break. I suppose I'm not the most natural person to have become talkative.

Unlike at my dad's house, at my mom's house, my mom, my sister Lena, and I rarely stopped conversing. As three women who got along well (most of the time), we had virtually no end of things to talk about. We ate dinner together nearly every single night and the entire point, especially in my mother's mind, was for us to talk. We were expert at weaving our stories together, at connecting the dots between our actions and beliefs and our experiences, at talking along with each other rather than over each other. We were a family of talking things out. If Lena or I got into trouble, our mom talked to us about it and asked us what the consequences *should* be. After I became an adult, many of the therapists I saw about my anxiety and depression expected me to use them as outlets for talking out my problems, but my mom, Lena, and I had already analyzed our family within an inch of its life for years. Anything the three of us couldn't figure out was discussed by any number of the many childhood therapists my mom tried to make me go to. And my best friends and I sorted out my adult problems together verbally, turning them over and over between us. I simply didn't need to talk more, to get things out; I wasn't waiting to unburden myself. If anything, I needed someone to tell me what to do for fifty-five minutes.* I'm not hesitant to talk to people close to me. In fact, I love doing it.

---

* Should I be continuing to look for a therapist who is perhaps a better fit? Yeah, but it's expensive and I'm tired.

When the pandemic arrived, I realized I even like talking to people I'm not close to. I am, as it turns out, into small talk. (Feel free to sigh for seventy-five straight minutes.) People love to brag about how much they despise small talk; the very dismissal of the practice serves, for some, as a shorthand for intellect. I can't tell you how many dating profiles I've seen that direct prospective partners to skip straight to "deep" conversations. Frankly, I think that's arrogant and juvenile. Is your plan to turn your attention to the person who's bagging your groceries and be like, "What was your parents' relationship like when you were a child and how do you think it affected you?" Absolutely not! The entire point of small talk is to create a rapport with someone so that you can eventually *get to* bigger topics, should you continue to see them in a context where that's appropriate. Small talk *is* meaningful, if not in content then in intent. After months of lockdown, I finally went back to my favorite café and caught up with the owners. It's not like we were dissecting Marxism or anything! We talked about their business and how the pandemic was for them and how crazy the world was. It was lovely! I had so missed getting to walk in and out of a place and see a new person and say a few words and then move on with my day with a little extra dose of friendliness, a reminder that there are other people around me living lives too. But no, according to the Smart People of the Internet, the Real Intellectuals, that interaction was grating and, furthermore, worthless.

I'd like to submit that what people consider small talk is gendered—or at least that what we consider "meaningful" conversation is gendered. When women talk to one another it is, almost by default, seen as guff. When we talk, it's gossip or chatter or fluff. We're catty or mouthy or vapid. The topics we converse about aren't as important as what men talk about, never mind that the topics people claim women discuss seem to be examples from the 1950s.

There's a quote misattributed to Eleanor Roosevelt—surely it is a rite of passage for any quote to have been wrongly said to come from her—that says, "Great minds discuss ideas. Average minds discuss events. Small minds discuss people." I used to see and hear that quote *a lot*. I feel like it has fallen out of favor with the dwindling presence of the chain email, but the quote is, not to put too fine a point on it, fucking ridiculous. Gossip is fabulous. Talking about people is *fun*. It doesn't have to be mean-spirited, it doesn't have to be cruel. It's connective. If I talk about how Ben Simmons's antics are fucking up the 76ers' chances of a championship, is that not talking about a person? Is that not gossip? How on earth is that different from, say, me talking about Kourtney and Travis's engagement? It's not. Also, *obviously*, women talk about sports and men talk about celebrity gossip, but we're trained from early on to find what comes out of women's mouths less important. To get back to Eleanor's supposed quote, when a man talks, it's about an idea; when a woman talks, it's about a person.* Not only do we think women talk too much, but we hate what women talk *about*.

If what women say is seen as meaningless, unimportant frippery, then it makes sense that people would want us to shut the fuck up. There is a very real perception—by people of all genders—that women talk more. Just look at all the words we have for loud women: *chatterbox, shrew, gossip, nag, harpy, fishwife, busybody*. If you think of someone who is talkative, I'm almost certain you imagine a woman. And yet, women do not talk more. We are, however, treated like we do, and perhaps, more important, we're reminded that it's a bad thing. Multiple self-help books over the years cited a study saying that women said twenty thousand words a day while men uttered a much more respectable seven thousand. (No word on how many nonbinary or gender-nonconforming folks spoke.) It

---

* Let's also just be very clear that the idea that there are great minds, average minds, and small minds is *incredibly* problematic!

turns out that was not a real study. There is no evidence that study was ever even done!

As feminist Dale Spender put it, "The talkativeness of women has been gauged in comparison not with men but with silence. Women have not been judged on the grounds of whether they talk more than men, but of whether they talk more than silent women." Studies consistently show that even when we talk less than men, people overestimate how much women talk.* In one study, men rated conversations between men and women as "equal" when women talked only 15 percent of the time, and when women talked 30 percent of the time, they felt that women had dominated the discussion. In reality, multiple studies have shown that who talks more depends a lot on the "sphere" in which the talking takes place. Women seem on average to talk more in "private" places like at home or among friends, while men routinely dominate conversations at school and in the workplace. And this divide is evident rather early on.

Teachers tend to assume that female students talk more and take up more classroom time, when the opposite is overwhelmingly true. At every single age level, teachers are more likely to call on boys and give them more time to speak, especially in regard to more difficult questions, reinforcing that they are the voices of competency. Boys get more time to answer questions than girls do, and teachers are more likely to move on to another (often male) student if a girl gets a question wrong, while when a boy gets a question wrong, they're more likely to give him the time to correct himself. This continues into college: male students speak 1.6 times as often as female students in classrooms where they don't have to raise their hands to speak. One anecdote came from a male science teacher who tried to balance the number of times girls and boys spoke in his class and

---

* Interestingly, people also overestimate how *fast* women talk. Which is, to me— someone who gets told I talk too fast all the time—hilarious.

when he did so, he felt like women were taking up 90 percent of the time. Additionally, the male students apparently complained.

On top of getting reduced speaking time in classroom and workplace settings, women get interrupted more and are more likely to yield to interruptions than to keep talking until they get their point across. Men consistently interrupt women more than they do other men, suggesting that they do not value what women are saying as much, or that in the more competitive style of conversation they tend to employ, women are "easy" targets to knock out of standing. My boyfriend is a chronic interrupter; in fact, I am too, but in a different way.* We both do it out of excitement to talk to the other person, but while my "interruptions" come at the end of sentences and tend to be supportive of the person talking—e.g., "Oh my God!" or "I can't believe he did that!"—his interruptions tend to be his trying to take a turn to talk. It drove (drives) me fucking insane. It got to the point that I brought it up in couples therapy. I will full-on stop the conversation and say, "I was talking." I know he doesn't do this to be rude—he has a lot better, easier ways of being rude to me if he wants to, and I know he doesn't want to! But when I have to stop him in front of friends, to publicly call out that he's interrupting me, I often feel the room tense up. I have become the bitch simply for wanting to finish my sentence.†

Yoshiro Mori, president of the Tokyo Olympic organizing committee, publicly claimed that women made meetings run too long because they talk too much, something he found "annoying." The comments were in response to the Olympic committee aiming to have 40 percent of the committee be female. Not even half! God forbid! A lot of studies focus on the workplace, which is unfortu-

---

* My way is—obviously—better. When he writes a book he can do a whole chapter on how wrong I am.

† Sometimes I wonder if I got into writing simply because you can't be interrupted.

nate, since work isn't (or shouldn't be) the only sphere that exists, but these studies do make clear the actual monetary cost for women that comes with talking. Research suggests that women putting forward positive solutions in the workplace or coming up with revenue-generating ideas get ignored, while men are rewarded for those contributions. And that neutral perception in comparison to a positive one for men isn't the basement—oh no, the bar can sink lower! Powerful women tend to face backlash for talking more; one study found that "female CEOs" (fake ones they made up for the study) who talked more were seen as worse leaders than ones who spoke less. And when those CEOs' names were changed to masculine ones? Magically all that talking was . . . great leadership! Woo! This is apparently fairly global, too. A group of researchers from Yale studied Malawian farming villages after teaching their citizens new agricultural techniques and found that while men and women understood the information equally (of fucking course), when women were communicating what they'd learned, people paid less attention.

To me, this isn't just problematic because it makes women feel the need to stay quiet, to make sure their mere presence isn't threatening, to navigate *incorrect* perceptions about themselves. It's not just bullshit because it means women simply do not get to be heard as often as men do (and certainly, cis straight white women are getting heard the most). It's also shitty because of how *fun* it is to talk. It's shitty because we're ignoring how connective talking is, or can be. This attitude—the belief that women talk too much and that talking too much is bad—undervalues the ways and places in which women are, on average, good at talking. We are really good at collaboration, at helping people feel welcome, at checking in on people, at including them. We're good at negotiating the needs of many; we're good at adapting, at helping others save face, at getting to the vulnerable roots of people.

To be sure, not everyone likes talking or is good at it, regardless of their gender or the sphere they're in. In an ideal, just world, we would not require people to adhere to rigid and often opaque social norms in order to be accepted into certain spaces or to get certain jobs. My argument here is not that we all need to get better at talking, or that we all need to talk more. I don't think everyone needs to become a skilled conversationalist in order to be kind or a good person by *any means*. I'm just saying that we undervalue certain *types* of conversation because we connect them with women. And we punish women for talking "too much," even when they aren't.

For my money, the best time to be had is getting a coffee with a friend or two and talking. Not coworking, not watching a movie together, not even going to a bar to dance (although that's another love of mine), but simply talking. And in order to be good at talking, you have to be good at listening, which often gets ignored. When people complain about how much they loathe small talk, what I hear is that they don't like *listening*. They have deemed certain pieces of information beneath them and therefore irritating. For some reason, the amount of carrots in your mother's famous pot roast recipe is less important than Joe explaining the most recent sales reports, despite the fact that at the end of your life, you're not going to be lying there wishing you could go to one more quarterly budget meeting. A lot of people enter conversations waiting their turn to speak, which, I argue, makes them *bad* at conversations. It makes sense to me that they think everyone else talks too much, perhaps especially women.

At some point in high school I realized that I wanted to get better at talking to people; this came after I had lost weight and more people were talking to me. (If you want to see who is *really* ignored in conversations, look beyond gender differences—look at intersections of race, class, gender, disability, and sexuality, but also look at perceived attractiveness. People love to ignore women they think aren't hot enough for them to listen to.) Depressingly, people talked and listened to me *a whole lot* more after I lost weight. And I had no practice. Well, I had a lot of practice in talking at home with a bunch of women; I was great at talking informally and quickly and collaboratively with my sisters and my mom. I was good at speaking over my siblings or knowing when to stay quiet for the sake of one of my parents, or to start a conversation to distract another one of them. At school, I was, I'm sure, seen as aggressive and annoying for how much I spoke up and raised my hand. For many years, I was undeterred by being seen as intimidating by my classmates. Until I lost weight, most people (especially boys) didn't talk to me anyway, so what the hell did I care if they also thought I was a freak?

But eventually my hormones took over and I wanted to learn to be attractive to other people, to be likable. (And of course, by this I mostly mean fuckable.) Talking to people made me nervous. It still very much does! But I figured I could learn to fake it. So, like the pathetic person I am, I googled how to become better at talking. I read that people liked when you remembered their names and repeated them, that people loved being asked questions, and that if you wait a minute or two and don't fill every silence, often people will continue to talk and that *that* is usually when you get to the good stuff. It turned out that so much of what made people good at talking was actually *listening*. And so, because I was desperate to be liked and because I assumed everything I read on the internet was true and helpful, I practiced those things.

At first, it was a conscious effort. I would actively focus on people and being a better listener and asking follow-up questions. It sucked! Or at least I sucked at it. No one had taught me before how to be a good listener other than simply telling me to wait my turn to speak. When your goal is to ask follow-up questions, or to remember someone's name, or to not jump into every silence, however, you *have* to listen. After a while (and I'm talking years here; it's slow work changing who you are), listening became easier and easier. It eventually became natural. I am not saying I'm perfect—I was still raised in a family of talkers who love the sound of their own voices, as most of us do—but I'm better than I was before. I am aware now of when people dominate conversations, when they talk about topics that not everyone in the group is privy to, or when they alienate others with their own conversation patterns, and I try to help correct course slightly. I try to ask people who aren't as easily included questions, I try to give people who hesitate the floor, I try to listen better.

And let me tell you, it makes talking *a lot* more fun! Who knew that not being self-absorbed might actually have positive consequences? Shocking! It's fun to learn about people, not just to impart Important Information. It's lovely to hear why someone loves *Dancing with the Stars* or how they got into pickling things or what new nondairy milk they endorse. Those things are important firstly because someone is sharing with you, which is in and of itself a kindness, but also because those conversations so often lead to the bigger things, *or* because, if you listen closely enough, they are *about* the bigger things. All I'm saying is that if we ever meet in person, expect me to learn and remember your name and then ask you a bunch of questions, and if we're an hour into a conversation and I don't know about your relationship with your mom yet, it would be a real shock.

Acknowledgments

While I am not a fan of introductions, acknowledgments are my favorite part of any book, so please lend me a little grace, as these thank-yous might go long. It does not help that I have approximately 9,428 immediate family members.

Firstly, thank you to my agent, Jessica Felleman, for taking a wildly disorganized call a few years ago and then spending months helping me actually create something cohesive; thank you for gently insisting that the book did in fact need to have a point. Thank you also for taking all the many, many calls and emails that came afterward and for calming me down about pretty much every step of the publishing process. Thank you endlessly to my editor, Rebecca Strobel, for making this book what it is now instead of what it was in the beginning. Rebecca, I can't thank you enough for the brilliant guidance you gave me and the wonderful vision you had for the book. It was so, so easy at every turn to trust you to make the book better, which is a dream. The biggest thank-you imaginable to both of you for all the times you laughed with me and encouraged me and not just because it was your job.

Thank you to the entire Gallery team who made writing a book a breeze, and who gave me so much of their time and hard work.

Thank you to Anne Jaconette and Rachel Brenner. Thank you to Jen Bergstrom, Sally Marvin, and Aimée Bell. (I still vividly remember Aimée mentioning Nora Ephron in the first meeting and knowing I wanted to work with Gallery.) Thank you to Polly Watson for making the book actually readable (and sorry for making you have to address the consistent spelling of come/cum in a professional setting). Thank you to Caroline Pallotta, Kaitlyn Snowden, Lisa Litwack, John Vairo, and Michelle Marchese for making sloppy Word documents from me into a beautiful, physical, actual book. Thank you to Carolyn Levin, who legally vetted this book and asked me if my family would care if I said they drank all the time and understood when I replied, "Oh no, they're Italian."

A big shout-out to everyone who has ever found me hot: thank you.

Thank you to the inordinately kind people who own and run Toasted and Roasted and Charlie's Coffee House, where I wrote a lot of this book before the pandemic.

An enormous thank-you to Josh Gondleman, who helped me every step of the way simply because he's one of those freaks who like to be nice to people. Josh, I could not thank you—or pay you—enough for all the guidance and kindness you sent my way.

To Lauren Larson, my first editor at *GQ*, who gave me way more mentorship and laughter than I could ever have dreamed of. Thank you also to Rosa Pasquarella for giving me my first real TV job. I'm here because of you two! Thank you!

If my dog Party could read, I would thank her for being a little rat who never lets me ignore her for more than eight minutes at a time. She's always coming up with such good excuses not to write.

To my friends who had to listen to me talk about this book in incredibly boring, vague ways for years; I wrote out a specific list of people to thank and then it turned into just a general list of people I'm friends with that kept getting bigger and bigger and it turns out I was just bragging about having lots of friends. Thank you especially to Kelsey for all the laughter and motivation and makeup help; getting ready with you is a highlight of my life. Adrienne, thank you for the pep talks and the pretzels and the encouragement. Thank you to Kev for letting me commandeer your friendship with Dave. Thank you to Margaux, Tyler, Sarah Beth, Alex, Devan, Tam, and Mia for being in this book and for being wonderful, dear friends. I will Venmo you each twelve dollars.

Also, as corny as it is, a massive thank-you to everyone I've ever followed on Twitter who is smarter and kinder and better than I am; I hope I've learned to be even an ounce more like you. I swear I will never log off.

To all the teachers I've ever had who put up with me in their classes: sorry I talked so much, but also you're welcome for my being such an engaged learner! Thank you especially to Penny Longnecker, Amy Barker, Nancy Menchhofer, Kelly Schneider, Sean McCarthy, Larry Anderson, Sarah Banet-Weiser, Jennifer Dieken-Buchek, June Bourque, Scott Warren, Anna Kalfus, Karen Ambhul, Florence Hughes, and many, many more. You were the best part of school for me; I would do any grade over in a heartbeat to learn from you again.

To my massive extended family, who have agreed to never bring up anything they read in this book ever. Even if they have something nice to say. We're all going to pretend this book didn't occur! The next time we see each other we can talk about how I'm trying to grow an orange tree on my back patio, or about Jimmy Butler, or what the best casserole is, but not this book. I love you all.

To my aunt Karen, who taught me how to read when I was three; you started all of this mess. You're who I've always wanted to be when I grow up. I'm so sorry I took only two years of French in high school.

To Jim and Katy, thank you for choosing to marry my parents. Being a good stepparent is often a thankless job; I know you both work incredibly hard at it. Thank you.

To Olivia, Angelo, and Giovana: God, I love you all so much. I will do pretty much anything you ask—even if it's not within reason. (Feel free to abuse that.) Thank you for all the joy. To Josh and Andrew and Ben, thank you for weaving into our family so well and so easily; sorry about all the crying we do! To Michael, God bless you for being such a good son-in-law; it really takes the pressure off Dave. To Emily and Lucy and Nicholas, thank you for being the brightest, most delightful people, for feeling like family should.

To Emilee, thank you for twenty-six years of the best friendship. Thank you for freaking out about climate change with me on Mondays and Wednesdays. Thank you for making it work across an ocean. Thank you for pouring seven drops of Dawn dish soap in the park pond to try to do "something bad" for once when we were sixteen. Thank you for knowing every line of *The Grinch* and *French Kiss* and for making me laugh so hard that I've peed multiple times. Ain't nothin' but a raw cheetah.

To Lena, for going through it all with me, for getting it, for making me laugh; you're the caviar garnish to my life. Thank you for teaching me everything from how to snap my fingers to how to curl my hair. Thank you for mostly being cool about me wanting to share a room with you. Thank you for letting me steal your *Cosmo* magazines and your *Sims* games and your clothes. Thank you for laughing with me at funerals. Thank God you were already there when I was born.

Thank you to my mom, who believes in me a truly disgusting amount and who says "Okay, Soph" when she doesn't. Mom, you taught me everything I know about how to treat people well. Thank you for letting us eat raw cookie dough and for saving our voice mails. Thank you for teaching me gratitude and compassion. Thank you for being my best audience. Sorry for at least half of my behavior. Thank you for your Saturday phone calls and love of birthday cards. I love you more.

Thank you to Papa, who really hoped I would be a hockey-playing astronaut and instead got a writer-comedian who lives in fucking California. (I promise I'm trying to carry myself back unspoiled.) Thank you for making me calculate the speed of light by hand and for drawing us diagrams after we fell off our bikes about where in the turn we should have accelerated. Thank you for passing down your devotion to family, your crewneck sweatshirts, and your love of language to me. Someday I hope to use the words *xis*, *itinerant chicken sexer*, or *Plato is a big fuckhead* in an email to my own children.

Thank you to Dave, who has, from the very beginning, let me mine our lives and make everything public on all kinds of platforms, who insisted he didn't care what I wrote about him in the book. (A mistake on his part, obviously.) God, you love me so well. Thank you for agreeing that my one and only flaw is that I sometimes get mascara under my eyes.

And to Jane Fonda. I don't know her or anything; she's just the best.

Notes

65 *general care for others overwhelmingly falls on women:* Gus Wezerek and Kristen R. Ghodsee, "Women's Unpaid Labor Is Worth $10,900,000,000,000," *New York Times*, Opinion, March 5, 2020, https://www.nytimes.com/interactive/2020/03/04/opinion/women-unpaid-labor.html.

65 *The gap in chores and household tasks starts:* Claire Cain Miller, "A 'Generationally Perpetuated' Pattern: Daughters Do More Chores," *New York Times*, August 8, 2018, https://www.nytimes.com/2018/08/08/upshot/chores-girls-research-social-science.html.

65 *mothers tend to do more work while men:* Wendy Wang, "The Happiness Penalty for Breadwinning Moms," Institute for Family Studies, June 4, 2019, https://ifstudies.org/blog/the-happiness-penalty-for-breadwinning-moms.

82n† *A hallmark of female conversation:* Amanda Montell, *Wordslut: A Feminist Guide to Taking Back the English Language* (New York: Harper Wave, 2020).

219n* *There is a nationwide shortage of gynecologists:* Hannah Smothers, "We're on the Verge of a Devastating OB-GYN Shortage," Vice, September 18, 2019, https://www.vice.com/en/article/j5yjq7/obgyn-doctor-shortage.

229 *Speculums haven't been updated much since 1847:* Brynn Holland, "The 'Father of Modern Gynecology' Performed Shocking Experiments on Slaves," *History,* August 29, 2017, updated December 4, 2018, https://www.history.com/news/the-father-of-modern -gynecology-performed-shocking-experiments-on-slaves.

241 *even with less money and less time than men:* "Gender Pay Gap Report for 2020," The State of the Gender Pay Gap 2020, PayScale, https://www.payscale.com/data/gender-pay-gap; Bruce Drake, "Another Gender Gap: Men Spend More Time in Leisure Activities," Fact Tank: News in the Numbers, Pew Research Center, June 10, 2013, https://www.pewresearch.org/fact-tank/2013/06/10 /another-gender-gap-men-spend-more-time-in-leisure-activities/.

242 *girls on average spend more time doing housework:* Gretchen Livingston, "The way U.S. teens spend their time is changing, but differences between boys and girls persist," Fact Tank: News in the Numbers, Pew Research Center, February 20, 2019, https://www .pewresearch.org/fact-tank/2019/02/20/the-way-u-s-teens-spend -their-time-is-changing-but-differences-between-boys-and-girls -persist/.

243n* *in straight partnerships where women earn* more: Olga Khazan, "Emasculated Men Refuse to Do Chores—Except Cooking," *Atlantic,* October 24, 2016, https://www.theatlantic.com/health /archive/2016/10/the-only-chore-men-will-do-is-cook/505067/.

279n* *stay-at-home dads do less childcare on average:* Greg Jericho, "Stay-at-home fathers do less childcare than working mothers, research shows," *Guardian,* May 15, 2017, https://www.theguardian.com /lifeandstyle/2017/may/16/stay-at-home-fathers-childcare-working -mothers-research-finds.

Bibliography

Advisory Board. "How Often Are Women Interrupted by Men? Here's What the Research Says." Daily Briefing, July 7, 2017; republished October 30, 2018. https://www.advisory.com/en/daily -briefing/2017/07/07/men-interrupting-women.

Alexander, Reed. "Women Who Speak Out at Work Get Ignored. Men Become Leaders." MarketWatch, November 7, 2017. https:// www.marketwatch.com/story/women-who-speak-out-at-work -get-ignored-men-become-leaders-2017-11-07.

Association for Psychological Science. "Women Face Backlash for Speaking up at Work." Association for Psychological Science, January 20, 2015. https://www.psychologicalscience.org/news/minds-busi ness/women-face-backlash-for-speaking-up-at-work.html.

Bonesteel, Matt. "Tokyo Olympics Chief Says Women Talk Too Much at Meetings, Calls It 'Annoying.'" *Washington Post*, February 4, 2021. https://www.washingtonpost.com/sports/2021/02/03/yo shiro-mori-tokyo-olympics-sexist-comments/.

Cutler, Anne, and Donia R. Scott. "Speaker Sex and Perceived Apportionment of Talk." *Applied Psycholinguistics* 11 (1990): 253–72.

https://pure.mpg.de/rest/items/item_68785_7/component/file_506904/content.

Dartmouth College. "College Classrooms Are Still Chilly for Women, as Men Speak More, Study Finds." ScienceDaily, January 19, 2021. https://www.sciencedaily.com/releases/2021/01/21011911 4452.htm.

Donnelly, Erin. "Do Women Really Talk More than Men?" Pimsleur. *The Science of Language* (blog). November 19, 2018. https://blog .pimsleur.com/2018/11/19/language-ideologies-do-women-really -talk-more-than-men/.

Gannett, Cinthia. *Gender and the Journal: Diaries and Academic Discourse*. Albany: State University of New York Press, 1992.

Goldberg, Susan. "Gender in the Classroom." *Today's Parent*, August 24, 2016. https://www.todaysparent.com/kids/school-age/gender -in-the-classroom/.

Hammond, Claudia. "Prattle of the Sexes: Do Women Talk More than Men?" BBC Future, November 11, 2013. https://www.bbc.com /future/article/20131112-do-women-talk-more-than-men.

Mobarak, Ahmed Mushfiq. "When Women Speak, Do People Listen?" Yale Insights, February 27, 2020. https://insights.som.yale.edu /insights/when-women-speak-do-people-listen.

Robb, Michael P., Margaret A. Maclagan, and Yang Chen. "Speaking Rates of American and New Zealand Varieties of English." *Clinical Linguistics & Phonetics* 18, no. 1 (2004). https://doi.org/10.1 080/0269920031000105336.

Spender, Dale. *Man Made Language*. London: Pandora, 2001.

Tannen, Deborah. *You Just Don't Understand: Women and Men in Conversation*. New York: William Morrow, 2013.

"Who Talks More, Men or Women?" *Sip Life Slowly and Enjoy It* (blog). July 25, 2017. https://siplifeslowly.com/2017/07/25/who-talks -more-men-or-women/.

Wiley, Mary Glenn, and Arlene Eskilson. "Speech Style, Gender Stereotypes, and Corporate Success: What If Women Talk More like Men?" *Sex Roles* 12 (1985): 993–1007. https://doi.org/10.1007/BF00288100.

About the Author

SOPHIA BENOIT is a writer and comedian who grew up in Missouri and was correctly voted "Most Likely to Never Come Back." She writes sex and relationship advice for *GQ* and has had bylines in *Allure*, *Refinery29*, the *Cut*, the *Guardian*, *Reductress*, and more. She writes an advice newsletter, *Here's the Thing*, in which she urges everyone to ask their crush out. She does *not* have an MFA in creative writing, but every couple of months she looks up graduate programs and becomes convinced earning an advanced degree will change her entire life. Sophia lives in Los Angeles with her boyfriend, Dave—but usually only spouses make it into author bios, so forget about him.